Echoes of the Holocaust
on the American
Musical Stage

Echoes of the Holocaust on the American Musical Stage

Jessica Hillman

McFarland & Company, Inc., Publishers
Jefferson, North Carolina, and London

LIBRARY OF CONGRESS CATALOGUING-IN-PUBLICATION DATA

Hillman-McCord, Jessica (Jessica H.)
  Echoes of the Holocaust on the American musical stage /
Jessica Hillman.
      p.   cm.
  Includes bibliographical references and index.

  ISBN 978-0-7864-6602-3
  softcover : acid free paper ∞

  1. Musicals — United States — History and criticism.
2. Holocaust, Jewish (1939–1945), in music.   3. National
socialism and music.   I. Title.
ML1711.H38 2012
782.1'40973 — dc23
                                            2012033486

BRITISH LIBRARY CATALOGUING DATA ARE AVAILABLE

Front cover: *Fiddler on the Roof,* Broadway 1964–1972 (Photofest)

Manufactured in the United States of America

McFarland & Company, Inc., Publishers
  Box 611, Jefferson, North Carolina 28640
  www.mcfarlandpub.com

Acknowledgments

This project grew out of work I did on my master's thesis and doctoral dissertation at the University of Colorado at Boulder. I wish to acknowledge the contributions of all of my distinguished committee members, including Professors Paul Shankman, Oliver Gerland, James Symons, and Beth Osnes. I'd particularly like to thank Bud Coleman for his encouragement and editorial skill, and Henry Bial of the University of Kansas for his advice and cogent feedback.

Colleagues at ATHE's Music Theatre/Dance focus group gave useful responses to this work along the way, and Jill Dolan and Stacy Wolf offered illuminating comments on the *Milk and Honey* chapter.

I'd also like to thank the faculty of the theatre department at State University of New York at Fredonia, particularly chair Thomas Loughlin, for their collegiality and for crucial support on the final stages of getting this project to print.

Finally, I also wish to thank Robert and Elizabeth Hillman for their continued love and advice, and Doug McCord for making this publication possible in so many ways.

Portions of chapters, in different form, have been published as:

"When Nazis Sing: Meta-Theatricality, Fascist Aesthetics and Transgressive Humor in Mel Brooks' *The Producers*." *Northwest Theatre Review* 12 (2006): 18–28.

"*Hope of the Homeless*: *Milk and Honey*'s Restorative Nostalgia for Israel." *TDR— The Drama Review*. Edited by Jill Dolan and Stacy Wolf. *TDR* 211 (55:3)

Thanks to Williamson Music, Hal Leonard Corporation, Alley Music Corporation and the Appletree Music Company for allowing the following lyric reprints:

"Milk and Honey" From *Milk and Honey*. Music and Lyric by Jerry Herman. © 1961 (Renewed) Jerry Herman. All rights controlled by Jerryco Music Co. Exclusive

Table of Contents

Preface

YouTube clips of Hitler (mistranslated from the 2004 film *Downfall*), comically and anachronistically ranting about everything from the iPad to Justin Bieber, receive millions of internet hits. *Hogan's Heroes* episodes are replayed every night on television. Serious films about the Nazi era and the Holocaust are almost continuously in theaters, often winning Oscars. Barely a week goes by without at least one Holocaust-related article in the *New York Times*. Fiction and poetry about the Nazi era and the Holocaust proliferates more every day. As just these few examples indicate, America cannot seem to rid its collective imagination of images and themes raised by the Nazi era. We find stylistically diverse reactions to the Holocaust from direct portrayals to more distant echoes across the media and the arts, and especially in the theatre. In some ways it is logical that the Broadway musical, a uniquely American art form, has been a venue for playing out our cultural obsession with Nazism and the Holocaust; however, the portrayal of such violent, hateful figures and events, or even allusions to those events, runs counter to our stereotyped perceptions of musicals as "fluff." What happens to the figure of the Nazi when placed on the musical theatre stage? How have portrayals of the Nazi era and its implications shifted, and how do those shifts inform the study of our changing mores and collective fears? On a larger scale, what can we discover about changing American attitudes towards the Holocaust through musicals?

Scholars of the Holocaust and theatre academicians alike have ignored musicals' response to Nazism and the events of the Nazi era. The explanation for this bias, that musicals are considered aesthetically inferior and therefore unworthy of study, remains unspoken. By perpetuating this absence the academy risks ignoring precisely those works that shed the most light on our culture's evolving response to a defining era. I hope to redress this inequity by focusing on the artistic responses seen by the greatest amount of people —

musicals — and which can therefore legitimately be argued either to trigger or to reflect changing American values and mores. Aesthetic or artistic value judgments are not my concern in this study. Nor are concerns regarding the morality of the commercialization of the Holocaust. I will try to avoid these judgments whenever possible, despite the complications inherent in that task. Instead I will explore the exchange between artistic response and cultural values. This exchange circulates in both directions, from societal interests to art, and from artistic work to cultural concern. This multi-directional flow presents an incredibly difficult process to quantify, but its examination helps to clarify the impact of the Holocaust on American identity.

This work addresses the question of how our attitudes have changed, and how popular theatre has changed along with them. The musicals examined fall into two categories. First are those that deal directly with the Nazi era: *The Sound of Music, Cabaret* and *The Producers*. These musicals demonstrate the changing American milieu in two seemingly opposite ways, first through an increasingly grim and "realistic" portrayal of the threat of Nazism and the Holocaust, and second through an increase in comic responses to that threat. These two reactions are very apparent in American cultural response to the Holocaust, as seen in popular art forms such as TV, film, and particularly theatre. The second category of musicals, *Milk and Honey, Fiddler on the Roof, Rothschilds, Rags* and *Ragtime*, are more indirect in their responses to the era. In fact they treat entirely distant periods — Israel in the 1960s, the Eastern European shtetl, early 19th century Europe, and the American immigrant age. Despite these disparate times and locations, all these musicals confront, in their own ways, the inescapable knowledge of the Holocaust. They do so through nostalgic yearning for distant or vanished times and communities, offering a sublimation or transference of Holocaust pain into new contexts.

All of these musicals, in both categories, emerge from a postmemory context — a world where those who did not live through the events of the Shoah nonetheless return to the events, directly or indirectly, as an inexorable part of their consciousness. Despite these two separate categories, the close readings of musicals pursued here will follow a chronological structure, as the evolution of American attitudes towards the events of the Holocaust is crucial to the manner in which these musicals approach the tragedy.

Musical Theatre

There has been distinct absence of scholarly response, in both Holocaust studies and theatre theory and criticism, to popular musical theatre and its often-pioneering treatment of the themes raised by the Nazi era. Much of this absence, I would argue, is due to an unspoken cultural elitism against musical theatre, an elitism somewhat conveniently tied to aesthetic and moral concerns. Robert Skloot displays a typical attitude when he asks, "Will the experience [of the Holocaust] be cheapened, trivialized, or exploited in the treatment it is given?" (*Four Plays* 11). For Skloot, and others, this understandable concern leads to an absence of consideration of representations of the Nazi era that reached the greatest amount of people. In addition to these concerns, musicals have fallen "between the cracks" of scholarship. Scholars such as Peter Novick, Lawrence Langer, Berel Lang and Helene Flanzbaum, who write about the "Americanization of the Holocaust," make relatively little mention of theatre, and no mention whatsoever of musical theatre. Even scholars who specifically take as their subject theatre in reaction to the Holocaust, including Edward Isser, Vivian Patraka and Skloot, do not refer to musicals even glancingly. In addition, the relatively new scholarly field devoted to musical theatre also makes only passing remarks concerning the Nazi subject matter of, or Holocaust echoes within, the musicals I will analyze.

This deficiency must be redressed. We must put aside understandable, but limiting, moral and aesthetic concerns, at least for the moment, in order to explore what these musical representations can reveal to us. As popular art, and indeed one of the few truly American art forms, musical theatre is in the unique position to reflect our often-unexamined cultural values and mores. As Russel Nye states:

> Popular art confirms the experience of the majority, in contrast to elite art, which tends to explore the new. For this reason, popular art has been an unusually sensitive and accurate reflector of the attitudes and concerns of the society for which it is produced [...] Historians have tended to neglect it as a means of access to an era's — and a society's — values and ideas [10].

How much can the neglected popular musical form tell us about our American attitudes towards Nazism and the Shoah? How many millions more people have seen *The Sound of Music* than some of the more dense, solemn and "elite" Holocaust plays? In the 1950s, when most artists were still silent on the subject of the Holocaust, popular theatre approached the taboo. Three years after the Broadway production of *The Diary of Anne Frank* in 1956 that helped begin the transition of American attitudes towards the Holocaust, *The Sound of Music* included a young leading man transformed into a Nazi in uniform. Perhaps the lack of scholarly attention to the musical format, considered inconsequential, allowed this subversively potent image to appear unremarked. Musicals present an entirely new artistic format for representations or more distant reflections of the Nazi era and the Holocaust, and one that, despite, or perhaps because of, its popularity with audiences, has managed in a large part to pass under the radar. This same acceptance that causes its dismissal in scholarly circles also creates a vast impact previously unacknowledged. Musical theatre combines various styles of Holocaust representation just as the format of the musical itself is a mix of disparate parts coalescing into a unified whole. The focus of this project therefore examines those widely accepted or disseminated Broadway musicals which both directly address the Nazi era, as well as those which do so through nostalgic echoes, metaphors and sublimations.

Case Studies

Chapter I traces the history of dramatic response to the Holocaust. Although European and Israeli reactions are briefly mentioned, I focus on American theatrical projects, in the context of their changing views of the Nazi era. The second half of the chapter places the musical case studies into two categories, "direct and indirect," by examining their commonalities and dissimilarities. I set up the terms with which we'll examine these categories, including the contradictory trends of grim realism and comedy, and nostalgic responses in view of fears of disappearing community.

Chapter II examines *The Sound of Music* (1959) as the first musical with staged Nazis or Nazi subject matter. The early time period in which it was produced, in addition to the clash of this serious material with a light, sweet Rodgers and Hammerstein classic starring nuns and children, makes this musical particularly fascinating to explore. The Von Trapp family at the center of the musical is conspicuously non–Jewish, although their dramatizers, Richard Rodgers and Oscar Hammerstein, were. No presence of Judaism exists in the piece, exemplifying the attempt at "Americanization" typical of this early approach. When we place the original production of *The Sound of Music* next to its film version and 1998 Broadway revival, we can trace an increasing grim realism, an interest in the imagery and regalia of Nazism and a growing use of swastikas and staged Nazi characters. Although *The Sound of Music* was not originally intended or read in any way as Holocaust drama, the modern associations of Nazism with the Holocaust cause the text to resonate differently today.

Chapter III examines *Milk and Honey* (1961), music and lyrics by Jerry Herman and book by Don Appell. Taking place in Israel, the show celebrates Zionism and American Jewish pride in that state, relatively new when the musical premiered. The musical on the surface seems to actively fight nostalgia, instead glorifying and exoticizing the present and future of an exciting new land. However, on closer examination several sources of nostalgia circulate in *Milk and Honey*. A straightforward "reflective" nostalgia focused outside the text, on *Milk and Honey*'s diminutive leading actress, Molly Picon, star of the Yiddish stage. This reflective nostalgia masked a darker disavowal process: restorative nostalgia for Israel in the face of the Holocaust. The musical offers the restoration of the biblical conditions of ancient Israel, sublimating the pain of modern loss.

In Chapter IV, we explore *Fiddler on the Roof* (1964) — book by Joseph Stein, music and lyrics by Jerry Bock and Sheldon Harnick, directed and choreographed by Jerome Robbins — as the quintessential "Jewish musical." At the same time, critics and audiences consistently refer to the musical as "universal," and the resulting tensions must be interrogated. I will examine the sublimated confrontations with the Holocaust in the work, through the central concern of memory and nostalgia that circulates within and around the show. *Fiddler* celebrates a way of life and a culture that has gone forever. The conflicted urge towards a "happy ending" seemingly required by the musical form confronts the knowledge that many of these characters themselves, as well as their descendants, would be victims of genocide within a generation. The show celebrates, in all their particularity, the "Traditions" and cultural practices of Jewish shtetl life in Eastern Europe at the turn of the century, and uses both ritual and its musical world to create a work of theatre in which memory functions as a counterstrategy to the pain of Holocaust.

Cabaret, discussed in Chapter V, was revolutionary for the Broadway musical stage in its form as well as content. Opened on Broadway in 1966, *Cabaret*'s representation of encroaching Nazism in the late Weimar Republic is consistent with the American decade in which it was produced. With the 1960s as a pivotal time of change, *Cabaret* emerged from this newly aware and yet still conflicted mindset. The musical both directly approaches the existential void of a postmemory generation by refusing a typical "happy ending," while still embracing older comic types and genres. The chapter addresses the question of how this precarious balance between comedy and tragedy affects the ultimate message of the musical. Additionally, the changing emphases and increasing grim realism of *Cabaret* productions are examined. Incarnations of the musical have shifted with the times, proving that *Cabaret* has radical potential, even fifty years after it was written.

In 1970, *Fiddler on the Roof*'s authors Bock and Harnick turned to a new project: *The Rothschilds*, story of the growth of the famous and wealthy Jewish European banking family. In Chapter VI we consider how *The Rothschilds* takes a much harsher and more direct look at the implications of the Shoah, in line with the era from which it emerged. By the 1970s "musical comedy" was becoming scarce and darker musicals were beginning to be in vogue. The 1970s were also a time of budding interest in the history and implications of the Holocaust. At times *The Rothschilds'* references to history were quite

explicit. Enough so in fact, that a critic, Walter Kerr, for the first time, acknowledged the Holocaust in a published response to one of these musicals. While
The Rothschilds ostensibly celebrates the great successes of the Rothschild family, both materially and socially, the show also traffics in Jewish stereotypes:
the title characters succeed through their excellence in banking, in managing
the money of Christian European leaders, and getting their hands dirty in
areas Christians were not allowed. While Mayer and his sons fight injustice,
they do so through methods that could be accused of being motivated by personal greed. The show presents a success story, and in theory an optimistic
one, but the very methods that insure the Rothschilds' success in 1818 not
only incur anti–Semitism in their own time, but were used as rationale for
genocide little over one hundred years later. In a postmemory generation,
oppression against Jews cannot help but be linked to the Holocaust, the single
most horrific anti–Semitic example in history.

Chapter VII examines two musicals, *Rags* and *Ragtime*, which both take
the same, very popular subject: life for the recent Jewish immigrant on the
lower east side of New York City at the turn of the century. *Rags*, book by
Joseph Stein, music by Charles Strouse and lyrics by Stephen Schwartz, only
lasted four performances on Broadway. The musical covers the spectrum of
Jewish immigrant types that existed in this period. Based on the 1974 novel
by E.L. Doctorow, the musical version of *Ragtime* (score by Lynn Ahrens and
Steven Flaherty, book by Terrence McNally) opened on Broadway in 1998.
In one of its three intertwining stories, Tateh (Yiddish for father), comes to
America with his daughter to make a new life, and finally finds the American
dream, inventing "moving books" and becoming a film director. Both *Rags*
and *Ragtime* share themes of nostalgic interest in the Jewish labor movement,
and attempt to unpack the mythic outlines of the American Dream and its
realities or falsities for Jewish immigrants. In doing so, both musicals employ
Holocaust echoes. A double layer of nostalgia, both of the immigrant for
home, and the audience for the immigrant community, can be read in terms
of Svetlana Boym's "mourning of displacement." She describes a nostalgic
desire to return home, complicated by the knowledge that "home" has forever
disappeared. The Holocaust assured that these immigrants could never go
home again. As with *Fiddler on the Roof* these works offer America as a solution
or an alternative history. The Jewish immigrant serves as a metaphor or sublimation in these musicals, offering an alternative happy ending or escape
from the Holocaust narrative.

In *The Producers*, discussed in Chapter VIII, Mel Brooks uses humor
as a weapon against Hitler. By the time the musical appeared on Broadway,
victory over the evils of Nazism has been so ingrained that we may now laugh
at all the trappings of a defeated regime. *The Producers* uses comedy to exorcize

the evil of Hitler, thereby allowing the existence of nostalgia. The musical traffics in nostalgia for the musical's golden age, while simultaneously risking offense to multiple ethnic or social groups. The chapter examines the transgressive clash of Holocaust humor, examining this popular culture piece in context of Holocaust theory and criticism which denies the possibility of laughter. The complexities created through this collision of styles are interesting to examine, particularly Brooks' equation of gay sexuality with fascism.

Finally, in my conclusion I raise moral and aesthetic questions that have emerged in reaction to the intersection of Holocaust art and popular culture, and look towards the future of musical theatre's examination of this topic. By examining the various modes of representation available to the musical theatre, we can begin the process of understanding American culture's past response to this defining event, and how this response continues to evolve. These are questions that must be addressed. Perhaps the musical, that most liminal and effervescent of forms, can contribute something valuable to the national discourse.

CHAPTER I

History and Context

Since 1945, when World War II ended and the horrifying facts of the Holocaust began to be disseminated throughout the world, critics and artists have debated and tested the "limits of representation." Can we, or in fact, should we, represent the Holocaust at all? If so, in what artistic terms can we approach this era? American theatrical culture has had its own particular response to these questions, intimately connected to the changing emotional response of Americans towards the events of the Nazi era. The tone of theatre in reaction to the Holocaust varies according to the period in which it was written. In order to analyze various artistic responses to Nazism, direct or indirect, we must first sketch a brief portrait of the changing nature of America's reaction to the events of the Nazi era, including the extermination of European Jewry.

Although America fought in World War II and took part in the liberation of the concentration camps, the nation's role in the Holocaust, as an event separate from the rest of the war, was primarily a bystander nation. Whatever the extent of its wartime knowledge of the massacre that was occurring, an issue which remains highly debated and politically sensitive, the United States government took little to no action on the Holocaust, instead focusing on other concerns. Shortly after the war, aims to redress Nazi crimes against the Jews were brushed aside in favor of new political concerns. Although American Jews would be expected to have a strong reaction to learning of the extermination of their brethren, Jews were, and remain, less than 3% of the American population. When, why, and how did the rest of America come to embrace the Holocaust as an American tragedy? How did we as a nation go from our far from spotless wartime record — suppressed information about the tragedies as they occurred, failure to bomb Auschwitz, restricted immigration for Jews fleeing Germany before the war and for Holocaust survivors — to a cultural embrace so pervasive that in the 1990s the American National Holocaust Memorial and Museum opened on the Washington D.C. Mall amongst the other American cultural monoliths? This fascinating and highly complex shift is partially due to, and certainly reflected by, popular culture.

American attitudes towards Germans and its Nazi leadership varied widely from Hitler's rise to power in 1933 until his suicide in 1945. Before the war, the more liberal segment of the population, including many play-wrights, warned that the Nazi regime was murderous and highly dangerous. The rest of the population had less interest in the matter, but once the United States entered World War II, public sentiment shifted strongly to patriotism and an anti-enemy mentality. Peter Novick, author of *The Holocaust in American Life*, argues convincingly however, that during the war Hitler's crimes against the Jews were not seen as unique or defining. Instead, they were one subset of his extensive crimes against humanity. Jews were not spoken of as being Germany's prime victims; instead various religious or political dissenters and POWs were perceived as the defining prisoners of concentration camps. In addition, Germany was not seen as the chief enemy of the war; the Japanese who had attacked America at Pearl Harbor took on that role. This makes the response of this era's playwrights all the more complex. In this period there were two separate dramatic genres addressing Nazi subject matter, differentiated by the extent of the projects' interest in the plight of the Jews.

Edward Isser, in his *Stages of Annihilation* (1997), names the first genre of plays focusing on the then current Nazi era, antifascist. This category includes popular plays, which during the war addressed Nazism, but from an uninformed perspective regarding the horrific events which were taking place. These projects focus on the adventurous, mysterious and even romantic side of fighting an "evil" enemy, albeit one whose evil was not fully understood. Many of America's most popular playwrights wrote antifascist plays, including Elmer Rice, Sinclair Lewis, S.N. Behrman, Clifford Odets, Robert Sherwood and even George S. Kaufman and Moss Hart. The more famous works include Claire Booth Luce's *Margin for Error* (1939). Maxwell Anderson's *Candle in the Wind* (1941), and Lillian Hellman's *Watch on the Rhine* (1941).

Despite the general American ignorance in this era of the extent of Nazi crimes, one segment of the population was aware of the horrific possibilities and put this awareness into artistic form in order to reach the public as effectively as possible. They chose as their format a fascinating subset of American dramatic genres, the pageant. American Jews staged four massive pageants during and just after the war, first to point attention towards the plight of European Jews, and directly after the war to campaign for the creation of the state of Israel. These pageants, including *The Romance of a People* (1933), *The Eternal Road* (1937) and *We Will Never Die* (1942), were spectacles including large casts, music and scenic effects, and were highly effective agit-prop pieces and fund-raisers. *A Flag Is Born* (1946) even took as its subject three Holocaust survivors, including Tevya and his wife (based on Sholem Aleichem's Tevye, as was the musically famous Tevye, in Bock and Harnick's *Fiddler on the Roof*). Given the post war debate concerning the extent to which American Jews kept silent about the Holocaust, these pageants are a fascinating example of the Jewish community's engagement with fighting Nazi crimes and American indifference. It is important to note, however, that these pageants were produced and supported by the more radical Zionist "Emergency Committee to Save the Jewish People of Europe," founded by Peter Bergson. This movement was not supported by mainstream American Jewish organizations worried about American anti–Semitism, and not eager to "rock the boat." This tendency became even more pronounced in post-war America.

Despite this initial dramatic activity, after the immediate post-war period American culture entered a period of silence in regard to the Holocaust. This silence has been attributed to various factors. Americans wanted to move on; almost immediately after their victory shifting their priorities to the Cold War. By necessity, the Soviet Union took over the role of "Enemy Number One" from Germany. The Nuremberg Trials became politically unpopular as mobilization for the Cold War, with Germany as first line of defense against communism, began. The segment of the American population that might have been expected to keep the matter alive, American Jews, now including the Holocaust survivors who had managed to make it to the United States, were busy with the new integrationist possibilities open to them and were not necessarily eager to stir up the specter of anti–Semitism. Additionally, talk of the Holocaust distracted from the priority of Zionism. In the emerging Cold War atmosphere, Jews were also eager to avoid the stereotypical association of their people with communism. By "dwelling" on the crimes of Germany, Jews were associated with the new American enemy, the Soviets. Even the presence of Holocaust survivors did not increase interest in the events of the Holocaust. Survivors were encouraged to forget, to "move on." Most tended to keep their memories or memorializing to themselves; America did not want to hear. American silence also held guilty overtones, as information, including the horrific images of liberated concentration camps, was released and Americans became aware of the extent of the crimes their country failed to halt. Additionally, the 1950s projected an overall positive image, at least on the surface. The country's prevailing mood and view of humanity did not admit tales of intense human cruelty and victimization.

And yet, in these same years, many Jewish Americans began the process of embracing their ethnicity. A "Jewish Renaissance" in literature began in the 1950s and 60s. The push to the suburbs helped to create a new, more secure and positivist outlook. And the construction of over six hundred new synagogues and temples in the late 1940s and 50s, Goren points out, "reflected their preeminent place in the suburban landscape as the accepted presence of a Jewish community" (295). Landmarks of political and cultural acceptance abounded in the late 1950s and 60s, and other popular culture forms, such as film and television, reflected the changes. Scholars point to *The Ten Commandments* in 1956, as a "Jewish" film (due to its Old Testament subject matter) and therefore groundbreaking. It grossed eighty million dollars, and was nominated for seven Oscars including Best Picture. Leon Uris' *Exodus*, about the birth of Israel, hit the best-seller list in 1958. The film, starring Paul Newman, was also popular two years later. A popular play, *The Tenth Man* by Paddy Chayefsky, set in a synagogue in Mineola, Long Island, opened on Broadway at the end of the decade, in 1959, and ran for six hundred twenty three performances.

In this same period, a shift in American attitudes towards the Holocaust took place. Among the first events contributing to that shift were the various incarnations of *The Diary of Anne Frank*. The English translation of *The Diary of a Young Girl*, published in 1952, created an emotional connection for Americans who had seen themselves as completely distant from events involving European Jews. Goodrich and Hackett's 1956 stage adaptation of the diary took the lead on post-war Holocaust drama, followed by the 1959 film version that continued the dissemination of the story. The diary stops short of the horrific violence occurring to the Jews, specifically to Anne and her family. The various incarnations of Anne's story in America in this period all addressed the universality of her experience rather than the specificity of her identity as a Jewish victim of the Nazis. In fact, in a large part the stage adaptation "de-Judaized" Anne and her family. In addition to a de-emphasizing of ethnic identity, and despite the still very wrenching and emotional impact Goodrich and Hackett's 1956 play version had on audiences, its method of presentation was softened a great deal. Both the play and subsequent movie version in 1959 appealed to American hopefulness by ending with Anne's statement, "In spite of all, I still believe men are good" (Goodrich and Hackett, 174).

Certainly in this early era artistic reactions did not address the harsher realities of the implications of the Holocaust on human nature. While the various *Anne Frank* incarnations were popular, the few other books addressing Holocaust issues were more or less ignored, school textbooks touched on the subject lightly, if at all, and mention in newspapers was rare. Therefore, although *The Diary of Anne Frank* can be identified as one of the first events to begin shifting American attitudes towards the Holocaust, in many ways the play adaptation of *Anne Frank* is more representative of the early period of silence, rather than reflecting interest in the issue. The tone and thematic concerns of this early staged *Anne Frank* serves to encapsulate American visions (or avoidance) of the Holocaust in the 1950s, and when compared to the incarnations of this same project in the late 1990s, clearly describes the shift of values and American attitudes towards the Shoah.

Attitudes continued to shift in the late 1950s and 60s, a change attributed to factors including Vietnam, the civil rights movement, Israel's Six-Day War, television and filmic representations of the Holocaust, and the pivotal Adolf Eichmann trial. These events, together with a new American concern with increasing anti–Semitism, helped to make awareness of the Holocaust more central. Smaller cultural markers occurred; first William L. Shirer's best selling non-fiction work, *The Rise and Fall of the Third Reich* (1960), which nevertheless devoted only three percent of the lengthy work to the Holocaust. Renewed anti–Semitism in Germany and in America, with the "American Nazi Party" led by George Lincoln Rockwell in the late 50s and early 60s, also gained attention. But the signal event most scholars point to was the capture of Adolf Eichmann by Israeli agents in Argentina, and his subsequent trial. Indeed, according to Peter Novick, the use of the term Holocaust, "first became firmly attached to the murder of European Jewry as a result of the trial" (Novick 133). The method of Eichmann's capture from Argentina by the Israeli Mossad incurred public debate, and the subsequent playing out of the trial, with its detailed description of the horrors of the Holocaust, occurred in full view of a fascinated world public. Hannah Arendt's series of articles about the trial in *The New Yorker*, later published as the book *Eichmann in Jerusalem: A Report on the Banality of Evil* (1963), also contributed to the furor surrounding the trial. Her thesis, centered on the very ordinary nature of institutionalized evil, confronted an America perhaps not quite ready for the bleak view of human nature it implied. Finally the very sensationalism of the Eichmann story, including his final evasion of the death sentence by committing suicide, helped to put the Holocaust on the cultural map.

Subsequent events in Israel also had a vast impact on American attitudes. In 1967, the Six-Day War contributed to the changing understanding of the Holocaust. Jewish concern with what looked like the imminent end of the State at the hands of its Arab neighbors, and then exultation with the dramatic Israeli victory, allowed a new attitude towards Jewish victimization. Novick argues that the war brought Jewish identity full circle, that the brave and triumphant Israeli Jew offered a "salvation myth" when combined with the events of the Holocaust. The longer and bloodier Yom Kippur War in 1973 complicated this myth. Israel was again in much peril, but this time enjoyed less support from the world, particularly America. American Jews read this declining assistance as a frightening parallel to the situation of German and Eastern European Jews in the Hitler era. Israel was no longer a safe haven for survivors.

These events, together with a new concern with increasing anti–Semitism, helped to make concern with the Holocaust more central in this period.

In 1964 (the same year *Fiddler on the Roof* opened on Broadway), a non–American play nevertheless presented an important event in the merging of American political and cultural concern. Rolf Hochhuth's German play *The Deputy*, a scathing portrait of Pope Pius XII and his inaction in the Holocaust, came to Broadway under a firestorm of controversy. In Europe the play had produced violent confrontations, and in America the Jewish community's official organizations were pressed to speak out against the production. Critically, the play was not a success, the Broadway production ran for 167 performances and plans for a national tour were cancelled, but the controversy once again underlines the potential for theatre to impact larger cultural ideas.

Other theatrical projects in this period demonstrate the changing attitudes towards the Holocaust. They include Millard Lampell's *The Wall* (1960), based on the John Hersey novel, and Arthur Miller's *Incident at Vichy* (1964). *The Wall* takes place in the Warsaw ghetto, and although the truth of the ghetto was that 300,000 Jews were deported and killed at Treblinka, Lampell chooses to emphasize the positive, those who stood and fought the Nazis. *The Wall*'s attempt at a heroic and positive telling of a Holocaust story places it in temperament closer to early works such as *The Diary of Anne Frank*, than works which were to come. Arthur Miller's *Incident at Vichy* can also be positioned closer to the early category of constrained representations, although it displays a level of moral ambiguity missing in *The Diary of Anne Frank*. Miller's play takes place in 1942 in Vichy France, and deals with a group of prisoners waiting to be sent to a death camp, in contrast to a mistakenly detained non–Jewish character. Like *Anne Frank*, Miller avoids direct representations of Nazi crimes. Critics have chastised Miller for perpetuating the stereotype of the helpless, coward Jew; for blaming the victim, and for factual inaccuracy. The emotion and debate surrounding both Miller and Lampell's plays and their conflicted moral stance are consistent with the 1960s when they were written, when attitudes towards the Holocaust were still in flux.

By the 1980s and '90s, the number of Holocaust and Nazi themed dramas had veritably exploded. In the intervening years since the 1950s cultural forces had shifted. Although American Jews had wanted to avoid the victim status incurred by the Holocaust, victimization was becoming arguably ever more of a status symbol in America. Starting with the civil rights movement, changing ideas about ethnicity and immigration meant that the melting pot mentality of America was shifting. The value of ethnicity was increasing, and Jews felt more freedom to speak of what made them unique, which included, unfortunately, and ever increasingly, the Holocaust. This fact is witnessed by the debate over the victims of the Holocaust. Six million Jewish victims are more or less agreed on as a number, but in the 1970s, eleven million, a number including Hitler's non–Jewish victims, was often mentioned, The fight over who would be memorialized as victims, particularly in the American Holocaust museum, emphasizes that many groups now wanted to be acknowledged for their part of the tragedy, while some Jews want the centrality of their suffering to be acknowledged.

In this saturated and tense time examples of popular art approaching the Holocaust are myriad. Film proliferated: *Schindler's List* (1993), *Life Is Beautiful* (1998) *The Grey Zone* (2002) and *The Pianist* (2002) *The Boy in the Striped Pajamas* (2008), *Good* (2008), *Defiance* (2008), and *Sarah's Key* (2011) are just the most obvious and recent examples of a thriving film genre. Television has also embraced the subject matter. Projects include Arthur Miller's *Playing for Time* (1980), *Escape from Sobibor* (1987), *War and Remembrance* (1988), and more recently *Uprising* (2001), *Conspiracy* (2001), and an updated *Anne Frank* (2001) which extended Anne's story through her death at Auschwitz. Most scholars, including Mintz, credit a nine-day mini-series produced for NBC (*The Holocaust* in 1978), as a defining moment in America's cultural appropriation of the events of the Shoah. Although many critics argue that the subject matter was denigrated by its melodramatic miniseries structure, the vast audience for the show — over one hundred million — made a large number of Americans vastly more aware of the facts, and indeed the existence, of the Holocaust. Not coincidentally, in the same year, President Jimmy Carter announced a commission to explore the creation of an American Holocaust memorial.

Later events kept the Holocaust in the news and in the media. In 1985, President Reagan visited the Bitburg cemetery in West Germany, and caused a controversy over his statement, "German soldiers buried in the Bitburg cemetery were victims of the Nazis just as surely as the victims in the concentration camps" (quoted in Novick 227). A year later the debate over the Austrian president Kurt Waldheim's Nazi past was in the news. The Justice Department's practice since the late 1970s of investigating and deporting American immigrants with Nazi pasts also has been in the news over the years. Because Steven Spielberg's *Schindler's List* and the American Holocaust Museum both opened at the same time, 1993 was termed the "year of the Holocaust." Most recently debates over Swiss banks and their horded Nazi gold has gained attention. This continued presence and changing attitudes in the media have been reflected on stage.

Literally hundreds of modern dramatic projects address the Holocaust and the Nazi era. These works can be fairly easily categorized by which aspect of the trauma they choose to illuminate. A majority of these works do not directly address or portray Nazi killings. Barbara Lebow's *A Shayna Maidel* (1984), Donald Margulies' *The Model Apartment* (1988), Jon Robin Baitz's *The Substance of Fire* (1991), Cynthia Ozick's *Blue Light (The Shawl)* (1994), and Jon Maran's *Old Wicked Songs* (1996) all address issues of Holocaust survivors. This category seems to be the most popular for American authors. Several plays choose ghetto life or ghetto uprisings as their subject matter, including Harold and Edith Lieberman's *Throne of Straw* (1973). Projects which deal with concentration camps are less frequent, and include Martin Sherman's *Bent* (1979), which addresses Hitler's homosexual victims, and Tim Blake Nelson's *The Grey Zone* (1996) which focuses on the life of a Sonderkommando, a Jewish concentration camp inmate forced to help the Nazis with the killing process of his brethren in order to remain alive. Despite these last few exceptions, most commercial modern American stage works do not address the Holocaust directly but rather work on the margins of the subject, by depicting survivors, ghetto life, the Nuremberg Trials — the film *Judgment at Nuremberg* was re-conceived as a Broadway production in 2001— and even Americans' reaction to the news of the Holocaust, such as Arthur Miller's *Broken Glass* (1994).

In fact, many plays, movies or television shows that share the more distant topics of some of the test case musicals here — early immigrant America, shtetl life, Israel, Jews in old Europe — could also be explored for Holocaust echoes and metaphors. As a full study of these projects lies outside the scope of this work, here we can merely point out the myriad Jewish themed works that address those periods, and that are likely to share a postmemory context with these musicals. In only the beginnings of such a list we can point out, in literature, numerous works from authors such as Roth, Malamud, or Ozick; in film, movies such as *Yentl* (1983), *Crossing Delancey* (1988), *Avalon* (1990), and *A Serious Man* (2009); in spoken word drama, Neil Simon's *Brighton Beach Memoirs* (1983), Tony Kushner's *Angels in America* (1993), and William Gibson's *Golda's Balcony* (2003); and in opera *Brundibar* (2003), newly adapted by Kushner and Maurice Sendak (this last was originally performed at Theresienstadt). Other musicals not addressed here could also be explored for these echoes, including Jason Robert Brown's *Parade* (1998), and Jeanine Tesori and Kushner's *Caroline or Change* (2004).

Holocaust Aesthetics

The musicals addressed in this book touch on the massacre of the Jews of Europe only glancingly, if at all. They instead focus on either the encroaching threat of Nazism, in the case of *The Sound of Music* and *Cabaret*, pure satire of Hitler and his regime in *The Producers*, or much more indirect or fleeting references, metaphors or substitutions, in *Milk and Honey, Fiddler on the Roof, Rothschilds, Rags* and *Ragtime*. Edward Isser states, "Holocaust drama is composed of works that represent or *allude to* the racial policies of the Nazis" (20) [emphasis mine]. Although the musicals I will examine do not directly represent the world of the Nazi extermination camps, they nevertheless exist on the fringes of the Holocaust dramatic genre. For even in projects most distant from the concentration camps themselves, I would argue that, today, the connection can still be made to the death of six million Jews at the hands of the Nazis.

The Holocaust has become so central a concern to American identity, and so many representations have appeared which link Nazi symbols or representations with the crime that now defines them, I would argue portrayals of the Nazi era cannot now exist without somehow evoking the Holocaust. Gilman contends most Americans cannot look at a swastika without immediately summoning to mind images from the death camps. As he observes, "The murder of the Jews moved from being one aspect of the crimes of the Nazis to being their central, defining aspect over half a century. Over the past decade or so, it has evolved from a specific, historical moment to the metaphor for horror itself" (279).

The shift in representations in the late '50s and '60s demonstrates that the perception of the Nazi era was changing, and that the Holocaust was attaining a more central role. As we have seen, by the '90s, with Holocaust education practically universal in public schools, with a museum in Washington D.C. dedicated to the Shoah, and with pervasive popular culture representations of the Holocaust, the death of the six million is now the defining event of the Nazi era. After various social and cultural events connected Nazi imagery with genocide in every American mind, after America had taken upon itself identification with the Holocaust as "an American tragedy," even a dramatic project most seemingly distant from the actual killing and horror of the Shoah could not escape from overtones of the genocide. This also means that projects that do not even take place in the era can evoke memories, associations and echoes of the Holocaust. The event was so large, so overwhelming, that some artists chose, either consciously or not, to respond to it through more distant metaphors, such as shtetl Jews, earlier European anti–Semitism, Israel as a refuge, or the immigrant survivor in America.

Can we approach the horrors of mass genocide through an artistic lens, or will art by its very nature diminish the reality of the unspeakable crimes perpetrated by the Nazis? Some argue that certain crimes and tragedies, like the Holocaust, are too tremendous to approach with anything but the most clinical or factual lenses. Nonetheless popular theatre has in many ways ignored the issues of artistic representation raised by scholars. As Peter Novick argues, the academic debate offers, "the question of whether all of this writing has influenced either the producers or consumers of mass media representations of the Holocaust. Probably not much" (212). The aesthetic question of whether the Holocaust *can* be represented is beside the point for projects that *are* representing events surrounding the Holocaust. Because these popular works are not hampered by scholarly debate, they are able to reflect, as much as possible, "real" American attitudes towards the Holocaust and how these attitudes have changed.

All of the projects examined here, in both categories, share a "postmemory" mindset. The emerging scholarly discipline of "History of Memory," emerged from poststructuralism's distrust of pinning down the "reality" of history. Postmemory — a Holocaust studies term — comes out of that new concern with the functions and modes of memory. The Holocaust takes a central place in the new concern with memory. Terrence Des Pres offers, "We live in the unrest of aftermath, and we inherit the feeling that something has been taken that cannot be restored [...]. The self's sense of itself is different now, and what has made the difference [...] is simply knowing that the Holocaust occurred" (17). The postmemory generation, particularly children of survivors, are forever influenced by Holocaust imagery and narratives and although they did not live through the events, will "remember" them nonetheless. Alan Finkielkraut introduced the term "imaginary Jews" to refer to the generation that identifies itself with the Holocaust without having gone through that event, calling the generation, "armchair Jews, since, after the Catastrophe, Judaism cannot offer them any content but suffering, and they themselves do not suffer" (15). Musical theatre offers one unexamined but highly potent way to engage with this loss for a postmemory generation.

Direct Musicals

Three of the eight musical we examine in this work, *The Sound of Music*, *Cabaret* and *The Producers*, take some element of the actual Nazi era as their subjects. These popular works demonstrate two trends, towards grim realism and towards comedy. These trends can be put into the perspective of the developments scholar George Mosse noted in post–World War I Europeans. In reaction to the horrors of that bloody war Mosse defined two cultural trends, both a process of sanctification, and of trivialization. These trends are united in their source, collective trauma, but branch out in their response to that source. These two reactions are very apparent in American cultural reactions to the Holocaust, as seen in popular art forms such as TV, film and particularly theatre.

GRIM REALISM

Popular Broadway productions have shown a very clear trend towards a grimmer realism in their Nazi portrayals. This development will be examined in the context of the succeeding productions (and briefly, film versions) of *The Sound of Music, Cabaret* and *The Producers*. A new production of *The Diary of Anne Frank* serves as a test case to demonstrate how attitudes changed. Revived on Broadway in 1998, director Wendy Kesselman was hired to "newly adapt" Goodrich and Hackett's text in order to match modern sensibilities to the Holocaust. The changes Kesselman made are telling. She re-emphasizes Anne's Judaism, mostly overlooked in the original version. More importantly, this much darker and tougher version ends with Otto Frank telling the traumatic details of Anne's final sighting in the Bergen-Belsen, where she died, days before being liberated. This more harrowing approach typifies one way American attitudes have shifted towards the Holocaust and how dramatic portrayals have shifted with them. Americans now appear ready for more complete and increasingly difficult information, including the horrific details of Nazi crimes. Instead of the older attitudes in the 1950s and 60s of finding some kind of "happy ending" or at least an underlying positive worldview such as "I still believe people are good at heart," the modern age seems less convinced that any positive portrayal is possible. In fact, many view the hope for happy endings, at least as regards the Holocaust, as illusion. The musicals examined in this category, through their production histories, demonstrate this need to confront the darker sides of the material.

THE COMIC REACTION

Robert Corrigan states, "Thus while tragedy is a celebration of man's capacity to aspire and suffer, comedy celebrates his capacity to endure" (3). But how does this ability to endure apply to the Holocaust, which, perhaps more than any one single event in the history of humankind gives the lie to the idea of man's enduring spirit? Given the difficulties in representing the Holocaust even in the most serious of ways, comedy must be, by its definition, an extremely complicated and risky method of approaching the Nazi era. Moral concerns raised by comic representations will be addressed in the conclusion. However the best comedy can be quite serious at heart and much of the comic treatment of Nazis in the musicals I will address serves a far more weighty purpose than might initially seem evident. Most of the musicals in this study do not attempt to approach the events of the Holocaust through a comic lens. Only *The Producers* necessitates a full consideration of the second trend towards comedy, and we will investigate this trend in detail in that chapter. However, with the musical theatre genre often still understood as "musical comedy" we must investigate the clashes of tone that occur when a musical project simultaneously resonates with the Holocaust while classified as a popular comic theatre genre.

Indirect Musicals

Our second category of musicals takes place even more distantly from the events of the Holocaust. *Milk and Honey* takes place in Israel in 1959, *Fiddler on the Roof* in the Russian shtetl of 1905, *The Rothschilds* in Napoleonic Europe and *Rags* and *Ragtime* in America at the turn of the 20th century. Why examine these works in a study of cultural responses to the Holocaust? Despite their chronological or spatial distance, all of these musicals resonate deeply with the events of the Nazi era and Holocaust. Though they each do so in their own unique way, they are unified by the use of nostalgia, as a direct metaphor or a distancing method.

Nostalgia

Through the process of nostalgic memory, the pain or difficulties associated with the original subject are erased. Nostalgia therefore acts as a powerful force in engaging with the problems of a postmemory generation in the projects I will examine. Nostalgia emerges, according to scholar Fred Davis, from an attempt to smooth over radical life changes, either individually or as a community. He states:

> Just as the phasing of the life cycle periodically entails status transitions that in their perceived discontinuity and attendant anxiety evoke nostalgic reactions from individuals, so do untoward major historic events and abrupt social changes pose a similar threat and evoke a similar response from people in the aggregate [102].

The events of the Holocaust, combined with fears of the reducing American Jewish population, led to fears of disappearing community. Nostalgia, with its ability to smooth over identity threats, helped to assuage the fear.

The term nostalgia first appeared in 1678, invented by Swiss physician Johannes Hofer. Its roots are Greek (*nostos* meaning homeland, and *algos* meaning pain/longing). Nostalgia began as a medical diagnosis, particular to Swiss soldiers at the front who were literally sick with homesickness. It has expanded into much more. Various scholars parse the definition for their own purposes. Ben Furnish, in a study of nostalgia in Jewish film and theatre, splits nostalgia into three subcategories, nostalgia for place or "home," nostalgia for time (lost youth) and nostalgia for relationships and family. We find each of these categories in the musicals examined. Svetlana Boym, in *The Future of Nostalgia* (2001), separates nostalgia into two discrete categories, first "restorative," which, as the name implies, looks to restore the past longed for, thereby denying itself as nostalgia per se, and "reflective," self-aware nostalgia which does not hope for restoration. Boym's categorizations will also shed light on musical theatre's use of nostalgia.

Nostalgia's dictionary definition, "a wistful or excessively sentimental yearning for return to or of some past period or irrecoverable condition" (http://www.m_w.com) offers several key terms: *wistful* and *excessively sentimental*. Nostalgia adds a cleansing sheen to problematic pasts, often inducing a sentimental or wistful urge to falsely remember them. Nostalgia clearly involves a yearning for the past, but that past does not have to be always personally experienced, nor accurate. Furnish argues, "Jewish-American artists increasingly created works that inspired and relied on nostalgic evocations of subjects that most of their audience members had never know in any literal way" (22). Furnish's point applies particularly well to Jewish musical theatre, where communal memory, or more removed nostalgia strongly circulates. Although distant or removed memory sources might seem to negate the current relevance of nostalgic representations, Fred Davis disagrees. In his *Yearning for Yesterday: A Sociology of Nostalgia* (1979), Davis examines the triggers for nostalgia, pointing out that causes of nostalgia always operate from the present, despite their concern with the past. He also argues, "Mass collective nostalgia is most likely to occur after times of severe cultural discontinuity" (102). The Holocaust operates as a central cause of this severe discontinuity in our case, and we will examine the mass nostalgia that occurs in the Jewish community as a result of the complex and intersecting trends of Holocaust "postmemory" and Jewish secularization.

This work will examine the varied uses of nostalgia in *Milk and Honey, Fiddler on the Roof, The Rothschilds, Rags* and *Ragtime*. In order to proceed we must recognize the signs of nostalgic techniques. Nostalgia as expressed through art operates on a subconscious level. Nostalgic works take place in the past, although temporal distance can change from piece to piece without affecting the extent of nostalgia produced. Period music and costumes, and verbal or visual references to historical events are all present in both straightforward historical works, as well as in nostalgic works, but the latter push the emotional responses to those elements. Davis describes theatrical techniques associated with nostalgia, "in theater [...] such means as scrim, half-light, echoes, distantly tinkling sounds, silhouetted figures, and body movements of particular deliberateness are employed to convey the protagonist's nostalgic recapturing of moments and matters past" (84). Some of the musicals we will examine use these techniques; others eschew visual techniques and depend of the resonance of their subject matter. Two other loci of nostalgic content in the musicals I will discuss are in their scores and in staged ritual. Musical references to the past, and the use of Jewish religious rituals in these shows are vital elements to examine. Most of the indirect musicals examined here contain, or at some point in the creative process contained, Jewish rituals. From weddings to funerals, Sabbaths to Sukkoth, communities come together to mourn or celebrate in these works. Why might this be a shared theme? Even truncated, what power do staged rituals possess? We will examine the various rituals in our case studies for their own particularities, keeping in mind that a nostalgic yearning for community unifies their meanings.

COMMUNITY

Jewish collective memory, post–Holocaust, encompasses intense complexity. Clearly history pre–Shoah can be rated as superior to the era of the Holocaust itself. However the American Jewish *present* offers a far superior world, at least in terms of personal freedoms and success. Why then nostalgia? The removal of various sources of community, including ancestral homelands, encourages fond and wistful memories of those sites. If American Jews are largely highly successful, what has been lost in the process? What do these musicals offer in exchange? Our test cases offer restorative nostalgia for biblical Israel, immigrant survivor substitution and the comfort of America as a solution or alternative history.

Social scientist Chaim Waxman, in his book *Jewish Baby Boomers*, points out that the spring of 1964 offered a pivotal moment for concern for the Jewish future, as two articles, "The Vanishing American Jew" by T.B. Morgan in *Look* Magazine and "Intermarriage and the Jewish Future" by Marshall Sklare in *Commentary* were both published in that year. Those two articles concerned the declining birth rate and increasing intermarriage rates of American Jews. These concerns, especially intermarriage, are still current in the Jewish community. It is significant however that these issues were beginning to be discussed in earnest in this era of *Milk and Honey* and *Fiddler*— the latter of which opened on Broadway the same year the articles were printed. This worry that the American Jewish population was declining made the need for nostalgia all the more potent. If community was disappearing, it needed to be remembered. This disappearance was compounded by the Holocaust and the death of six million European Jews. Although these events had happened twenty years previously, awareness of this loss was coming to the forefront. Nostalgia in this context acts not just as a memorial to the lost, but also fights the loss of community, by pointing to "simpler" times where kinship and unity flourished.

How was the Jewish community shifting — and was it declining? Traditional definitions of Jewishness were changing, and have continued to do so. Secular Judaism, as opposed to a stricter religious identification, was on the rise. As an alternative to more traditional forms of Jewish identity such as attending synagogue, joining Jewish organizations, or reading Jewish papers, magazines or literature, Waxman discusses the idea of "symbolic ethnicity." In a 2001 sociological study, he found that on most of his chosen indicators of ethnicity, Jewish baby boomers, "manifest ethnicity to a more limited extent than their predecessors, even as they assert that their group identity is important to them" (150). He offers as one explanation of this discrepancy Hebert Gans' theory of symbolic ethnicity, "Symbolic ethnicity has neither the social nor the psychological depth of traditional ethnicity. It is a matter of personal identity-construction in which one chooses if, when, and how to be ethnic" (150). Waxman, in order to further explicate this idea of symbolic ethnicity, offers the example of "Sam Silverman" who defines his Jewish ethnicity through his identification as a Democrat and Dodger fan. In other words, Jewishness does not have to be expressed through religious belief, but instead through political, cultural or artistic preferences, even, for example, through an affinity for musical theatre. The concept of third generation reclamation, where grandchildren care about the ethnicity of their grandparents, an ethnicity their parents abandoned, combines with symbolic ethnicity to initiate its own kind of Jewish revival.

Scholars caution of the dangers of symbolic ethnicity. Martin Peretz warns, "What the revival means mostly, even among very involved Jews, is more sentiment than substance. There's the Holocaust and there's Israel, to be sure; and then there's ignorance" (2). Despite these arguments, clearly Jewish ethnicity has experienced a widening of definitions, and the idea of symbolic ethnicity informs our topic here. If one can define Judaism through political affiliation and sports fandom, why not through being a *Fiddler* fan, or going to see Broadway musicals, particularly those whose subject matter underscores your ethnic concerns? These musicals therefore function on several levels — through the communal experience of attending or making theatre (traditionally an activity Jews, in particular New York Jews, took part in) and through the specific Jewish themed material of the musicals we discuss in this project.

Both these categories of musicals, direct and indirect, share an intense grounding in the postmemory generation's response to the Holocaust. By beginning close readings of these eight specific musicals, we can hope to shed light on larger questions regarding America's evolving response to the Nazi era.

CHAPTER II

———————————————

The Sound of Music

"Who are we going to offend — people who like Nazis?"
— Howard Lindsay (quoted in Nolan 206)

The Sound of Music (1959) has reached iconic status in America. The original New York production broke advance box office records and was one of the longest running Broadway musicals in its time, while the film remains one of the most profitable and popular movies of all time. But fascinatingly, what made *The Sound of Music* unique has been largely ignored to date. Several stage musicals had addressed weighty themes before *The Sound of Music*, however these musicals' subjects were arguably less surprising than Rodgers and Hammerstein's melding of the rise of Nazism, the shorthand for evil, with singing nuns and children. This tonal clash, which stretches the boundaries of traditional musical comedy, has created a fascinating, though largely unexamined, reflection of societal attitudes. The unique nature of *The Sound of Music*'s content becomes especially apparent when viewed in the context of America's changing relationship to Nazism and the Holocaust.

In the late 1950s, as discussed, America was only beginning to come out of a period of prolonged silence about the Nazi regime and their crimes. The Cold War was still raging, and West Germany was now an American ally. The Holocaust was largely avoided as a topic of conversation, survivors kept quiet. *The Diary of Anne Frank* was the first widely released artistic response to Nazi crimes, not yet termed the Holocaust. Anne Frank's diary came to America in 1952, the stage production in 1956, and the film in 1959, the same year *The Sound of Music* opened on Broadway. It was a year before Eichmann was abducted, two years before he was tried. Although it is rather surprising that the Nazi Anschluss was taken as a subject of a "musical comedy," the aesthetic approach to the Nazis in *The Sound of Music* was in keeping with American attitudes at the time. As the Holocaust was not yet considered central to the Nazi era at the time of the original production, the Holocaust was in no way alluded to or could be read into the original text. As the times have changed, however, the Holocaust has become a more central American concern. Therefore a trend towards grimmer realism can be seen in succeeding productions of *The Sound of Music,* most clearly in the 1997 Broadway revival. This chapter also addresses the musical comedy format of the musical; *The Sound of Music's* combination of comedy and Nazis in the same project provides an example of the early absence of comedic representations of Nazism.

Background, History and Productions

The original production of *The Sound of Music* was the brainchild of director Vincent J. Donohue, in response to a 1956 German film, *Die Trapp Familie.* The film depicted the life of Baroness Maria von Trapp, a former postulant who had fled Vienna before the Nazi Anschluss with her husband and stepchildren. The family became a successful singing group in America, and to this day owns a ski resort in Stowe, Vermont. The movie was the largest box-office hit in Germany since World War II. The film was based on the English-language autobiography of Maria von Trapp, entitled *The Story of the Trapp Family Singers* (1949). Donohoe saw the story as a star vehicle for Mary Martin, with whom he had worked on a televised production of Thornton Wilder's *The Skin of Our Teeth* (1955). Martin agreed, and became co-producers with Leland Hayward and her husband Richard Halliday. They hired book writers Howard Lindsay and Russell Crouse, who had Broadway successes such as *Life with Father* (1939) to their credit. This team originally envisioned the show as a play with music, perhaps using the folk songs of the von Trapp family singers. When they decided that perhaps a few original songs should be interpolated as well, Martin suggested Rodgers and Hammerstein, whom she had worked with on *South Pacific* (1949). The famous musical team responded that "musical plays" seldom succeed, and that the idea of combining original songs with other music was misguided. They would write a complete score or nothing. The creative team agreed and decided to wait for Rodgers and Hammerstein to finish their work on *Flower Drum Song* (1958) before beginning the new project. Meanwhile Halliday began the search to secure the rights to the von Trapps' story, hunting down the von Trapp children across the globe and finally locating Maria von Trapp in a hospital in Innsbruck where she was recovering from malaria, contracted in New Guinea as a missionary. With the rights secured, the writing process went swiftly, and the project was almost ready only six months after *Flower Drum*

Song opened. The creative team prepared in widely varied ways. Rodgers researched liturgical music for a Preludium, the first time he had done musical research in his career. Mary Martin became friends with Maria von Trapp, who taught her how to cross herself and play the guitar. Hammerstein, on the other hand, was told by doctors that he had incurable stomach cancer during the process. *The Sound of Music* was Rodgers and Hammerstein's last musical collaboration, and "Edelweiss" their last song written together. Hammerstein died a year after the opening of the show, in August of 1960.

Although the vast cultural impact of *The Sound of Music* means that plot summaries are redundant, it is important to point out the basic story and differences of the original stage production from the more widely known film version. *The Sound of Music* opens with a "Preludium" of Latin liturgical music (channeled through Richard Rodgers) after which the nuns realize their rebellious postulant Maria has not returned to the Abbey for the evening. In the next scene Maria, romping in the Alps, swings onto stage on the limb of a tree and sings the title song ("The Sound of Music"). The nuns, unable to curb Maria's zest for life, debate her future in the Abbey ("How Do You Solve a Problem Like Maria"). Maria returns to the Abbey, and the Mother Abbess, after singing a duet with Maria ("My Favorite Things"), decides to send her as a governess to the seven von Trapp children, who are being raised by their Navy captain father. After Maria arrives at the von Trapp villa she begins to win over the suspicious and rambunctious children by teaching them to sing ("Do Re Mi"). Liesl, the eldest daughter, sneaks out at night to meet her suitor Rolf, and they sing of her precocious youth ("Sixteen Going on Seventeen"). Maria, after catching, then establishing trust with Liesl, comforts the children during a thunderstorm by singing a mountain folk song ("The Lonely Goatherd"). Weeks later Captain von Trapp returns home, bringing his friend Max and love interest Elsa von Schraeder with him. Elsa and Max muse on the problems of a marriage between millionaires ("How Can Love Survive?"). The children interrupt a fight between Maria and the Captain, where she upbraids him for ignoring his progeny, singing a song prepared for Elsa ("The Hills Are Alive"). The Captain's heart softens, realizing what music can bring back to his family. At a party where the children perform ("So Long Farewell"), Maria and the Captain dance together and realize their love for each other. Maria flees back the Abbey in confusion, only to be sent back to the villa by the Mother Abbess, forcing Maria to face her fears ("Climb Every Mountain").

Act II opens with Elsa and Max's encouragement to the Captain to acquiesce to the oncoming Nazi regime ("There's No Way to Stop It"). When Elsa and the Captain recognize their political views are too divergent, they call off their engagement. Maria returns and she and von Trapp confess their love

("An Ordinary Couple"). They are then married. As they are on their honeymoon, the Anschluss (the Nazi invasion of Austria) occurs. The couple returns early to find that the Nazis are requiring von Trapp to accept a commission in their Navy. The family uses the cover of the upcoming Salzburg Music festival as an excuse for more time, and escape to the Abbey after they perform in the concert ("So Long, Farewell" and "Edelweiss"). They are discovered in hiding by Rolf, now a Nazi convert, but he does not alert the Nazis to the von Trapp's presence, allowing the family to escape over the Alps into Switzerland ("Climb Every Mountain").

The Sound of Music tried out in New Haven and Boston, and opened on Broadway at the Lunt-Fontanne Theatre on November 16, 1959. It had a record breaking box office advance, ran almost four years —1,443 performances — and won 8 Tony Awards, including Best Score, Best Leading Actress for Mary Martin — who beat Ethel Merman in *Gypsy*— and Best Musical. The original production spawned a national tour starring Florence Henderson, and a London production at the Palace Theatre which ran for six years, making it the longest running American musical in London at that time. The Broadway show was more of a popular than a critical success. Critics tended to attack its sentimentality, which Rodgers responded to angrily, stating that only "a fake intellectual" (quoted in Hyland 256), would not like the show. Hammerstein also took exception, "Sentiment has never been unpopular except with a few sick persons who are made sicker by the sight of a child, a glimpse of a wedding or the thought of a happy home" (quoted in Nolan 220). Critics called the show "stereotyped" or "hackneyed" and "conventional," and likened it negatively to operetta, an allusion strengthened by the show's Tyrolean setting. Walter Kerr summed up the critical tenor when he cuttingly stated, "What might have been an impressive and moving entertainment will be most admired by people who have always found Sir James M. Barrie pretty rough stuff" (Kerr 228). Kerr seemed to object most to the cuteness factor incurred by the presence of seven child actors. He argues, "I am not against tots. But [...] must they wear so many different picture-book skirts, and smile so relentlessly, and give such precocious advice to their elders so often?" (Kerr 228). The critical response was not all negative; many critics remarked on the beauty of the score and enjoyed Mary Martin's performance. Much of the praise, however, was couched in rather indifferent terms, calling the show "agreeable," "charming" and "adorable" (228).

Despite this critical dismissal, the show remained a popular hit, and reached immortality when the film version was released. The movie, produced by 20th Century–Fox in 1965, starring Julie Andrews and Christopher Plumber, screenplay by Ernest Lehman, and produced and directed by Robert Wise, has been touted as second only to *Gone with the Wind* (1939) as one of the most popular and profitable movies ever made. It is certainly the most popular film musical ever made. It grossed $79 million dollars pre-inflation and became not just financially successful, but over time has encouraged an almost cult-like following. *The Sound of Music* devotees watch the movie far more than once. For instance, the record as of 1988 was 940 times for one woman. Often attendance records for a city vastly exceeded the city's population. The original release of the film lasted a record-breaking four and a half years. *The Sound of Music* was nominated for 10 Oscars and won half of that number, including Best Picture. The film retains much of the original stage score, while changing the order in which the songs are sung; for example instead of Maria singing "My Favorite Things" with the Mother Abbess, the song takes the place of "The Lonely Goatherd" in the storm scene. Additionally as Hammerstein had already passed away by 1965, Richard Rodgers wrote both the lyrics and the music for two additional songs, "I Have Confidence" and "Something Good," to replace "An Ordinary Couple." This last song was not the only one to be cut, both of Elsa and Max's songs were excised as well, most importantly, "There's No Way To Stop It," about encroaching Nazi evil.

Since its release, this film's impact has been evident throughout American culture. In 1976, ABC showed the film for one night only on television. The program was rated number one in the Nielsens, and ranks eighth in the top ten most watched films on television. Spin-off marketing includes a special *Sound of Music* vacation tour in Austria, a *Sound of Music* Dinner Theatre, a *Sound of Music* record store, *Sound of Music* commemorative plates and music boxes, a children's book, and a "Barbie as Maria" doll. The Broadway soundtrack won a Grammy, and the soundtrack to the film has gone Gold, subsequently Platinum, and has sold over ten million units around the world to date. A recent trend makes the continued fascination with this movie quite apparent: the touring "Sing-Along *Sound of Music*," an audience-participation event. Attendees sing along with the film's score, come dressed as the characters and are encouraged to make other participatory gestures, including barking at Rolf, "ahhing" at Gretl, cheering for Maria, and tellingly, booing the Nazis. This production, which began in London, has enjoyed long runs in cities such as New York and San Francisco, and several national tours. Finally a British television show, *A Problem Like Maria* (2006) cast Maria in the Andrew Lloyd Webber produced West End production of *The Sound of Music* (2006) through audience votes. All of these products illustrate the extent to which *The Sound of Music* has become an integral part of the American cultural landscape (www.foxhome.com/soundofmusic/wra/wram.html).

The Rodgers and Hammerstein Theatre Library reports that over 450 productions of *The Sound of Music* are staged every year in the United States and Canada, and hundreds more around the world. Productions in native tongues have been staged recently in Japan, Sweden, Greece, Great Britain, Australia, and Israel. The influence of the film is felt in production choices of the stage show. Often productions attempt to more closely follow the film version by changing the order of the songs, adding the film's two additional songs, and often cutting the three songs that do not appear in the film. (This is often done illegally, as the Rodgers and Hammerstein Organization licenses the original stage version).* A London production in 1981, starring Petula Clark, followed the film blueprint exactly, and when the New York City Opera staged the original libretto in 1990, starring Debbie Boone, the differences from the movie were surprising to many audiences and critics. The 1997 Broadway revival, starring Rebecca Luker, found a happy medium between these extremes, keeping both the additional film songs as well as Elsa and Max's numbers. Critics received the production well, again commenting on the sentimentality of the show. Vincent Canby, in *The New York Times*, called the original libretto, "an operetta so sugar-frosted that its Nazis would not have looked out a place as tiny attendants on a wedding cake" (250). This production, however, directed by Susan Schulman, did extensive research into the period and brought out the themes of incipient Nazism in a way which had not been done before. These changes were arguably due to the shift in American perception towards the Holocaust and thus towards the Nazi period.

Grim Realism

In order to trace changing American attitudes towards Nazism and the Holocaust on the stage, and in *The Sound of Music* in particular, we must isolate specific characters and moments which most clearly illustrate these shifts throughout the various productions. I am not arguing that there are references to the Holocaust in *The Sound of Music*. Indeed, there are no Jews. In fact, the piece is heavy with Christianity, peopled by praying Nuns. After seeing the original production, Noel Coward remarked in his diary:

> There were too many nuns careening about and crossing themselves and singing jaunty little songs, and there was, I must admit, a heavy pall of Jewish-Catholic schmaltz enveloping the whole thing [quoted in Hyland 255].

Coward hits on a fascinating point: the complexity of Jewish creators, Rodgers and Hammerstein, writing such a heavily Catholic show. The musical opens with a Latin Preludium, sung by nuns in the interior of the abbey. The stage

---

*See Hillman, Jessica. "*Tradition or Travesty?* Radical Reinterpretations of the Musical Theatre Canon." *Theatre Topics.* 20:1 (March 2010): 1–10.

directions describe the set as complete with vaulted arches, stained-glass win-
dows, and an altar with lighted candles, and during the music nuns kneel at
the altar in prayer. The Mother Abbess, as a religious figure, has ultimate
authority, taking on the frequent Rodgers and Hammerstein character of the
"old sage." The Mother Abbess points Maria in the correct direction both literally and figuratively, helping inspire Maria to return to the Captain and the
family and to make the treacherous mountain climb that ends the musical.
Her anthem, "Climb Every Mountain" encompasses the moral power of the
show with sweeping musical intensity. The abbey and the nuns remain a presence throughout the show, and play a vital role in protecting the family from
the Nazis and guiding them to safety over the Alps. This presence of Catholicism as the ultimate moral force in the show is noteworthy, given the
Judaism — albeit highly assimilated on Rodgers' part and conflicted on Hammerstein's — of its creators. It is true that nuns are present in the original
factual story, while no Jews are. However the artistic team had a choice in
how much to emphasize Catholicism. How much can this emphatic Judaic
absence be compared to the de–Judaizing of Anne Frank's story on Broadway
in 1956, three years earlier? In some ways the comparison is strained, for of
course, *The Sound of Music* is not a Holocaust story. Consistent with the time
period in which this musical was created, the attachment of Holocaust
thoughts and images were not connected to Nazi imagery in the way they are
now. *The Sound of Music* in its initial form had no interest in confronting the
kinds of issues that Nazism could potentially evoke, and would evoke in later
years. How Rodgers and Hammerstein, American Jews, felt personally about
portraying Nazi characters who had committed crimes against their fellows
in religion, we do not know. Their thoughts were likely consistent with a
period where the Holocaust was not yet fully or directly spoken of.

Despite the lack of a link between Nazi portrayals and the Holocaust in
this period, the subject was still sensitive enough to occasion cuts from the
original production. Although at first the 1959 production included swastika
clad Nazi guards, these were taken out of the show during tryouts in New
Haven and Boston. The creative team and / or the producers decided the
swastikas and the Nazi characters on stage were too severe. The exact changes
are hard to ascertain. Theodore Bikel, the original Captain von Trapp, told
the *New York Times* that swastika armbands were cut. Historians Green and
Hyland write that Nazi supernumerary characters were removed. The script,
as printed in 1960, demonstrates that Nazis were primarily an offstage presence
in the original production, but also indicates that a few Nazis may have been
seen. At the end of the concert scene, when the family has escaped, the stage
directions indicate first a commotion offstage when the family fails to appear
to claim their prize:

OFFSTAGE VOICES:
Where are they — the von Trapps?
They've gone!
[...] Call the guard!
Hauptmann, take the first road, Ullrich, block the driveway!
Steinhardt, call district headquarters!
(*The commotion mounts*)

MAX: (to the orchestra) Play something!

(*He exits hurriedly. The lights dim almost to blackness.* **Three men in SS uniform
 run across the stage.** *Whistles and shouting voices are heard*)
Blackout [136; my emphasis].

The answer to the question of exactly what was changed in the previews
is likely a combination of the two explanations: swastikas were taken off the
Nazi characters that remain in the script, including Zeller, Von Schreiber and
Rolf, while the Nazi guards with no lines were taken out of the concert scene.
At first librettist Howard Lindsay believed that the Nazis should be kept on
stage, stating, "Who are we going to offend, people who like Nazis?" (quoted
in Nolan 206). But ultimately Richard Rodgers explained the rationale to
remove them, "The end result is that there's more menace without seeing
them than there was when they were onstage in those musical comedy uniforms. Having them off-stage exerts more pressure on the situation than seeing
them did" (quoted in Green 165). Rodgers' choice of the phrase, "musical
comedy uniforms" is particularly fascinating here: what exactly does he mean?
Were the costume choices already watered down from the actual Nazi uniform?
Or was Rodgers acknowledging a shift in perception when a uniform went
from history to the stage, particularly a musical stage? Was he himself ques-
tioning the power of figures of evil on the musical comedy stage? The incon-
gruity of the meaning of such uniforms combined with the associations of
the light Broadway musical theatre form may have struck the creative team.
Or perhaps it was the contrary, that Nazis embodied on the stage would have
been a phenomenologically strong image, one which had actually not yet been
attempted in the post-war climate. In *The Diary of Anne Frank* the Nazis are
also kept offstage, indeed this seems to be the preferred stylistic choice of the
era. Although Rodgers' argued that absence holds more power to frighten,
perhaps the unacknowledged impact of an embodied Nazi offers a stronger
explanation. Perhaps Nazis onstage were simply too frightening, too real, in
an otherwise light musical about singing children.

In the 1959 production, Nazis are treated almost peripherally, as only a
modest obstacle to the romantic story of the heroine and her new family.
Opening night critic Richard Watts, in the *New York Post*, sums up the atmosphere that prevailed in the de–Nazified production:

It might seem odd to say that any show dealing with the arrival of the Nazis and the flight from them of an entire family was charming, but that is one of the striking things about *The Sound of Music*. These scenes have their suggestions of menacing evil, but they manage it reticently and without interference with the gracious mood of sentiment [229].

Another critic, Frank Aston, in the *New York World Telegram*, even remarks on the helpfulness of the Nazis in getting rid of Elsa, Maria's romantic opponent, "It looks as if a rich, totalitarian dame will get him. But the Nazis, otherwise loathsome, are a big help fixing up this detail" (230). These critics help to sum up the unthreatened American attitude towards Nazism that prevailed in the period. But perhaps this stance covered a slightly more ambiguous attitude. There are tantalizing hints that the original production team wanted something a bit stronger politically than what they were left with. The original scenic production notes of librettists Lindsay and Crouse demonstrate few changes from the show as it was eventually produced, but they do offer one startling example of the extent to which the writers wanted to emphasize Nazism. Their notes on the setting for Act II, Scene I, where Elsa and Max attempt to convince the Captain that there is "No Way To Stop It" (the Nazi menace), state:

In this scene we go into twilight, and on the mountains on the backdrop we want the effect of one or more bonfires in the shape of swastikas. This can be on St. John's Eve, June 23, or perhaps the bonfires may be a personal warning to Captain von Trapp [quoted in Nolan 212].

Needless to say, this effect did not make it into a production where swastikas were removed from costumes. But it does allow us an interesting glimpse into the original artistic vision of the show, and the great pressure from the producers to change it in the face of the current American attitudes towards Nazism.

Despite the fact that most of the "superfluous" Nazi characters were removed from the stage, specific named Nazi characters remain. The events of the Nazi takeover of Austria are much more central to the plot of the staged *Sound of Music* than in the better-known film version. Lindsay and Crouse included extensive discussion of the Anschluss — the Nazi invasion of Austria — before and after it occurs. The minor character of Franz, the butler, makes the first mention we hear of Nazi Germany in a fairly innocuous comment in Act I, Scene 4. In response to a late telegram he remarks, "Well that's one thing people are saying — if the Germans did take over Austria we'd have efficiency" (25), Frau Schmidt, the housekeeper quickly retorts, "Don't let the Captain hear you say that" (28), immediately establishing the Captain's political views. This incident is followed by various political discussions amongst the Captain, Elsa, Max and Rolf. By Scene 11, the party at the villa, Nazi foreboding has reached a peak. Herr Zeller, a neighbor with pro-German sympathies, and for all intents and purposes the villain of the piece, conducts a "spirited argument" (73) with Baron Eberfeld, another neighbor:

ZELLER: You have German blood, haven't you?
EBERFELD: I am not a German. I'm an Austrian.
ZELLER: There's going to be an Anschluss, I warn you and everyone like you —
and that goes for our — (73).

Zeller's embarrassed wife and the entrance of the Captain cut off the exchange. Zeller returns after the Anschluss, now working for the Nazis as the civic authority for the region, to order that the Nazi flag be flown, and again later in the same scene with the German Admiral von Schrieber to order the Captain to join the Navy of the Third Reich. These actions force the Captain's decision to flee Austria. An event in a later scene brings the portrayal of the encroachment of Nazism full circle. After the Anschluss, Rolf comes to deliver a telegram. The butler, Franz, who made the first reference to Germans in the show, salutes Rolf and shouts "Heil" (125). A shocked Maria states, "Even Franz" (125). The conversion of this seemingly innocuous and incidental character, a typical servant musical chorus character, to Nazism, is a particularly jolting move. It gives a face to evil, demonstrating how easily it can spread, and proving that Nazism is not limited to faceless storm-troopers, or offstage voices.

The political pragmatists Elsa and Max also provide examples of how evil can encroach. Although not Nazis themselves, they provide the main opposition to the Captain's idealistic anti–German ideals. Elsa and Max's stance begins to emerge immediately after their arrival at the villa. Regarding a possible party, Captain von Trapp remarks, "I wouldn't know who to invite. Today it's difficult to tell who's a friend and who's an enemy" (59). Elsa responds, "This isn't a good time to make enemies. Let's make some friends" (59). Later, when the Captain remarks that Max has received several calls from Berlin, Max responds:

Georg, you know I have no political convictions. Can I help it if other people have? [...] This is the way I look at it. There was a man who was dying. They were giving him the last rites. They asked him, "Do you renounce the devil and all his works?" and he said, "At this moment, I prefer not to make any enemies" [101].

When the Captain declares his intention to defy the Nazis if they invade, Elsa and Max, shocked, try to dissuade him, first by stating, "Nothing you can do will make any difference" (103), and later trying to lighten the atmosphere by singing "No Way To Stop It." Musically this song veers from a jarring rhythm and minor key on the verses, on lines which alternate the Captain's angry refusal to yield with Max and Elsa's urging the Captain to keep his head down and let the events pass. In the chorus the music shifts to a falsely jaunty melody repeating the title words and Max and Elsa's increasingly insistent and frenzied refusal to worry. The Captain exposes their argument by demonstrating this attitude's essential selfishness. The imagery of the song, of stars and planets, places petty political events as minuscule in comparison. The Captain turns this imagery on its head, accusing his friends of feeling that the stars and planets revolve around them. Ultimately Elsa and the Captain realize their essential disagreement will not change, and the Captain realizes his love for Maria, and together they call off their engagement. Max later tries to enlist Maria's help in encouraging the Captain to cooperate with the Nazis, but she too stands strong in the face of danger.

Although Elsa and Max's arguments are not unreasonable, the structure of the libretto and their characterization makes clear that resistance to the Nazis is the moral choice, while compromising with evil is wrong. The script portrays Max as a shallow hanger-on, remarking, "I like rich people. I like the way they live. I like the way I live when I'm with them" (58). Elsa, on the other hand, is portrayed as a pragmatic businesswoman, a rather shocking role in both the era the story takes place in and in 1959 when *The Sound of Music* was written. Much is made of her business sense, for example, she remarks that she looks after her deceased husband's estate, and the Captain responds:

CAPTAIN: I thought that was a corporation now.
ELSA: It is and I'm president.
CAPTAIN: You president of a corporation!
ELSA: After all, I managed Heinrich's affairs for years before he died.
CAPTAIN: I can't see you sitting behind a desk.
ELSA: Well, of course, I wear a business suit and smoke a big cigar [56].

Elsa's wry duet with Max about the difficulty of love between millionaires, "How Can Love Survive," also helps to place her as a foil to the feminine moralism of Maria, who just wants to be "An Ordinary Couple" and share the simple joys of marriage and family with the Captain. The de-feminization of Elsa helps to undercut the potential appeal of her political compromising. Max, despite his self-serving compromises with the German government of the Third Reich, eventually shows that his heart is in the right place by helping to delay the announcement of the winners of the final contest in order to give the von Trapps more time to escape.

The Captain and Maria, in contrast to Elsa and Max, are consistently and unyieldingly idealistic and uncompromising. When most are silent in the face of the Nazi regime, arguing, as the characters Elsa and Max do, that there is "no way to stop it," the Von Trapps, strengthened by the power of family, music and nature, refuse to acquiesce to that devastating ideology. Maria, who after her marriage has lost much of her irrepressible freedom, now makes all her responses as a supportive and unquestioning wife. However, the Captain, throughout the musical, has only one moment of worry and doubt about his political response to these events. When he receives the telegram demanding he join the German navy, he tells Maria:

> CAPTAIN: I can't just brush this aside. I admit it would be exciting to have a
> ship under me again. What I mean is it would be a relief, and a comfort and
> to know that you and the children are safe. But it would also mean... Please
> Maria, help me.
> MARIA: Georg, whatever you decide, will be my decision.
> CAPTAIN: Thank you, I know now I can't do it.
> MARIA: Of course not [126–7].

This moment also reveals Maria's true political views, despite her heavy pall of wifely duty. The Captain apparently needs this unconditional spousal support to reaffirm his strength in the face of danger. At the concert, he sings "Edelweiss," the ultimate statement of Austrian nationalism, a brave stand in front of an audience full of Nazis and Nazi sympathizers. He breaks down and can't go on briefly, but with the support of his family has a defiant finish.

The implications of the Captain's politics were complicated in the original production by the actor bringing them to life, Theodore Bikel. Bikel was born an Austrian Jew, raised since the age of thirteen in Palestine. He began his career as an actor in the Habimah and Israeli Chamber Theatres. He was famous later as one of the most prolific interpreters of the role of Tevye in *Fiddler on the Roof.* Bikel was well known by 1959, and so his background could not have helped but inform the readings taken from the Captain's firm and upstanding political convictions in the show. Bikel's presence also complicates the absence of Jewishness in the original production, as discussed earlier.

The children, like their father, and in contrast to the compromising adults Elsa and Max, represent purity and moral innocence, and thereby clearly demonstrate the evils of Nazism. Brigitta, the child who Maria describes as "noticing everything," and who indeed points out the love between Maria and the Captain before they know it, innocently remarks of the fight at the party between Nazi sympathizers and their opponents, "Father I don't think these people are having a very good time" (74). The musical continually sets the children's innocence and intelligence against the Nazi menace. When Zeller returns after the Anschluss to order the Nazi flag to be flown at the villa, Brigitta asks, "You mean the flag with the black spider on it?" (118). When Zeller leaves, barking "Heil," little five year old Gretl asks, "Why was

The Sound of Music (stage). Music by Richard Rodgers, lyrics by Oscar Hammerstein, book by Howard Lindsay and Russel Crouse. Shown from left: John Voigt as Rolf, Marissa Mason as Liesl.

he so cross?" (119). When the family is hiding out in the Abbey from the Nazis, Gretl asks, "Isn't this God's house" (138)?

Rolf, on the other hand, leaves childhood and innocence behind during the short time presented by the musical, and actually joins the Nazi movement. Rolf presents the most fascinating case of the portrayal of Nazism in *The Sound of Music*, as he subverts the typical musical comedy role of the young lover or leading man. Political foreboding disrupts the scene of an otherwise traditional courtship of the young lovers Rolf and Liesl before their song, "Sixteen Going On Seventeen." In discussing plans for how they could meet, Rolf inadvertently lets slip that a Colonel is secretly in Salzburg from Berlin. He warns Liesl not to tell her father. Liesl asks why not and Rolf responds:

> Well, your father's pretty Austrian. [...] Some people think we ought to be German. They're pretty mad at those who don't think so. They're getting ready to — well, let's hope your father doesn't get into any trouble [40].

He appears shortly after his song, in Act I, scene 9, and salutes the first "Heil Hitler" of the show. The Captain responds angrily, "I am an Austrian, I will not be Heiled" (63). Later, after the Anschluss, Rolf has turned completely to Nazism. Unrecognizable from the young ingénue who sang the love song "16 Going on 17," he proves unmoved by Liesl's emotions or affection, and threatens the Captain:

> If he knows what's good for him, he'll come over to the right side. And if he doesn't he'd better get out of the country — there are things that happen today to a man like that. He'd better get out quick. Cry all you want, but just remember what I said before it's too late [125–6].

Despite the shocking nature of the young love interest turning evil, the original artistic team did not fully Nazify Rolf. In the original libretto, Rolf finds the von Trapp family hiding in the Abbey, entering, according to the printed libretto, in SS uniform — likely without a swastika in the original production. Rolf first draws his pistol and calls for the Lieutenant, however:

> (*As Rolf's head turns back his flashlight beams directly on the face of Liesl. There is a hushed moment as she looks pleadingly at Rolf. From a distance we hear the Lieutenant's footsteps as he approaches. The sound draws nearer and nearer. Suddenly Rolf turns and calls through the door*) No one out here, sir! [139].

The libretto saves Rolf on the brink of complete de-humanization. This plot point presents one of the most distinct differences from the film.

In the 1965 film version, certain members of the production team wanted to complicate the overall sweetness of the musical and to make a political statement. William Wyler, who was originally supposed to direct the film, wanted to emphasize the Nazi invasion. Richard Zanuck, chief of Fox studios, recalled, "He wanted tanks. He wanted a real invasion, blowing up the town and everything. I didn't see the need for all this right in the middle of a musical" (quoted in www.trappfamily.com). Zanuck's surprise at Wyler's wish for serious content within the musical format is consistent with attitudes which persist today. The film, produced in 1965, without going as far as Wyler intended, still surpassed the stage production in terms of its realistic visual treatment of Nazism, though not in the amount of time granted to the subject. The film's date presents an important consideration, for by 1965 American attitudes concerning Nazism and the Holocaust were beginning to shift. Eichmann had been captured and tried and a new openness towards exploring the tragic events was beginning to take effect. The Holocaust was not yet intimately connected to Nazism, but attitudes had begun their shift in that direction. Like stage productions considered earlier from this period, *The Wall* (1960) and *Incident at Vichy* (1964), the film of *The Sound of Music* exhibits a somewhat confused and ambiguous attitude towards Nazi representations.

Certainly the presence of Nazi figures and swastikas present one difference from the original stage musical. Maria and the Captain return from their honeymoon to discover a large Nazi flag hanging from their house which he immediately drags down. The audience at the final concert is filled with swastika clad soldiers who pursue the family in frightening detail. Additionally the portrayal of Rolf is quite different; a later time period enabled the producers to make the more pessimistic choice of a Rolf who fully gives over to the Nazis. Instead of letting the family hide unnoticed, as in the original libretto, Rolf shouts the alert, betraying the family's presence and forcing them to run to the mountains. This moment is undercut in its impact however, by the comic shtick it enables: the Nuns stealing the Nazis' spark plugs out of their cars.

Despite this harder line drawn in the film, interestingly Nazis become less of a focus throughout the movie. Although the imagery saturates the end of the film, the screenplay eliminates most of the political discussion in the first half, keeping the Nazi section rather limited. This allowed the film to be cut in a politically sensitive Germany, showing only the first two thirds and ending with Maria and the Captain's marriage. Nevertheless, the film bombed in Germany. Additionally, the film softens Elsa and Max's political bent. Although Max still believes in dealing with whatever political group happens to be in power, Elsa has very little to say on the subject. Instead of breaking off the engagement herself due to von Trapp's politics, she is portrayed as a spurned lover, losing out to Maria despite catty maneuvers. Both Elsa and Max's musical numbers are cut, most significantly "No Way to Stop It."

On March 12, 1998, *The Sound of Music* was revived on Broadway for the first time, directed by Susan Schulman. This production showed the passing years and the changing attitudes towards Nazism quite clearly. Tellingly, it opened in the same year as Wendy Kesselman's "updated" *Diary of Anne Frank* and Sam Mendes' revisionist production of *Cabaret*. Mervyn Rothstein, in the *New York Times*, noticed that in all three of these productions, the "goose stepping was louder" (1), in other words, the Nazi imagery and attitude towards the Holocaust embraced a grimmer realism than had been seen in the original productions of all three texts. This was particularly true of *The Sound of Music*. Swastikas were back on Nazi uniforms, and Nazi characters came directly onstage, on several occasions. In particular, during the final concert three large, red, shocking swastika banners were the backdrop for the singing of "So Long, Farewell" and "Edelweiss." Schulman stated:

> I wanted to deal with the subject in a more authentic way. In the 50s, nobody wanted to upset anybody — especially in a musical. World War II was still very

real for many people. There was a fear about musicals dealing with such heavy subject matter [quoted in Rothstein 1].

Schulman and the other artists involved in these 1998 revivals cited the changing times and an "end of the millennium feeling" (Rothstein 2) that allowed a grimmer aesthetic to prevail, and be commercially successful. James Young, author of "The Texture of Memory: Holocaust Memorials and Meaning," (1994) states, "plays reflect the temper of the time. And the temper of our time is without illusions" (quoted in Rothstein 2). Feelings about World War II were not the only thing that had shifted since the 50s; attitudes towards the limits of the musical form had also shifted. Serious material has been more and more accepted within musicals, *Cabaret* stands as one landmark in this journey. Musicals can now address difficult topics such as murder, social inequality, or political rebellion. Therefore Schulman was able to contrast her production of *The Sound of Music* to the earlier stage and film incarnations. She made sure the look was authentic to the 1930s rather than the 1960s look of the film. She also wanted to emphasize the gradual encroachment of the Nazi threat, "The show introduces Nazism a little bit at a time, as it was introduced in Salzburg, very insidiously, like bacteria — one little flag, then it grows and grows" (quoted in Rothstein 2).

Despite Schulman's intentions, which were noticed by the critics primarily in the swastika banners, the essential sweetness of the show still undercut the attempts at seriousness. The much loved but simple musical score cannot support as many interpretive variations as the more musically complex *Cabaret* for example, or even Rodgers and Hammerstein's own more challenging scores such as *Carousel* or *South Pacific*. Additionally, the lasting impact of the much loved film version takes responsibility for the impossibility of the show shaking its sugar sweet image. As Ethan Mordden states, "Even the Nazis aren't real by the time the 'bright copper kettles' effect sets in" (213). The reviews for the stage revival make this association clear.

USA Today critic David Patrick Stearns remarks, "Bland platitudes evoke anti–Nazi idealism. It's *Up With People* with swastikas" (1). Vincent Canby remarks in the *New York Times*:

> Except for the pesky 1938 Anschluss when Hitler occupied Austria, the Trapp family [...] would have lived ever after on their estate. [...] But even this ending is sunny. If the family hadn't left Austria, they never would have ended up as successful innkeepers in Vermont [251].

It is therefore apparent that this overall sunny atmosphere overwhelms even attempts to strengthen the underlying Nazi threat. The strength of the basic melodramatic and humanistic structure is in keeping with the worldview of its creators and the time it was written.

Comedy

The Sound of Music does not represent the comic Nazi, but rather the very absence of Nazi related humor, again in keeping with the period in which it was written. One would not expect the Nazis to be in any way funny in this piece, indeed they are impressive in their absolute lack of humor. The Nazis are set up as a foil to the morality of the central characters: Maria, the Captain and the children. The show limits humor to the non–Nazi characters, most particularly Maria and the children. The nuns, bastions of morality, are allowed gentle humor as well. The fascinating aspect of this split is the inclusion of these non-humorous, non-musical comedy characters in what is essentially a musical comedy. Not only are the Nazis not comic, but they do not sing. In *The Sound of Music* singing demonstrates absolute moral goodness. Maria asks the Mother Abbess for permission to sing, sings away her fears, and teaches the children and their father to love again through song. Rolf, on the other hand, sings before his conversion, when he still only flirts with Nazism, a young lover still more interested in Liesl than politics. Once he has gone over to the party however, he becomes a non-singing character with the rest of the Nazis. Zeller, Von Schreiber and Franz the butler are all speaking, non-singing characters, as are the largely silent Nazi guard characters. The final scenes makes the centrality of this metaphor clear, when singing becomes a statement against oppression in a show which centers on freedom: Maria's freedom to be an individual, freedom to sing, freedom from grieving, and most particularly freedom from oppressive governments. The Captain's patriotic "Edelweiss," as a sly statement of independence in front of an audience of Nazis, makes clear the thematic concerns and moral stance of the show, and the central concerns of Rodgers and Hammerstein musicals: community responsibility, and the need to earn your own happiness. Even if the factual von Trapp family left Salzburg because of patriotic concerns and love for Austria, not because of a moral stance against the Nazi government and the crimes it had yet to commit, their story has been made into the ultimate statement of personal courage in the face of evil. The more evil becomes attached to the government they fled, the more resonance the story incurs and the more complex readings the material can receive.

Certainly Rodgers and Hammerstein had included serious thematic concerns throughout their career, and thus the meaningful content of *The Sound of Music*, their last show, does not surprise. They had dealt with spousal abuse in *Carousel* (1945) and attacked racism in *South Pacific* (1949). But the musical was still viewed as a genre that could not truly make a political statement, disappoint an audience looking for a simple moral message, or impinge on a positive worldview. Certainly *The Sound of Music* was not taken in a way that threatened positive humanism, nor was it intended to do so. It fits the tenor of the time from which it emerged. However, the potential to undercut this liberal worldview with the implications of the figures it portrays, the Nazis, with their ever-increasing association with the horrific crimes of the Holocaust, remains just under the surface, ready to disturb.

CHAPTER III

Milk and Honey

"This is the place where the hopes of the homeless and the dreams of the lost combine. This is the land that heaven blessed, and this lovely land is mine!" [I-3-26]

These lyrics — from the title song of the 1961 musical *Milk and Honey*— encapsulate the multi-layered political and cultural implications contained in this seemingly simple Broadway musical. With their call to both the recent and ancient past, and their vigorous claim of ownership in the present, Jerry Herman's words, mirroring the musical as a whole, negotiate a delicate balance between pride and sorrow. With music and lyrics by Herman and libretto by Don Appell, *Milk and Honey* was the first major Broadway musical to take Jews as its central characters, presenting a then unique setting and subject matter: the new state of Israel. Its pioneer status situates *Milk and Honey* as a cultural document demonstrating American Jewish attitudes toward the young country, and one of the central causes of its existence, the Holocaust. Through old-fashioned Broadway escapism and exoticism, *Milk and Honey* superficially glorifies the present and future of an exciting new land. More deeply, as a reaction to sublimated grief and disavowal of the Holocaust, we find both "reflective" nostalgia for the Yiddish stage, and "restorative nostalgia" for Israel's roots in the biblical homeland, the titular land of milk and honey.

Background

Herman was a young composer in his twenties with an Off Broadway revue called *Parade* to his credit when the idea for *Milk and Honey* emerged. In his autobiography, Herman recalls producer Gerard Oestreicher attending

42

Parade and talking to the composer, who also played the piano for the revue. Oestreicher, likely inspired by the huge success of *Exodus*, both the Leon Uris novel published in 1958, and the film version released in 1960, was searching for a composer for a musical about Israel.* Herman, later famous for razzle dazzle Broadway musical spectacles focusing on larger-than-life diva roles (*Hello Dolly!* [1964], *Mame* [1966], *La Cage aux Folles* [1983]) was at this point young, unknown, and eager for his Broadway break. According to Herman's memoir, Oestreicher asked if he could handle Jewish material for a show set in Israel. Herman recounts:

> Well, [...] I'm, *not* going to admit that I didn't know the first thing about Israel. So I said right away: "You have come to *exactly* the right person. I grew up in a Jewish home and I had a Jewish mother who taught Hebrew music at the YMHA in Jersey City. [...] I know *all* those Hebrew songs. And more important than knowing the music, I grew up with that heritage all around me" [*Showtune*, 37–8; emphasis original].

Apparently a Jewish background offered an important stamp of authenticity required to work on the show, for Oestreicher promptly hired the young composer. Soon thereafter Jerry Herman and librettist Don Appell were flying to Israel together. Oestreicher arranged the two writers' trip so that they could witness Israel's thirteenth Independence Day celebration. He wanted them to soak up the atmosphere and emerge with an idea for a show that had no pre-existing source material. Israel's government treated the authors "like royalty" according to Herman (39). Oestreicher had contacted them, and told them

> We were coming to write this very happy and very positive show about their country. The government was thrilled about the whole idea, of course, because Israel still had an image problem in 1960 and publicity wasn't all that terrific [39–40].

As Herman remembers, "The Israeli government people were so thrilled that we weren't going to write a play about Israel-embattled-with-gun-in-hand, but rather one that might encourage tourism, that they rolled out the red carpet and had a black limousine at our hotel every morning" (quoted in Citron 48). Herman, disappointed that their tour only included government-approved sections of Israel, snuck away with Appell to tour the country on their own, including its border towns. Herman saw some elements of the state that concerned him, but admits that very little that was not positive made it into the final show, calling it a "valentine" to Israel (41).

Herman and Appell decided to center their show on a second chance

---

**Milk and Honey, when completed, resembled *Exodus* in its adoring and inspirational tone. The lyrics quoted above also echo a song from the *Exodus* soundtrack, "This land is mine, God gave this land to me."

love affair between two American Jews visiting Israel, and soon they were hard at work on drafts, casting, and hiring artistic personnel, including director Alfred Marre, scenic designer Howard Bay and costume designer Miles White. Herman insisted on hiring Hershey Kay as orchestrator, and Richard DeCormier's vocal arrangements added to the richness of the score. Finally, Donald Saddler was hired as choreographer. As for casting, Patricia Morrison was considered for the lead role of Ruth, but according to Citron:

> She lacked the ethnic quality for the role. At last Mimi Benzell, the Metropolitan Opera coloratura, who was Jewish, was given the role. Herman felt that Benzell resembled his mother, who was the prototype for the role [57].

Robert Weede, also a Met Opera star, who had appeared on Broadway in *The Most Happy Fella*, was hired to play the male lead Phil. Tommy Rall played Phil's son-in-law David. Most importantly, Herman flew to Miami to recruit Yiddish theatre star Molly Picon for the cast. After he showed her a song written for her character, Clara Weiss, called, "Hymn to Hymie," she accepted. Many cuts and additions were made to the musical during previews in New Haven and Boston before the musical made its way to New York.

Milk and Honey opened on Broadway on October 10, 1961, at the Martin Beck Theatre, receiving mixed to positive reviews. Walter Kerr, in the *New York Herald Tribune*, wrote the most negative review, declaring the musical, "not only homespun; it is too home-movie" (241). Molly Picon, however, received universal raves. John Chapman typified the reaction when he wrote in *The Daily News*, "in her first performance in a Broadway musical, she exhibits all the skills and charms she has learned in something like a half century on Yiddish and vaudeville stages" (238). John McClain, in *The New York Journal American*, displayed a typical shocked approbation of Picon's dance skills, stating, "her acrobatic contribution to some of the company production numbers [...] defy both the Christian and Hebrew calendars" (238). Tommy Rall's performance, Donald Saddler's choreography, and the scenic and costume design were also highly praised.

Most reviews seemed to find the novelty of the musical's milieu to be its most effective and intriguing element. John Chapman called the setting a, "picturesque 'new' locale, Israel" (238). As Richard Watts, Jr., said in the *New York Post*, "Although the book is a minimum of help to *Milk and Honey*, the drama of Israel is always there intriguingly in the background" (240). In fact, in several reviews, Israel as a country seemed to be more under consideration than the show itself. *The New York Times'* Howard Taubman declares, "The brighter flame is fed by the spirit of affirmation represented by Israel and its dedicated people, who are working to make real the ancient dream of a land of milk and honey" (239). Similarly, Norman Nadel, of the *New York World*

Telegram, spends at least a third of his article reviewing the state of Israel, with no mention of the musical, and ends, "It makes you understand why people believe in Israel, and love the country. As this proud, fierce love comes through, *Milk and Honey* is as its bright best" (241).

Milk and Honey cost $300,000 to produce; the best orchestra seats sold for $4.40 and $6.60. The box office was strong, with $16,000 in sales the day after opening — higher than *My Fair Lady* that week — and was still taking in $50,000 a week by its thirty-fifth week. But when Molly Picon left to star in a film, producers hired British actress Hermione Gingold to replace her. *Milk and Honey* almost closed without Picon. After the film wrapped she returned, and ticket sales improved again, but when Picon was sidelined by appendicitis, the musical again faltered. *Milk and Honey* closed on January 26th, 1963. Despite its popularity and success, the show paid back only ninety percent of its investment. High salaries, expensive sets and slow sales during Picon's absences had damaged the show commercially. Herman states, "Picon's leaving throttled the show. It took a year off the life of the musical" (quoted in Citron 63). Nevertheless, the musical lasted two years, or 543 performances, according to Herman, "a long run in those days" (quoted in Horwitz 1).

Synopsis

Milk and Honey remains comparatively unknown today, necessitating a synopsis. The show opens on the streets of Jerusalem, outside the King David Hotel, on the eve of the Israeli Independence Day celebration. A quarrel between a Yemenite shepherd boy and a hotel porter about the right to take livestock through the street causes a commotion ("Sheep Song"). Ruth Stein, part of a group of American Jewish widows touring Israel, and Phil Arkin, visiting his daughter and new Israeli son-in-law, meet when he translates the scuffle. Phil proceeds to teach Ruth the one word of Hebrew she truly needs to know ("Shalom"). Clara Weiss, one of the traveling widows, enters and officially introduces Ruth to Phil, prying to find out his potential as a marriage prospect (her major concern while visiting Israel). Phil's daughter Barbara enters and suggests that Ruth tour Israel with she and her father that day. Ruth, though worried about the propriety of traveling with Phil, accepts. That evening Israelis party in the streets to celebrate the country's Independence ("Independence Day Hora"). Clara Weiss gets caught in the middle, and despite her age, shows everyone up in the dancing department. During the commotion Barbara encourages Phil to invite Ruth to the Negev Desert. Ruth accepts the offer. With Ruth offstage we discover that Phil is still married, although he has not lived with his wife for twenty years. The next scene opens several days later with a spirited work dance at Barbara and her husband David's moshav (privately owned farms operating within a cooperative). The dance demonstrates the reclaiming of Israel's barren land by the Jewish settlers. Adi, a disgruntled native Israeli, would prefer luxurious, air-conditioned America to living in the Negev, but he is shortly due to be married to his very pregnant fiancée Zipporah in a triple wedding ceremony. Phil tries to convince David to move to America. But David is a proud "Sabra" (native Israeli) and extols the virtues of his homeland in the title song ("Milk and Honey") to which Adi provides cynical counterpoint. As time passes, Ruth enjoys living on the moshav, learning Hebrew and sewing wedding dresses for the upcoming triple wedding. With their attraction growing, Phil tries to convince Ruth to stay longer, singing ("There's No Reason in the World"). David encourages Phil to buy land in Israel, where no one will care about his marital status. Clara Weiss and the group of widows have arrived on the moshav as part of their tour, and are impressed to see the fine specimens of Israeli manhood on display. Clara sings about the widows' motives for visiting: hoping to take home a husband as a souvenir. When the men turn out to be married, Clara sings an inspirational march to the widows ("Chin Up Ladies"). In the next scene Ruth jubilantly tells Phil she's decided to ignore staid strictures and to stay in Israel with him ("That Was Yesterday"). Barbara worriedly tells Phil not to tell Ruth about his marriage. When Phil disagrees, Barbara lashes out at David about her unhappiness and fear of living in Israel. After Phil has told Ruth about his marriage, he sings to her to stay with him regardless ("Let's Not Waste a Moment"). The scene dissolves into a Yemenite wedding ceremony, complete with three brides and grooms, a cantor, Hassidim, bridesmaids and a maid of honor performing a ceremonial dance of love ("The Wedding"). As the curtain closes on Act I, Ruth and Phil climb the stairs together to his bedroom above the barn.

A jubilant Phil, feeling much younger than his age, opens Act II. Ready to start a life as a farmer in Israel with Ruth he sings ("Like a Young Man"). Barbara tells him that Ruth has left for Tel Aviv early that morning, unable to reconcile her conscience with Phil's marriage. Phil goes to find her, and David comes to tell Barbara that he will move to America and become a businessman for her ("I Will Follow You"). He performs a solo dance expressing his conflicting loyalties to Barbara and to the land of Israel. Clara Weiss meets widower Sol Horowitz, who to her great pleasure trades in diamonds. But before she can accept his dinner invitation, she must ask the permission of her dead husband ("Hymn to Hymie"). After their dinner — Hymie gave permission — Clara finds Ruth, who explains that her own marriage was far from fulfilling, and she's never had feelings like she has for Phil ("There's No Reason in the World," reprise). Back on the moshav, Zipporah gives birth and Adi jubilantly leads a chorus of the title song, while the chorus satirically reminds him of his previous misgivings ("Milk and Honey"). Phil has returned without finding Ruth, but soon we see that she too has come to the moshav. Phil argues she shouldn't stay, but Ruth sings that she needs him ("Just as Simple as That"). The last scene takes place in the airport, where our central lovers part, hoping that Phil will manage to get a divorce from his wife, so that they will be able to at last be together ("Finale").

Too Jewish?

Milk and Honey was the first Broadway musical that dealt primarily with Jewish characters and themes. Although musicals had contained Jewish characters before 1961, *Milk and Honey* was unique in its scope, and was thus a trailblazer. There was a definite shift in the 20th century in allowable subject matter of Broadway musicals. If in the first half of the century, as Andrea Most argues in her *Making Americans* (2004), Jews used musical theatre as means for jumping into the melting pot; for purposes of assimilation, a clear shift happened in the second half of this century. If, in the Broadway musical's early years and the "golden years" (usually argued to span the decades of the 1940s and 50s) Jews wrote about nuns, frontier folk, and the King of Siam, writing songs like "White Christmas" and arguing "We know we belong to the land." During the 1960s, beginning with *Milk and Honey*, Jewish authors of musical theatre turned their gifts onto subjects closer to home. It seems that an Israeli background or themes were now welcome in this era as well. Critic John McClain opined, "It would seem inevitable that somebody should undertake an Israeli musical — echoes of its restless rhythms and dances have already reached us" (238). Nevertheless, there were serious fears about the subject matter, whether it would appeal to general audiences or would simply be "too Jewish." Cast member Molly Picon reminisced about meeting producer Martin Beck backstage at her debut on Broadway in 1940, in the Jewish play *Morning Star*:

> He told me he liked the play, but personally wouldn't have touched it with a ten-foot pole. He explained: "Who wanted to see a Jewish play on Broadway?" Now we were beginning a [musical] about American Jews in Israel and would play it in his theater [the Martin Beck Theatre on Broadway]. Beck's words came back to me, of course. I wondered whether we would prove him wrong. I desperately wanted to [217].

Picon felt the consequences of the creative team's concern. Don Appell, the book writer, encouraged Picon to play Clara "sweeter" during the rehearsal process. Picon rebelled and thought something else lay behind the coaching:

> The real problem, I suspect, was not so much that the producers didn't want Clara to be too funny [...] they were afraid I would be too "Jewish." They kept cautioning me about using my hands and even removed a rhinestone buckle from my hair because Hadassah [the Jewish women's organization] might find it gaudy! [219].

Costumes and physicality were not the only culprits, "At one point, someone decided I should speak without inflections. 'But the dialogue is written that way,' I reasoned and, thankfully, prevailed" (221). Picon's confidence prevailed over any worries or doubts the musical's creators had. She persisted, "As my role increased, little by little, so did my gestures and comedic interpretation. And if it seemed 'Jewish,' so be it" (219). Audiences and critics offered universal praise, vindicating her assurance.

Other actors also bore the brunt of worries regarding the musical's Jewish material. Although ethnic stereotypes were at stake with Molly Picon, religion also offered a site of anxiety. Through successive drafts, the lead female Ruth was made far less religiously Jewish. Early drafts painted Ruth as a deeply devout Hebrew schoolteacher. By the time *Milk and Honey* opened, the character could not speak Hebrew, and references to her faith were expunged. For example, in an early draft, Phil appeals to the, "one who made the world," to keep Ruth from compromising her values. Appell removed this line. Most importantly, a long scene where Ruth appeals to a Rabbi to assuage her moral concerns was cut from the show during previews. According to Picon, the New Haven tryouts convinced the authors to lighten the tone, and so they began cutting the text: "The first to go, thankfully, was a synagogue scene which had never worked. Mimi [Benzell, as Ruth] had been given this long speech where she went to temple to beg God's forgiveness. That was out" (219–220). Cutting this scene entailed financial loss for the producers, as it meant losing an already constructed set. Ruth's solo in this scene called "Give Me a Word" was also deleted. Herman felt that the number was "too serious even for an operetta" (quoted in Citron 59). The cut scene's stage directions demonstrate the ambivalence toward Judaism displayed by the show's authors, at least book writer Don Appell. The scene took place in the rabbinical chambers, described thus:

> The feeling we should get about this room is that it dwarfs everyone who enters. [...] One small window high on the wall allows the light to stream in from the outside world. It is a room that is devoted to meditation and learning, but *it can be frightening to an outsider* [II-3-17; emphasis mine].

The script later describes the window as "prison-like" (II-3-20), and describes the rabbi dramatically, "his body is huge and his face seems to be chiseled out of stone. He is at once godlike and majestic in appearance. When he speaks his voice is rich and warm and comforting, but it is at the same time authoritative and unyielding" (II-3-17). Ron Holgate, who played the rabbi (and in a revival, Phil), "felt his scene was the only one the Boston critics cited as 'ringing true'" (Citron 59). It seems that the potential that religious display might be "frightening to an outsider" prevailed. It's seriousness and religiosity may have been simply "too Jewish" for *Milk and Honey's* creators.

Over thirty years later, in 1994, the only major professional revival [as of this writing] of *Milk and Honey* opened at the American Jewish Theater. (A two week staged reading ran in October 2011 as part of the "Musicals Tonight" series at the Lion Theatre, Off Broadway.) With the passage of time, the musical required an entirely new book, according to the artistic director Stanley Brechner and director Richard Sabellico. They rewrote the libretto, taking away the "glitz, starting with what Brechner called the 'fantasy world' atmosphere" (quoted in Miller 23). The musical's treatment of ethnic stereotypes had also dated. Referring to the widows, Sabellico argues, "The script's caricatures borders on the offensive" (quoted in Miller 25). The director employed other rewrites to "soften some of the propaganda" (quoted in Miller 25). Significantly, Brechner argued, "You cannot discuss Israel without a political context. We no longer consider Israel the land of milk and honey" (quoted in Miller 23). The AJT directors added an Arab character, deepened the Arab / Israeli conflict and tried to flesh out the characters. Ron Holgate, who starred in the revival and made his Broadway debut in the original production, argues that in 1961 the musical, "succeeded on the score and the performance. [...] Additionally [...] at that time Israel was a romantic and exciting place" (quoted in Miller 23). America's idea of Israel has continued to change since it's founding in 1948, the original production in 1961, and the revival in 1994. We examine these shifts when considering the types of nostalgia at work in *Milk and Honey*, and how they interact with a buried or sublimated reaction to the Holocaust.

Israel and American Jews

From the time of its creation, Israel offered a complicated construction for American Jews. *Milk and Honey*, ostensibly about Israel, more deeply examines the state of American Jewry. As Grose tells us, "The creation of the new state [of Israel] in 1948 had an immediate, profound, and confusing impact on the Jews of America" (304). Ben Gurion, an instrumental founder of Israel and its first Prime Minister, called on young American Jews to immigrate to Israel. According to Grose:

> The elders of the Jewish establishment were shocked; this violated the old understanding that the state would serve the needs of downtrodden Jews living under oppression, but had no personal claims to make on the secure Jews of America [305].

America had offered its own promised land for the Jewish population: American Jews were experiencing financial and cultural success at significant levels by the time of Israel's creation in 1948. Grose tells us, "Polls of American Jewry through the 1950s and early 1960s revealed nearly unanimous support for Israel — 94 percent of adults, in one study — but no more than 4 percent ready to immigrate" (306). Instead, according to some scholars, Israel was thought of as an "insurance policy" for American Jews worried about recurring anti–Semitism in America (Grose). But, with current success, they were not ready to collect on that policy; American Jews were happy to support Israel, but in this era were less interested in living there. Audiences could feel an allegiance to or affection for Israel, enough to crave exposure to the country without making the commitment to leave their established, comfortable lives. Instead, they could experience Israel through theatre, which offered an outlet for ethnic identification without significant effort. By watching a Jewish themed musical like *Milk and Honey*, an audience member could identify with their Judaism through secular means. *Milk and Honey* offered support for this identification by offering a guided tour of the biblical homeland. As Walter Kerr in the *New York Herald Tribune* points out:

> *Milk and Honey* has the sunniness of a travel poster, and, when it is singing, the bursting energy of a whole town meeting the boat. But its libretto seems to have been written by that stiff and self-conscious fellow who composes tourist guidebooks [240].

The musical acted as a travel brochure by peppering the text with tourist facts of interest, pointing out that, for the Israelis, the Independence Day celebration, "is the 4th of July" (I-2-14); that Israelis eat ham, contrary to kosher laws; and that "We don't have a Y.M.H.A here in Israel" (I-1-10). These bulletin points of interest address two distinct audiences. They teach outsiders, or non–Jews, but they also provide a service for insider audiences, who could take a trip to an ancestral land without leaving midtown Manhattan.

Milk and Honey's tour book function necessitates a positivistic outlook. Even Herman's attempt to dampen the show's unfettered praise of Israel seems rather meek. He gives one character, Adi, the cynical Moshav dweller, counterpoint to the patriotic eponymous hymn, "Milk and Honey," where he references the aridity of the climate, and pointedly, the political tensions and attacks from neighboring Arab countries. Herman states:

Something rubbed me the wrong way about saying how absolutely marvelous everything was in this country, if I could not mention the things I saw that were not marvelous. The show came out a valentine, but I was proud of that gray shadow that made it truthful [40–41].

But we cannot grant Adi's rant overmuch status, as the text marginalizes his solo voice against the group. Adi later repents and the community embraces and absorbs him. By the reprise, the vocal line assignments have switched, the chorus jokingly reminding him of his countermelody while Adi happily sings the anthem. After his son's birth he has been converted to the ideals of the group and no longer offers a threat. Adi's brief reminder of the hostile Arab population surrounding Israel stands virtually alone in the finalized libretto. Early drafts offered more awareness, but became successively sunnier. By the time *Milk and Honey* opened the Arab threat has been reduced to a sexualized joke. When the widows express their fears of living in the desert, one of them worries:

MRS. PERLMAN: In the middle of the night when everybody is sleeping, a big Arab can come and pick you up in his arms and take you away to his harem.
MRS. WEISS: You should only be so lucky [I-4-42,43].

Only one moment of intensity about the danger of living in Israel remains in the final libretto. When Barbara reveals to David her true feelings about working on the moshav, she cries:

Is this what you call a life? Working sixteen hours a day! Hoarding every drop of water and waiting for a rain that never comes. Surrounded on three sides by seven million enemies and the only way out is into the sea! [...] I hate it here! I hate it! [I-5-59].

As with Adi's dissent, Barbara's fears are ultimately negated. Her potentially disturbing observations are drowned out by reprises of the patriotic title song and her own repudiation in favor of loyalty to her husband. With these voices silenced, *Milk and Honey* can continue to offer a rosy, often nostalgic picture of a land triumphantly restoring in front of our eyes.

ANTI-NOSTALGIA: MORALITY, EXOTICISM AND AUTHENTICITY

On the surface, *Milk and Honey* acts as a valentine for the emerging country of Israel, celebrating new possibilities rather than old memories. The musical seemingly insists on a forward-looking and resolutely non-nostalgic perspective. The Israeli government's support of Herman and Appell's visit to their country seems to have paid off, for *Milk and Honey*'s façade offers a glossy advertisement for the new state of Israel. As critic David Richards argued in his review of the original in *The New York Times*, "The book [...]

can easily be mistaken for a travel brochure when it is not serving as a pep rally for what was then a young, idealistic state" (n. pag.). The central moral themes of the musical also belong in the realm of anti-nostalgic sentiment.

Milk and Honey strikes us today as having a particularly out of date moral stance. Its traditional minded exploration of the state of marriage and strict stance towards the definition of infidelity can be seen as the last gasps of a 1950s style morality, appearing on a Broadway oblivious to a world on the cusp of radical change. However, when examined closely, the musical's contrast of Israeli and American values presents an interesting twist. Although ideas were clearer in first draft, the final libretto nevertheless negatively contrasts the fussy morals of the Americans — Ruth, Phil, and Clara — to the new Israeli world. Traditional societal mores do not apply in this new virile society, and although American values win in the end, the confused morality of the older lovers and their bittersweet hope to be together seems to privilege freer Israeli mores. As David urges Phil, in Israel no one will care if the lovers are unmarried, for the new society places the patriotic upkeep of the land far above antiquated moral ideas. For instance the pregnant Zipporah does not marry until the end of Act I. The libretto underlines Israel's freer ideas towards the state of marriage. Much of this emphasis may emerge from the personal stories of *Milk and Honey*'s creators. As Citron argues, Appell (and Herman's) sexuality influenced their perspectives on Israel, "Having had to camouflage his sexuality all his life, Appell admired the Israeli people's freedom from restraint enough to make it the raison d'être of his musical" (49). The outdated, much criticized moral center of the libretto also serves to forward the idea of a brand new, anti-nostalgic world.

Efforts to provide "authenticity" also serve to fight nostalgic sentiment. Critics were aware of *Milk and Honey*'s attempts to create a genuine atmosphere, and were largely convinced. Critic Howard Taubman typified the reaction by stating, "Although a musical is not a documentary, there is a ring of authenticity in the atmosphere" (239). The choreography tried to incorporate real Israeli dances. Juki Arkin, an Israeli actor who played Adi, also acted as the "ethnic dance advisor," demonstrating the artistic team's attempts at authenticity, which the critics accepted. John McClain explains, "All the dance numbers are energetic and indigenous to the raw and lusty character of the new nation" (238). Walter Kerr argued that attempts at authenticity erred on the side of guidebook mentality, "The air of deliberate illustration persists: a goat must be milked to show us how it is done, [...] and brochure rhetoric seems to invade dialogue and lyrics as well" (241). Extreme scenic realism also contributed to attempts at authenticity. Live animals, including the goat milked on stage, a genuine tractor, bales of hay: these were bits of business for novelty, but also served to demonstrate the musical's attempted "liveness," robust immediacy and realism. Production photographs are particularly fascinating evidence when reading the musical's attempts at authenticity. Photos of the chorus show young, virile, scantily clad dancers in the face of stormy desert backdrop. Critic Norman Nadel, in a sexualized review not likely to make it to press today, illustrated this atmosphere:

> The men are indeed handsome, muscular and virile. The girls have strong, healthy, glowing bodies, beautifully formed, with long lithe legs and the best of all other requirements. You are permitted to see this, as they dance in work shorts and halters or twirl in short, full skirts [241].

Nadel's reaction brings up another pervading aesthetic in *Milk and Honey*, one that seems to be contrary to authenticity: exoticism. The words "exotic" and "authentic' both recur in the reviews. Richard Watts, in the *New York Post*, typifies this uneasy marriage, "There is a happy feeling of authenticity in the depiction of the atmosphere of the new state, and it is skillfully carried out by [...] the imaginative choreography [...] which can be exultantly vigorous and picturesquely exotic in turn" (240). Exoticism and authenticity are contrasting ideas today, but in the 1960s, dependent upon the audience and their extent of knowledge of the subject matter, their union seemed to be accepted. The "Independence Day Hora," brings us immediately into a foreign world with a dance that seems, certainly to the uninitiated, exotic and yet accurate. Audiences likely understood the world of the musical as foreign and exciting. Production photographs show *Milk and Honey*'s set prominently displaying Hebrew lettering on large signs, taking the upper half of the stage's visual picture. This lettering must have seemed both alien and genuine to an un-initiated audience, perhaps even to American Jews only slightly familiar with this "new" language, revived from the ancient world for use in Israel. The music also contributed to this atmosphere. In his memoir Jerry Herman gives credit to "Richard DeCormier, who did amazing things with the vocal arrangements to give the music a rich sound and an exotic ethnic flavor" (44). Exoticism and authenticity both act in this musical as signposts of a forward-looking world that has no need of the past, in the face of a vibrantly exciting future.

Memory and Nostalgia

Despite this surface impression, memory and the past are in fact central concerns at work in this musical. "Nostalgia's" definition encompasses homesickness and wistful sentimental longing. With the Diaspora as a defining characteristic of Judaism, the idea of homesickness for Israel has lasted for thousands of years, and wistful or sentimental longing for the biblical past has been elaborated through centuries of Jewish literature and culture. The constructed concepts of both Israel and nostalgia, however, are equally intricate and problematic. Svetlana Boym's definitions, in *The Future of Nostalgia* (2001), can help to contextualize *Milk and Honey*'s perspective towards Israel. Boym separates nostalgia into two categories, the first, "reflective" nostalgia, is self-aware and does not hope for restoration. This more "traditional" or straightforward form of nostalgia circulates in *Milk and Honey* through the echoes of the disappearing Yiddish theatre, ghosted on stage by Molly Picon's performance. Boym's second category, "restorative," nostalgia, as the name implies, looks to re-establish the longed-for past and denies itself as nostalgia. Boym argues, "Restorative nostalgia does not think of itself as nostalgia, but rather as truth and tradition" (xviii). She continues: "Nostalgia is an ache of temporal distance and displacement. Restorative nostalgia takes care of both of these symptoms. Distance is compensated by intimate experience and the availability of a desired object. Displacement is cured by a return home, preferably a collective one" (46). We find restorative nostalgia for biblical Israel circulating strongly in *Milk and Honey*. Both of these kinds of nostalgia in Herman's musical, one more directly than the other, can ultimately be connected to sublimation of Holocaust loss.

MOLLY PICON, YIDDISH THEATRE AND REFLECTIVE NOSTALGIA

Molly Picon (1898–1992), the child of immigrants, was born in America and raised in Philadelphia. She began her career in vaudeville, but she switched to the Yiddish theatre when she toured Europe with her husband Yonkel's Yiddish theatre troupe during the Depression. When they came back Picon and her husband opened a theatre on Second Avenue, and Picon became a bona fide Yiddish theatre star. Just under five feet tall and able to play children into her thirties, Picon was best known in her early career for playing plucky orphan characters. This kind of childlike character finds an older version in *Milk and Honey*'s Clara Weiss. Picon's American success story, as well as her transfer from the Yiddish to the Broadway stage, serves as a major foci for nostalgic sentiment in *Milk and Honey*'s 1961 audiences. Picon's performance resonated with a potent source of Jewish communal memory, the moribund Yiddish theatre. Whereas the Promised Land offered a site for restorative nostalgia, Picon and the Yiddish theatre fit into Boym's category of "reflective" nostalgia. According to Boym, reflective nostalgia is self-aware, and does not hope for restoration. Memories of the Yiddish theatre invoked by the musical do not take the aim of restoring Second Avenue to theatrical life. Instead, watching Molly Picon could invoke bittersweet but passive memories of the glory years of that theatrical form.

Milk and Honey (1961–1963 Broadway). Music and lyrics by Jerry Herman, book by Don Appell, directed by Albert Marre. Shown center, held aloft: Molly Picon as Clara Weiss.

Herman writes in his memoir that Molly Picon was a central part of *Milk and Honey* even at its very beginning stages:

> We started talking about the actresses who could play the widows. The name Molly Picon popped out of both our mouths at the same time. I knew about Molly Picon from my parents, but Don had actually seen all her performances in Yiddish theater pieces and he absolutely adored her. [...] He said, "I am going to write a part for Molly Picon and it will be so delicious that she won't be able to turn it down." (39)

Picon did not turn it down, and her performance received the best reviews, more or less single handedly insuring the run. Picon's trademarks made their way into *Milk and Honey*, demonstrating the continuity between her Yiddish theatre persona and her character in the musical. Picon describes struggling in her initial rehearsals of "Hymn to Hymie," "The song needed something flip, especially when Clara cried: 'Look Hymie, I'm young!' Finally I negotiated with Jerry and I worked my somersault in! It was my best move" (218). But her trademark gymnastic trick apparently was not enough for Molly. As

Picon continued, "The dance routines ate up hours, but we still seemed confused. At one point, I put in my own step and soon the entire company was doing my *pas de Picon*" (218). With this signature dance move from Second Avenue, a piece of Yiddish theatre nostalgia took pride of place at the center of an exotic "new" Israeli dance. The "pas de Picon" also made its way into the published stage directions, one of the few references to a particular actor still in the licensed version of any musical libretto. This demonstrates the impact Picon made on the show, and the extent to which her presence, in view of her past, was integral to the show. Picon's dancing, much remarked upon by critics, demonstrated that the Yiddish tradition was alive and well, albeit in a new context. Picon's vitality implied vigor in the Yiddish theatre, even though the historical form had virtually disappeared. The tensions created by this contradiction created a bittersweet nostalgia.

In 1962, during the run of *Milk and Honey*, Picon recalled, "I did an extra benefit after one show for the Yiddish actors who seemed mostly old and sick. [...] The benefit left me feeling very depressed and I wondered: Am I going Broadway or what?" (224). Picon's depression marks the serious transition that had taken place from the turn of the century, the height of the Yiddish theatre in New York, until 1962, when the theatre was largely dead. In the 1960-61 theatre season, when *Milk and Honey* opened, the Yiddish theatre in New York offered only one dramatic presentation. During its heyday it would have offered hundreds more. The epicenter of the Yiddish theatre was Second Avenue on New York City's Lower East Side, the neighborhood packed with recent Jewish immigrants.

The Yiddish theatre took pride of place in this neighborhood from its very beginnings, as a nostalgic vehicle. As Shipow argues, "Thus, being Jewish was often reduced to an exercise in nostalgia, the occasional comfort of ethnic congregation, when one had the time and money. A major avenue was the Yiddish theatre" (44). Jewish immigrants were thrown into a new world where their traditions, language and culture were constantly vulnerable to change. The theatre allowed them space to recall the world they came from, as well as connect to others that valued that world. David Lifson states, "In Yiddish theatres immigrants were able to revel in a nostalgia for the home country while the theatre provided them with a feeling of belonging in this new land" (n. pag.). The Yiddish theatre went into massive decline after 1940, but the process had begun even earlier. In the twenty years from 1928 to 1948 the number of Yiddish theatres in New York City reduced from fourteen to three. According to Lifson, the forces pitted against Yiddish theatre included socioeconomic depression, a loss of audience (due to both immigration limits in the 1920s, and flight to the suburbs), film and radio competition, lack of internal organization or artistic innovation, and internal financial issues.

The disappearance of an increasingly Americanized and assimilated audience helped to bring on the end of the Yiddish theatre, and offers a central explanation for nostalgia. A theatre form, and the lifestyle it represented, had gone. Integration does not have to entail forgetfulness however. In fact, it can intensify memories of the world left behind. The heyday of Yiddish theatre in America disappeared. But its echoes remained in Broadway musicals, and quite directly, in *Milk and Honey*. Herman's musical recalled the Yiddish theatre for a steadily integrating Jewish audience. If Second Avenue theatre was nostalgic to begin with, the removal of a generation and transference to another genre could only make that nostalgia more powerful.

Picon's performance offered a direct memory cue, and *Milk and Honey*'s text also contained Yiddish theatre resonances in its structure and form. Critic Howard Taubman calls attention to the fact that portions of *Milk and Honey* were directly beholden to Yiddish theatre: "Although its comedy is not sparkling and often recalls commonplace routines of Second Avenue, it does not play false with its characters" (239). The musical's comic style indeed recalls Second Avenue. For example, when we first meet Picon's character Clara Weiss, she tells Phil:

> MRS. WEISS: We come from different places. Ruth is from Cleveland. I'm from New York. But we have one thing in common.
> PHIL: I know. You're all Jewish.
> MRS. WEISS: No. We're all widows. Jewish also, but widows! (I-1-8)

Phil's assumption that the women are Jewish does not offer a stretch, given the locale of the musical. However, Phil's comment would have likely been a laugh line, due to Picon's well-honed Second Avenue performance style, marking her as a readily recognizable Jewish type. The original performers recognized that the Yiddish theatre influenced portions of *Milk and Honey* were the strongest in the musical. Into the run, Weede and Benzell were, according to Picon, "kvetching [complaining]. The score was a very difficult one to sing eight times a week and they didn't have my Second Avenue tricks to fall back on" (224). Picon was well aware of the kind of performance she offered. When concerned about taking a film role, she argued that onstage, "I could always rely on my Yiddish *shtick*: the singing, the dancing, the tricks, which I knew could keep me going on the stage for years" (235). *Milk and Honey* offered the perfect venue for her shtick, and brought it to a wider audience.

Who made up *Milk and Honey*'s audience? Ken Bloom, editor of *Jerry Herman's Lyrics*, summarizes the run of *Milk and Honey*, "The mainly Jewish audience took the show to heart and kept it running for 543 performances" (18). The musical also offered Jewish jokes that only a specific audience would understand. According to Herman, the audiences consistently loved one line in the show: "How hard it is to make a tsimmis, just for one" (II-2-16). Tsimmis, Herman explains, "is this elaborate stew that Jewish mothers would make in huge batches for their families" (49). This reference would be understood only by a Jewish audience, although this kind of ethnic cooking belonged largely to the old neighborhood, rather than the rapidly Americanized suburban Jews who came to see *Milk and Honey.*

Milk and Honey seems much less universal and more obviously aimed at Jewish audiences than some of the later projects we will examine. However, an entirely Jewish audience presents a statistical impossibility. The musical must have offered something to gentile audiences. What did Herman's musical offer to its varied audiences? Non-Jewish audiences were offered the usual pleasures of a Broadway musical: comedy, singing, and dancing. They also would have experienced the appeal of the exotic that we have discussed, compounded. Molly Picon certainly believed in the universality of, at the very least, her *own* appeal:

> We still had SRO audiences in Boston, 80 percent who weren't Jewish. Not that these figures stopped the critics from chastising our script. Local critic Eliot Norton pulled the play apart by saying it was only for limited audience. And I said, "I get most of my mail from unlimited audiences" [220].

Preview audiences challenged the idea of universality. Picon recounts occurrences on the road before the show opened, noting Philadelphia's audiences were still good, with groups like Friends of Mt. Sinai and Israeli El Al booking tickets. But in other cities with smaller Jewish populations there were challenges. Picon recalls:

> And when you did your best and the audience didn't respond, you'd lie awake trying to figure it. [...] are we off because it's Passover? Maybe the audience was anti–Israel? [...] We had to make them like our show, and we often did. But we weren't getting to general audiences [234].

Clearly Jewish audiences were important to the reception of the show. But the producers and creative team had made sure to hedge bets where audiences were concerned. After opening to glowing notices on Broadway, Picon pointed out that the other leads had a publicity agent while she did not:

> Naturally, I had asked where was mine. Oh, you don't need one, I was told. But the real message I got was that nobody wanted to publicize me too much for fear it would scare away the gentile crowd. They had been proven wrong. [...] The audience was coming to see me [222].

Indeed they were. Picon was nominated for a Tony, ticket sales flagged every time she left the production, and the commercial fate of the musical seemed to rest in her hands. Picon stayed with various productions of *Milk and Honey* for years after the tour closed, from the Paper Mill Playhouse, the

Coconut Grove Theatre and other large regional houses, to the "tent circuit" throughout the United States. Clearly, according to box office, as well as her own estimation, Picon was the show. Without her the productions have fallen off almost completely until the Off Broadway revival in 1992, with no major production since. Without Picon as a potent source of reflective nostalgia, the wooden libretto and dated material allowed the musical to fade into obscurity.

Restorative Nostalgia

Boym's second category of nostalgia circulates even more strongly in *Milk and Honey*'s text. The extent of the musical's Israeli patriotism implies a restorative nostalgia for the Promised Land, granted to first Abraham, then Isaac in the book of Genesis. Rather than ache for a distant past, the Israeli characters in the musical fight to restore the conditions of that past, to intimately experience their connection to the land, and thereby to return to a collective home. In the early years of Israel's existence, optimism and collective memory for biblical Israel emphasized that restoration of the biblical past was possible. With pride in their God-given birthright, Israelis worked to make the desert green again, bolstered by Jews around the world sending money to plant trees. *Milk and Honey* reflects this hopeful and industrious atmosphere, displaying the hope to reinstate the glories of the land of Canaan.

Milk and Honey's content, as well as its form, argues for restorative nostalgia. The title song's lyrics that opened this essay offer hints of the emotion behind the musical's fervent Israeli loyalty. The song opens by praising the abundance, strength, youth, happiness and musicality of the land and continues with the lyrics with which we opened:

> This is the place where the hopes of the homeless
> And the dreams of the lost combine.
> This is the land that heaven blessed
> And this lovely land is mine! [I-3-25].

This song acts as an anthem, glorifying the ideas upon which Israel was founded. Its imagery insists on youth, strength, happiness and moral certitude. Importantly it ends, "and this lovely land is *mine*" (italics mine), a defiant claim of ownership not to be denied. The lyric, "hopes of the homeless and the dreams of the lost," offers the historical view of Jews, homeless since the Diaspora.

The phrase "milk and honey" first appears in the bible in the book of Exodus 3:8 and refers to bounty of the land of Canaan, promised to the Jews.

Therefore the title itself offers a restorative nostalgic perspective. Early drafts were titled *Shalom*; the shift to *Milk and Honey* cannot be a coincidence. The new title sums up the historically laden thematic concerns. Israel was the land of milk and honey thousands of years ago, and although that agricultural abundance had been lost, *Milk and Honey*'s characters, through energy, lust for life and hard work, demonstrate the road back to that ancient success. Israel offers an active site of nostalgia, despite its temporal remove of thousands of years. This historical distance offers no impediment to the restorative nostalgic argument, we do not have to long for the past; instead, we can rebuild it.

Milk and Honey's choice of language offers an example of restorative nostalgic practices. The show makes frequent use of Hebrew, an ancient biblical language restored by Zionists in Palestine, largely as a symbolic break with traumatic recent history. The musical opens with an extended argument in Hebrew (first in dialogue, then in song) between a porter and a Yemenite boy who wants to bring his sheep into the street. The second song, titled "Shalom," takes as its purpose translating Hebrew, and we hear that language throughout the score and the spoken text. It is used for religious purposes in an elaborately staged Yemenite wedding ceremony scene, and a reprise of "Shalom" takes pride of place as the central theme in the musical's finale.

The creative team's aforementioned efforts to provide immediacy, "liveness," and authenticity to *Milk and Honey*'s production served to glorify and celebrate modern Israel's progress towards restoring the biblical past. For example, in several work dances Donald Saddler's noteworthy choreography symbolized the spirited, though backbreaking work involved in rejuvenating the land. Stage directions in the title song read, "*Suddenly ALL burst out into song as several men carry on three enormous trees representing the planting of the desert*" (I-3-30). The inhabitants of the moshav exhibit a nostalgic need for dry and barren Palestine to be returned to the fertile and bountiful land God promised, and the musical, with its eponymous anthem, cheers them on.

Milk and Honey's score also encourages nostalgic identification. The score was "authentically Israeli" enough to almost deprive Jerry Herman of his next, career-making job. After *Milk and Honey* Herman had to convince producer David Merrick that he was "American enough" to compose his next show, *Hello Dolly!*. Herman was offended by Merrick's intimations that he could only compose "ethnic" music, but he recalls responding:

> I don't blame you, Mr. Merrick, after seeing *Milk and Honey*, my Israeli operetta, for thinking I'm a little Jewish kid who can only write this kind of music — but aside from that show all my other work has been as American as apple pie [quoted in Citron 4].

"I Will Follow You," David's song to his wife, remains the most consistently Middle Eastern or Hebraic in the score, and according to Citron, "The quasi-Hasidic minor key melody has a liturgical ring which makes it sound like a Hebrew incantation. The tessitura is purposely high, cantorial" (55). Though there are various nods to Israeli or Middle Eastern music, and to Jewish religious melodies, Herman's score also belongs to his typical oeuvre of all-American show tunes. Nevertheless, theatre critics were easily convinced and conferred upon the score the stamp of authenticity. Norman Nadel, in *New York World-Telegram,* stated, "Herman is not at his best with ballads, though his derivative music (drawn from Israeli folk and dance forms) is tremendous" (241). And more importantly, some members of the Jewish community seem to have accepted the music. Several songs from *Milk and Honey*, along with those from *Fiddler on the Roof,* appear on a CD produced by Hebrew National in 1996, called "Kosher Classics: 'Music that Answers to a Higher Authority.'" The CD advertises, "Whether a habituate of the synagogue or not, Hebrew National Kosher Classics will certainly please fans of stage and screen music" (http://www.allmusic.com/album/r239172). Authentic or not, the score has become accepted into the secular and commercial Jewish music canon. *Milk and Honey*'s musical influences would have encouraged nostalgia in its first audiences. Herman's score recalls restorative nostalgia for the Promised Land, with its misty and non-specific allusions to Middle Eastern music. It can also act as a cue for personal religious memories, the cantorial melodies reminding audience members of their synagogue. Music, one of the most evocative forms for memory, can act as a direct call to nostalgia, and does not need to be accurate to call up emotional response. Even the most glancing musical references could act upon memories for audience members wistful for, and hoping to restore, a disappearing community.

Postmemory

Why might audiences crave reflective or restorative nostalgia, and why might the nostalgic aspects of *Milk and Honey* contribute to its success on Broadway? According to scholar Fred Davis, "Mass collective nostalgia is most likely to occur after times of severe cultural discontinuity" (quoted in Furnish 2). I argue that the Holocaust acted as this severe discontinuity in the Jewish community, and encouraged the nostalgia we find in *Milk and Honey*, both reflective and restorative. First, reflective nostalgia for the dying Yiddish theatre, ghosted through Picon's performance, could offer a sublimation of pain into a success story, a period of Jewish thriving in the safe space of America. The loss of Yiddish theatre offered a less painful decline of a

Jewish tradition, a decline by choice, rather than through violence. The world of Second Avenue offers immigrant nostalgia (as we'll find in *Rags* and *Ragtime* in Chapter VII) as a substitution, an alternative history. Secondly, although Boym does not discuss restorative nostalgia as a reaction to trauma, in *Milk and Honey* the loss, pain and agony of the Holocaust function as the central, if obscured, argument for restoration. The characters work hard to restore the conditions of biblical Israel in order to return not just a land, but also a people, out of agony, to glory. Through the wish to forget the pain of the Holocaust, trauma can be sublimated into cultural achievement — making Israel green again. In the process of sublimation, loss becomes channeled into artistic or cultural achievement, thereby serving a higher purpose. Instead of dwelling in pain, Israelis fight to return to a better time, before trauma. *Milk and Honey*, a product of a period just beginning to grapple with the Holocaust, demonstrates this process. The musical's celebratory tone results directly from the sublimation of the Shoah. This sublimation demands "valentines to Israel." In the early 1960s, in reaction to pain, Israel and its people could be portrayed, without ambivalence, as morally justified, exciting, strong, healthy, virile, and young. The musical takes part in creating a mythic structure, morally unambiguous and comforting, an image worthy of being restored.

Herman's musical opened on Broadway at a time of quickly shifting attitudes towards Jewish assimilation and the Holocaust. Scholar Andrea Most's work describes the assimilationist task taken on by musical theatre writers of the first half of the century. As she explains, expounding on ethnic concerns ran counter to the aim of "melting" into society. Instead, Jewish authors in this era offered veiled portraits of otherness, addressing outcasts from society, but never specifically Jewish characters. Additionally, as Jones argues, "There was also a tacit assumption around Broadway that explicitly Jewish musicals had no chance of commercial success" (206). Add to this the climate engendered by the HUAC blacklists, McCarthy hearings, and the Rosenberg trials, making explicitly Jewish themes too risky on the commercial stage.

As we have seen, in this period, the Holocaust as a subject appeared more or less off limits. In America, the 1960s were a transitional period for attitudes towards the Holocaust. Post-war Americans largely preferred not to discuss or think about the horrors of World War II, including the death of European Jews. A marked silence prevailed on the subject after the initial shock of the death camps, until at least a decade later. A shift to increasing awareness of the Holocaust took place in the late 1950s and 60s. A corresponding shift in artistic and popular culture representations — in theatre beginning in the mid–1950s with *The Diary of Anne Frank* (1955) — demonstrates that the perception of the Nazi era was changing, and that the Holocaust was attaining a more central role in the U.S. cultural imagination. *Milk and Honey* thus arrived on

Broadway at a time of seething change. The musical uneasily rides the waves of those changes by tentatively beginning to approach the realities of the Holocaust while persisting in deep denial, sublimating the pain into restorative nostalgia.

The creation of Israel owes itself in large part to the revelation of the horrific facts of the Holocaust. As Lenni Brenner says, "Much of Western opinion felt that the creation of a Jewish state would be the belated silver lining after the black cloud that was the Holocaust" (87). Fear of massive immigration to America in the absence of a national homeland offers a slightly less beneficent motivation for support of the country. According to Brenner, "A mixture of deep shock, feelings of guilt, and perhaps even a touch or more of anti–Semitism led to the support of the U.S. Army for Jewish emigration from Eastern Europe to a country the Jews wanted to build up as their own" (88). In 1961, as *Milk and Honey* was being created, one of the most pivotal events in the history of Israel's relationship to the Holocaust occurred: the sensational capture of Eichmann by Israeli agents in Argentina and his subsequent trial. As we've seen these events were instrumental in turning American attention towards the events of the Holocaust. The trials occurred between April 11, 1961, and May 31, 1962, and *Milk and Honey* opened on October 10, 1961. Eichman's trial, death sentence and suicide must have had an impact on both the shaping of the musical and its reception, affecting the view of Israel presented in and taken from the piece.

On the surface, *Milk and Honey* ignores the existence of the Holocaust. The only direct reference occurs in scene in a Tel Aviv café, where a widow asks one of the patrons, "Mrs. Weinstein, Tell me, were you born here or are you a refugee?" (II-2-9). Certainly, many of the inhabitants of Israel would have been refugees or survivors, although the widow's line offers the only direct acknowledgment of that fact in the entire text. But a glancing reference to the Holocaust appears in the title song, which, as I have noted, offers, "This is the place where the hopes of the homeless / and the dreams of the lost combine" (I-3-25). Although these lines, especially the term "homeless," resonate with the historical Jewish Diaspora, more specifically they encompass Holocaust imagery, most concretely with the simple word, "lost." The Shoah had made very clear that European homes, in the true sense of the word, no longer, or had never truly, existed for Jews. Jewish survivors made their way to Israel for solace and new beginnings. Grose argued, "Israel has succeeded in its primary mission: providing a home and a refuge for those of its people in need" (316). By acknowledging those in need and the reasons why Israel was created, *Milk and Honey* would have encouraged the most positive sense of restorative nostalgia, nonetheless tinged with sorrow, loss, and pain. The song continues after these lyrics: from a quicker jubilant pace it suddenly slows to offer, "For this is a state of mind we live in / We want it green, and so it's green to us / For when you have wonderful plans for tomorrow / Somehow even today looks fine" (I-3-27). These lines offer solemn hope for survivors living in Israel: *even today* will be fine with the glorious future ahead. The presence of these Holocaust resonances in the eponymous song indicates the relevance of these ideas, bubbling beneath the surface of the seemingly straightforward musical.

The restorative nostalgia in *Milk and Honey* looks back towards a golden era, when Yehovah promised the Jews the rich land of Canaan and made them his chosen people. It remembers a time when Jews successfully led kingdoms, when they were a political power in the region and when the land offered its riches to them, flowing with the milk and honey of the title. *Milk and Honey*, by referencing history thousands of years old, demonstrates the possibility of restoring biblical conditions, by emphasizing powerful modern Jews reclaiming that glorious time through the sweat of their own brows. Alisa Solomon points out that the musical echoes the tenants of central Zionist figure Max Nordau, and his belief in a "muscular Judaism" which, with its emphasis on physical rigor and strength, would help to counter the stereotype of the weak, scholarly Jew. Nordau wrote before the helpless Jewish victim label engendered by the Holocaust irreversibly multiplied this stereotype. *Milk and Honey* actively fights this negative imagery by including many Sabra characters: strong, virile, native Israeli fighters who have defeated the odds to beat back their enemies and win their own country. The character of David in *Milk and Honey* presents the ultimate Sabra figure. When his father-in-law Phil wants him to come to America, David and his wife Barbara counter:

DAVID: But your son-in-law happens to be an Israeli.
BARBARA: And a third generation Sabra at that! [I-3-25].

When Phil asks him the difference David replies, "Pride. In myself. In my country" (I-3-25). David, handsome, virile, and strong, loves his country deeply. Powerful warrior Jews like David were an image worthy of grasping, an image to hold up against the conflicting pictures of victims helpless in the face of evil, the embodiment of health, wealth and power to contrast with the death camp photos still fresh in people's minds. David is not alone in his physical beauty and power. The imagery remarked upon by critics of the sexualized, strong and tan dancers' bodies, acts as a visual counter to images of the Holocaust. The musical's insistence on health, vitality and strength, offers a welcome contrast to images of Jews as victims, helpless in the face of evil. If, as the malignant stereotype presented, Jews could not fight back against the Nazis, and largely went to the slaughter unresisting, the people of Israel resisted, won the land that was their God given birthright, and would not be seen as victims again. *Milk and Honey* glorifies the restoration of the land and of its people.

American Jewish reactions to Israel remain unstable, volatile, and challenging. In view of the highly complicated political and moral questions Israel engenders today, *Milk and Honey*, with its trademark Jerry Herman sincerity and simplicity, looks quaint, idealistic, and highly naive. Most importantly, however, through its innocence, *Milk and Honey* offers a window into early attitudes toward Israel — how they came about and how they are maintained. The ways the musical packages Israel are meant to encourage Jewish pride, and offer a tribute to and advertisement for the country and Jewish culture as a whole, in the face of unthinkable loss. By offering two major sources of nostalgia, both reflective for the closer-to-home Yiddish theatre and restorative for ancient Israel, *Milk and Honey* offered Jewish audiences a source of community and counteracted the horrifying implications of the Holocaust, only just beginning to be explored.

CHAPTER IV

Fiddler on the Roof

"[*Fiddler* is] not really an accurate depiction of the *shtetl*, it's more like having false memories of a longing for community."
— Sheldon Harnick (quoted in Rosenbaum 6)

Fiddler on the Roof became the longest running American musical when its original production closed in 1972, after 3,242 performances. It has played in at least 32 foreign counties, been performed in at least 16 languages, had at least 18 cast albums recorded, and, as of the early 1990s, had grossed over twenty million dollars internationally. Clearly *Fiddler* has been and remains a force to be reckoned with, offering more than just commercial records, but also significant cultural impact. *Fiddler on the Roof* presents a clear-cut case of nostalgic renderings on the musical theatre stage of pre–Holocaust Jewish life. It has, since it's opening in 1964, increasingly helped to define and shape American conceptions of a particular Jewish past, a past almost erased by the Holocaust. Accordingly, nostalgia functions on various imbricated levels within *Fiddler*, while simultaneously privileging an absent but implied world: America.

Production History

Writer Sholem Rabinowitz (1859–1916) wrote under the pen name Sholem Aleichem (a Yiddish greeting). Born in Kiev, the author briefly moved to America in 1906, and permanently immigrated upon the outbreak of World War I. Sholem Aleichem's most famous stories — those concerning "Tevye the Dairyman"—were first printed in 1895. Numerous Tevye stories, written in Yiddish as Tevye's monologues, were published independently between that year and 1916 and were only unified as Volume 5 in the author's collected works, published between 1917–1925. A 1939 film directed by Maurice

Schwartz and Off Broadway plays produced by Arnold Perl in the 1950s were based on Sholem Aleichem and the Tevye stories, but by far the most famous Tevye iteration was the musicalized *Fiddler on the Roof.*

The Civil Rights movement and a dawning awareness of the Holocaust characterized the early 1960s, when *Fiddler on the Roof* first emerged. American Jews were enjoying the possibilities of increased financial success, stability, and assimilation. All these factors were pivotal to the creation of the musical. The genesis of *Fiddler on the Roof* can be traced to lyricist Sheldon Harnick reading the Sholem Aleichem novel *Wandering Star* (1909–10), about a Yiddish theatre troupe. Both Harnick and his writing partner, composer Jerry Bock, were excited about the possibility of musicalizing the novel. When they took the idea to librettist Joseph Stein, he told them the novel was structurally too large to translate to the stage but, intrigued, they agreed to look at other Sholem Aleichem material. The Tevye stories became their next logical step.

The creators went about securing the copyright and worked on the musical alone before attempting to secure a producer for the project. Stein explains, "I couldn't conceive of going to a producer and saying, 'We have this idea of a show about a lot of Jews in Russia. You know, they have a pogrom and get thrown out of their village.' A producer would have just stared at us" (quoted in Stone 12). Bock and Harnick worked on finding the right moments to musicalize, going through several drafts, while all the collaborators searched for the thematic thread that would tie the show together. With draft in hand the creators approached producers and were "turned down endlessly" according to Jerry Bock (quoted in Stone 15). One producer brought up a theme that plagued the creators until the show opened, the overt Jewishness of the material, stating, "I love it, but what will we do when we run out of Hadassah [Jewish woman's organization] benefits?" (quoted in Stone 15). For despite *Milk and Honey*'s modest success with audiences (having closed in 1963, just a year before *Fiddler* opened), overtly Jewish material was still believed to have a limited audience and shelf life. Certainly Herman's musical's financial failure could not have encouraged producers.

Ultimately producer Fred Coe became interested in the material. Coe put the creators in touch with Jerome Robbins, who was to greatly impact the project. Robbins became part of the creative process and continued to push the authors to define the central themes of *Fiddler on the Roof*, then still tentatively titled "Tevye." Finally, according to Harnick, "*somebody* said, 'Do you know what this play is about? It's about the dissolution of a way of life'" (quoted in Stone 17, orig. emphasis). Out of this idea emerged the opening number, "Tradition." Producer Hal Prince, of German, rather than Eastern European, Jewish heritage, who had initially turned down the project due to the foreignness of its subject, eventually rejoined the team, partially due to the participation of Robbins. Prince states, "The entire time *Fiddler* was in rehearsal I was like a stranger to it. It was just so removed from me; the atmosphere of it, the whole genre, seemed foreign [...] the beauty of those people eluded me until much later" (quoted in Altman 107). When casting began the team faced a challenge. It was important to them to find cast members who, according to Harnick, "would look as though they could conceivably be linked with this community at that time" (quoted in Stone 19). In other words finding a cast who "looked Jewish" was important to the creative team. Eventually a cast was found, led by the actor Zero Mostel (son of a Rabbi) as Tevye. Mostel apparently added much to the role in rehearsals, though he proved difficult to handle once performances began. The production previewed in Detroit and Washington D.C. before heading to Broadway, opening on September 22, 1964.

Fiddler on the Roof, despite the inarguable classic it has since become, originally received mixed reviews. Reviewers gave glowing notices to Zero Mostel (which apparently made the already difficult actor impossible to work with). Walter Kerr, in his decidedly mixed review in the *Herald Tribune*, after managing to admiringly call Mostel a "Jewish dolphin," summed up his primary argument thus:

> *Fiddler on the Roof* dips below its own best possible level by touching character too casually, and sometimes soiling it, with the lesser energies of easy quips, lyrics that stray too far from the land, and occasional high-pressure outbursts that are merely marketable [216].

Howard Taubman, in the *New York Times*, put the same argument somewhat more positively, "If I find fault with a gesture that is Broadway rather than the world of Sholem Aleichem, if I deplore a conventional scene, it is because *Fiddler on the Roof* is so fine that it deserves counsels toward perfection" (216). John Chapman, in the *Daily News*, on the other hand, was completely positive, stating, "It is one of the great works of American musical theatre. It is daring, touching, beautiful, warm, funny and inspiring. It is a work of art" (217). The musicals' creative team remembers the reviews somewhat wryly. Sheldon Harnick recalls, "As I remember it, John McClain said, 'It would have been a nice show if they hadn't put that damn pogrom in'" (quoted in Stone 26). What McClain in fact said, in the *Journal American*, was:

> It seemed to me there was an overabundance of self-pity displayed and that the show wouldn't have been hurt, might even have been helped, if the first act curtain could have fallen on Robbins' brilliant wedding celebration instead of running on into the anti-climactic persecution incident which followed [215].

Norman Nadel of *The New York World-Telegram*, offered the most famous review, advertising that, "You don't have to be Jewish to love Tevye" (214).

This statement sums up the debate between universality and specificity that still rages today. On July 21, 1971, *Fiddler* overtook *Hello Dolly!* as the longest running musical in history. Peter Stone describes it, "After eight years it ran out of people. Everybody in the world had seen it, so it closed [in 1972]" (Stone 10).

After the success of the Broadway production, the producers fielded various offers to mount foreign productions. They first accepted a production in Tel Aviv, Israel. Richard Altman, the original production's assistant director hired to recreate various international productions, recalls:

> We were sure it would have a shattering effect in Israel itself, where theatre audiences would be filled with immigrants like Yente, or their descendants. And since the creators of *Fiddler* had all been Jewish, it was appropriate that the first foreign production was to be in Israel [123].

Altman was surprised by the Israeli production. The cast, self-proclaimed "new Jews," wouldn't grow beards, and the Israeli interpreter largely mistranslated the script. Additionally, says Altman, "the Israelis were more forgetful of Jewish ritual than any other cast I worked with" (131). Nevertheless, *Fiddler* enjoyed great success in Israel, and as Altman notes, "many Israelis who themselves or whose forbears had survived the Russian pogroms and the Nazi Holocaust came to the Alhambra Theater two and even three times" (133). Altman recalls that he traveled throughout the world recreating *Fiddler* productions. Everywhere he went, people worried the production wouldn't transfer successfully, and everywhere it went, *Fiddler* was a hit. With the musical steadily achieving success around the world, it follows that a film adaptation would eventually appear. In 1971, the Mirisch brothers — who produced the film — hired director Norman Jewison to bring the work to the screen. The brothers first contacted Norman Jewison to direct the filmic musical because they believed his surname described his ethnicity. When he told them in their first meeting that in fact he was not Jewish, they were initially taken aback, according to the director ("Fiddler on the Roof" *www.imdb.com*). The producers hired Jewison despite his background, but the story remains illuminating. Clearly the ethnic / religious pedigree of artistic personnel remained central to the hiring process. Jewison's gentile background seems to have affected his choices nonetheless. Peter Stone surmises, "I think that, in a sense, Norman [Jewison] (who is gentile in all things except his name) was so nervous about the responsibility of doing this very Jewish piece and took it so seriously that a great deal of the humor that had been in the stage version was missing from the film" (27). Perhaps due to these "nerves" Jewison was more careful and respectful than the original all–Jewish stage production team, and included far more specificity of ethnic and cultural detail. The film version will be discussed incidentally throughout this chapter, but the focus of this work must be the musical stage.*

Synopsis

Fiddler in the Roof centers on Tevye the dairyman, who lives with his wife and five daughters in Anatevka, a small *shtetl* within the Russian Pale of Settlement (area in which Jews were restricted to live by the Tsar) in 1905. The musical opens when Tevye introduces the audience to the shtetl inhabitants and how they "keep their balance" ("Tradition"). We then see his family at home preparing for the Sabbath. Yente the matchmaker brings word that Lazar Wolf the butcher desires to marry Tzeitel, Tevye's eldest daughter, who instead has pledged herself to marry her childhood friend, Motel the tailor. The three eldest daughters sing of their expectations and fears of marriage ("Matchmaker"). Tevye brings home Perchik, a starving young revolutionary, who will give lessons to the younger daughters in exchange for food. The family then gathers for the weekly celebration of the Sabbath ("Sabbath Prayer"). After Sabbath, Tevye's wife Golde persuades him to go to the tavern to speak to Lazar Wolf. Despite misgivings Tevye agrees to allow the marriage and they celebrate in a raucous number that eventually includes the local Russians ("L'Chaim [To Life!]"). The next morning Tzeitel, horrified to learn of the marriage planned for her, begs her father not to force her to marry the butcher. Tevye relents, but his boundaries are pushed farther when Motel arrives, declaring himself a match for Tzeitel. After some consideration, and a personal discussion with God — a relationship maintained throughout the musical — Tevye yields and allows the marriage. Motel and Tzeitel celebrate ("Miracle of Miracles") and Tevye plans an elaborate ruse to persuade Golde to approve of the match ("Tevye's Dream"). Before Tzeitel's wedding, Chava (the third daughter) meets the non–Jewish Fyedka and they strike up the beginnings of friendship or romance. Russians interrupt Tzeitel and Motel's traditional and joyous wedding celebration ("Sunrise, Sunset"), with a pogrom, bringing down the curtain on Act One.

Act Two opens several months later. Perchik awkwardly proposes to Hodel, Tevye's second daughter, after telling her he must leave Anatevka to fight injustice ("Now I Have Everything"). They ask Tevye's blessing, but not his permission, pushing his allegiance to tradition even further. Eventually he relents, but this new idea of love prompts him to question his wife Golde

*Various scholars, including Lester Friedman and Patricia Erens have written in-depth studies of the depiction of Jews in film, including musical films.

about her feelings for him ("Do You Love Me?"). Yente delivers a letter to Hodel from Perchik telling her he has been arrested and sent to Siberia; the news spreads and grows ("The Rumor"). Tevye accompanies Hodel to the train station to join her fiancée ("Far From the Home I Love"). Tzeitel and Motel celebrate their "new arrival"—a sewing machine (as well as a new baby)—and we hear that Chava and Fyedka now intend to marry. Chava tries to introduce the subject to her father, but here he refuses to bend, forbidding her to see Fyedka ever again. Time passes and Golde finds Tevye to tell him Chava has run away and married Fyedka. Tevye proclaims that Chava will now be dead to the family. In a dance sequence he remembers Chava when she was a child ("Chaveleh"). When she appears and begs him to accept her, Tevye cannot bend that far and leaves Chava sobbing in the road. The Russian constable tells the villagers of an edict forcing them to leave their homes, and they sing of the little details of their village that they will miss ("Anatevka"). The family packs to leave. Tzeitel and Motel will be staying in Warsaw until they can join the rest of the family, who are emigrating to New York to live with their Uncle Abram. They receive last visits from Lazar Wolf, traveling to Chicago, and Yente, who will make her way to the Holy Land. Chava and Fyedka come to say goodbye, telling Tevye that they will go to Krakow because, "we cannot stay amongst people who can do such things to others" (164). Tevye studiously ignores the couple, but prompts Tzeitel under his breath to tell them "God be with you." The family finishes packing and all the villagers begin their march away. Tevye beckons the Fiddler to join him on his exit, thus bringing a bit of his "Traditions" with him to America.

Authorial Identity

Not coincidentally, the creators of *Fiddler on the Roof*—Jerry Bock, Sheldon Harnick, Joseph Stein, and Jerome Robbins — were all Jewish. The show resonated with and emerged from personal history for all of them. Says Jerry Bock, "I think we dedicated this show to something personal in our lives — our fathers, our grandmothers, whatever" (quoted in Stone 27). As all in the team were at least second-generation immigrants, and not therefore personally acquainted with the world they were bringing to life, the group performed research, visiting Orthodox communities in Williamsburg, Brooklyn, and attending a Hebrew Actors Union benefit on the Lower East Side. These visits greatly impacted their choices for the show, for instance influencing the "cantorial" syllables in "If I Were a Rich Man." Director / choreographer Robbins (born Rabinowitz), had a troubled relationship with his Jewishness throughout his life, and came to *Fiddler* with the stated intent of examining and working through his feelings towards his first generation immigrant parents and his heritage of Eastern European shtetl Jews. Robbins had visited his grandparents' shtetl in Poland when he was six and the experience greatly affected him. As Maria Karnilova, the original Golde, said, "It was a very emotional show for Jerry. As far as [he] was concerned, this was *his* family back in Russia" (quoted in Lawrence 337, orig. emphasis). In fact, after the opening night of *Fiddler*, Robbins' father, Harry Robbins, tearfully asked his son "How did you *know* all that?" (quoted in Lawrence 346, orig. emphasis). According to Sheldon Harnick, Robbins was horrified by the thought that his ancestral shtetl that he had visited when he was six could well have been destroyed by the Nazis: "[Robbins] told us that one of the reasons he had agreed to direct "Fiddler" was that it would give him the chance to resurrect that shtetl world and give it an additional life onstage of 25 years or so. It's sad that he's not around to see that he's given that shtetl world an additional 45 years of life and, thank God, "Fiddler" still seems to be going strong" (personal communication).

We will speak to that need to redress the devastation of the Holocaust shortly, but first we should note that all the creators felt a personal connection to that destroyed community, despite their distance from it. They also felt that their connection made them a natural fit with the material of the show. For instance, Jerry Bock states:

> With *Fiddler* it wasn't a matter of specifics so much as a conglomerate spiritual feeling that this was an area I could express myself in. And, right up to the last, I felt that I would never run dry, because it was so much a part of me [...] I'm sure Sheldon and Joe had the same inner sense of the material's being right for the writer. It's not that any of us is Orthodox; it was the association, the comfort of having that instinctive knowledge about things [quoted in Altman 36].

That sense of connection resonates with nostalgia. Bock states that a "spiritual feeling" prompted him to express himself creatively in this arena. Bock was not himself from the shtetl, so he expresses here not a factual memory of this world, but received memory, and a quasi-religious attraction to the subject matter. Robbins and Bock were not the only creators dealing with personal nostalgia during the creation of *Fiddler on the Roof*. Sheldon Harnick relates, "while I was writing the lyrics for "Fiddler" [...] I was highly aware of my Jewish identity. I was constantly dredging up memories, painful and otherwise, of growing up Jewish in Chicago. [...] For years I was very self-conscious about being Jewish. I probably didn't feel fully at ease with my Jewishness until after I had served in the army" (personal communication). Whether through Harnick's identity struggles, or Robbins and Bock's ancestral meaning, authorial identity contributed to Fiddler's nostalgic narrative, which we will shortly examine in detail.

UNIVERSALITY

Fiddler on the Roof takes place in a remote world of the insular Eastern European shtetl, removed by time, geography, cultural traditions and belief systems. Despite this remoteness, *Fiddler* has been widely and famously acclaimed by its authors, critics and audiences alike as highly "universal," perhaps surprisingly, given the specificity of the authors' personal connection to the material. Nevertheless claims to universality have entered legendary status. Stein tells a famous story about the Japanese production:

> Sheldon and I were in Japan for that opening. We thought that culture was as remote as we could get from the material of the show. Then, at the run-through, the Japanese producer turned to us and said, "Tell me, do they understand this show in America?" I said, "What do you mean?" He said, "It's so Japanese!" [quoted in Stone 27].

The collaborators were proud of the implications of this story. They worked intensely not only to portray the shtetl world accurately, but also to allow the musical to appeal to a broader audience. *Fiddler* could be interpreted as "Japanese" because it addressed the universal difficulty of traditional societies undergoing painful change in the face of a modernizing world. Harnick states:

> We didn't want the show to only play to Jews, and, at the same time, we had no ambition to teach the world about Jews. We worked very hard to concentrate on universal values. Ultimately it was a story that just happened to be about Jewish people. What *Fiddler* did was show that basically Jews are just like everybody else [quoted in Rosenbaum 4].

The creative team held to this aim of universality in various ways. For one, as Harnick states, "Parenthetically, we were very careful not to have any Yiddish words either in the book or in the score, except for 'l'chaim' and 'mazel tov' which *everybody* knows" (quoted in Stone 21, italics mine). Harnick's words are telling in this context, implying a specific audience. While certainly numerous gentiles would know the phrases "l'chaim" (to life) or "mazel tov" (a general greeting / blessing), it is perhaps unlikely that outside specific areas of higher Jewish population density, "everybody" knows those phrases. In fact, perhaps due to *Fiddler,* more know the meanings now than when it first was written. Nevertheless the creative team strove to attain universality in the face of their worries that the musical was too specifically Jewish. Harnick admits the fears of the collaborators regarding the specificity of Jewish material on Broadway:

> I must say I was running scared most of the time because here we had a show that seemed to be long, that was Jewish and was very serious. I thought, "Will an audience accept this?" In light of what happened to the show, it seems that we should have known they would [quoted in Stone 21].

Harnick suggested they cut the serious ending of "If I Were a Rich Man," and the creators considered adding a comic dance number, or a comic song sung by the Rabbi, "When The Messiah Comes," where the song "Anatevka" now resides. All these attempts shared the aim of making the musical more "palatable" to a mass audience. Most compromises were *not* made, and according to the team, they decided to brave the potential reaction in order to stay true to the material. Years later, Harnick has a more defiant view towards the Jewishness of the material. He states:

> After "Fiddler" was a success, on several occasions Jewish people I met commented on how brave we were [...] to have risked so much time and energy on a musical about Jews. [...] In my mind I was thinking: multitudes of Jewish servicemen served in the armed forces that defeated Adolf Hitler. We have earned the right to acceptance and respect. Anyone who looks down on us for being Jewish is a fool who deserved only our contempt [personal communication].

Despite this retrospective feeling, the authors were nonetheless concerned about the audience *Fiddler* would find when it opened. Stein explains:

> That first night was a benefit for some Jewish organization. I heard a number of people in the lobby saying, "Well, we like it, but I don't know it *they* will like it." The next night "they" came because it was a benefit, I think, for the Red Cross, and "they" did like it! So we felt we had something rather special [quoted in Stone 23, orig. emphasis].

Fiddler on the Roof offers a Sabbath meal and blessing, a Jewish wedding, and traditional shtetl characters such as Yente the matchmaker and Nachum the town beggar. These details raise the question of the musical's intended audience. Does *Fiddler* aim to entertain Jewish Americans, who might recognize the particularities of these practices or characters, and subsequently might find them comforting or familiar? Or the more general American public who would find the traditions of lighting of the Sabbath candles, the chuppah (the wedding tent), and the breaking of the wedding glass to be quaint, to necessitate explanation, to mark the characters as "Other?" Henry Bial's theory of "double coding," or "the specific means and mechanisms by which a performance can communicate one message to Jewish audiences while simultaneously communicating another, often contradictory message to gentile audiences" (3), proves useful to examine these questions. *Fiddler* allows one set of readings for the larger audience, while offering separate associations for a Jewish audience. Indeed, there exists no one single "Jewish" audience due to the lack of a concretely defined Jewish community. Additionally, while Jews created *Fiddler*, their audiences were not all Jewish. Therefore, *Fiddler* needed to function on several levels of specificity and universality. For instance, Bial argues that in the Chava sequence the global message may be that adaptation to changing traditions is necessary, while a more specific Jewish message might be less accepting of intermarriage. *Fiddler's* plot points, dialogue, thematic concerns and visual choices can similarly be diversely coded for varying audiences. To critic Norman Nadel's famous statement about universality, Bial responds, "This kind of denial of cultural specificity is itself an example of double coding, for in the same breath the claim of universality is accompanied by the act of identification. The unspoken coda to 'You don't have to be Jewish to love Tevye' is 'but it helps'" (71). Bial's formulation certainly helps to make the universality debate less immediately pressing. *Fiddler* does not have to be merely universal or specific, it can be both. The debate nonetheless informs questions of nostalgia and postmemory.

Postmemory

Post–Holocaust Jewish culture necessitates concern for vanishing ethnic community. *Fiddler* recalled the shtetl community, destroyed by the Shoah, for those that felt its loss. The creators of *Fiddler on the Roof* were American Jews, who did not suffer the horrors of the Shoah personally, but were nevertheless deeply affected, having lived through the pain of World War II and been witness to the discovery of the Holocaust. That event, as the defining moment for modern Jewry, colors and intensifies *Fiddler's* privileging of community, for the community it celebrates was destroyed with finality by the Nazis. A need to address this destruction was vital to the origins of *Fiddler on the Roof*. *Fiddler* takes place in 1905, only thirty some years before the Holocaust. If we extended the trajectory of the plot in history, Tevye's descendents, if not his family directly, would be caught in the firestorm of Europe in the 1930s and most likely perish. The musical's final scene brings attention to the destinations of characters expelled from Anatevka, many of which have clear and deathly Holocaust associations. Harnick recalls, "It occurred to all three of us [Harnick, Bock and Stein], that Tzeitel and Motel, who go to Warsaw at the end of the show, might have lived long enough to be destroyed in the Holocaust, had they stayed there" (personal communication). This shocking reality resonates strongly at *Fiddler's* finale.

When *Fiddler* opened, a more cautious approach to speaking of the Holocaust still reigned. Critics in 1964 seem aware of the implications of the Holocaust on *Fiddler's* subject matter. However, consistent with the level of silence concerning the Holocaust in the 1960s, they address it only distantly. Reviews allude to the tragedy only through the lens of the less extreme violence done to the Jews of Anatevka, and emphasize the sunnier outlook on the material. As Nadel offers:

> No one who knows or suspects the life of a Russian Jew less than a century ago expects a boffo finale to a musical such as this. But [...] even at the final moment [...] *hope* comes through like sunlight [214; emphasis mine].

Critic John Chapman in the *Daily News* echoes this positivist outlook, in a slightly more condescending manner, discussing, "the spirit and bounce of these far-off Russian villagers, who find joy where it can be found and turn their backs on dejection" (217). One might think that *Fiddler's* anti–Semitic characters and events would call up at least a mention of the recent extreme case of anti–Jewish hatred, the Holocaust. But not one review in 1964 makes a direct reference. This avoidance of the specificity of the tragedy that befell Jews, and the emphasis on a hopeful reading of the musical, matches America's approach to the Holocaust in these early years.

    Fiddler's creative team was aware of the Holocaust's significance to their project, even if it was not directly addressed in the musical's production. Jerome Robbins incorporated a series of improvisation exercises regarding different types of hatred into the opening rehearsals with his actors, in order to teach the cast the significance of prejudice. Hal Prince remembers, "The second day [of rehearsal] it was a concentration camp; Fyedka and Chava were playing Nazis and Jews" (quoted in Altman 97). The connection between Russian hatred of shtetl Jews and Nazi murders of European Jews was made to the original company and in the minds of the creative team.

    Audiences in 1964 were surely at least subliminally influenced by the resonances of the Holocaust on the material. With some of the first widespread popular and accepted portrayals of Jewish characters, *Fiddler* demonstrates the fear the community lived under, the injustice done to them and the constant threat and eventual realization of violence and forced evacuation. Rosenbaum argues, "it was through these haunting images that many Americans first became introduced to Jews" (2). *Fiddler's* pogrom in particular resonated with the Shoah. At the height of the joyous celebration of Tzeitel and Motel's marriage, the Russians burst into the wedding. The constable offers:

> I see we came at a bad time, Tevye. I'm sorry but the orders are for tonight. For the whole village. *(to the musicians)* Go on, play, play. All right men.
>
> *(The Russians begin their destruction, turning over tables, throwing pillows, smashing dishes and the window of the house. One of them throws the wedding gift candlesticks to the ground, and Perchik grapples with him. But he is hit with a club and falls to the ground)* [109].

Significantly, there are no pogroms in Sholem Aleichem's source material; Stein added the event. He also placed it as the first climax structurally, right at the end of Act I, alerting the audience that the material would get far darker in Act II than in the rather cheery first act. The sudden violence, anger and senseless injustice of the moment subverts the sweetly comic portrayals of the shtetl world to this point. Several moments in the scene offer particular Holocaust echoes. The musicians that continue to play over the destruction offer a parallel to concentration camp orchestras that played cheery music as a backdrop to the tortures and killings enacted there. Additionally, Perchik's attempted defiance brings up the anger and debate over Jewish resistance, or lack thereof, to Nazi brutality.

Early drafts of the musical shed light on the extent to which the creators linked the Holocaust to their work. In one draft, Tevye offers an eloquent response to the constable's order to leave his shtetl. His powerful and moving argument offers ironic Holocaust resonances and foreshadowing:

> You who are willing, for a crust of bread and the right to be called "your honor" to carry out an injustice. [...] I have news for you, your honor. We are not strong, we have no power in the government... but we have a special talent... we have the talent to survive. We are a peaceful people, we do not win great wars, but we survive... we flourish and survive! (Bock Collection NYPL n. pag.)

Perhaps tellingly, this speech was cut, in favor of a more stoic and comically accepting characterization of Tevye. Another cut piece, a song written during the drafting process, eloquently speaks to the creator's liberal urge towards universality and equality:

> Why Jew and why gentile / Why gentile, why Jew?
> We could have been one / and instead we are two
> This riddle is not / for me to pursue
> Dear God, please forgive me / But what did you do?
> [Bock Collection NYPL n. pag.].

These lyrics, particularly the last line, also resonate strongly with Holocaust trauma. The creators fought to balance the extent to which the musical brought these images and associations to the surface.

In 1964 *Fiddler* produced a more direct, one-to-one relationship. Many American Jews, including the artistic team, were either first or second-generation immigrants themselves and had more direct connections to the shtetl world. But soon thereafter world events altered the kind of associations the show engendered. Events in Israel in 1967, including the capture of the West Bank, the Gaza Strip, and other territories, overturned the toxic stereotype of helpless Jewish victimization. One moment in *Fiddler* sums up this change of attitudes. After the pogrom that ends Act I, Tevye performs a gesture to God that sums up his feelings as the curtain closes. As performed by Zero Mostel and directed by Jerome Robbins, Tevye crosses downstage and helplessly shrug to God, seemingly asking him "Why?" When Altman directed Chaim Topol in the London production, during rehearsals the actor instead made a defiant fist to God. When asked why, he said, "I must play it that way, [...] because I'm tired of the 'poor Jew' who's always bowing and scraping to God. That's the European World War II Jew, and I'm a Sabra. I've got more guts than that" (quoted in Altman 167). Indeed, Topol had been in the Israeli army, and portrayed a stronger, more defiant Tevye overall. Altman instructed the actor not to keep the rebellious gesture, but his impulse offers a cogent example of the change occurring in Jewish thought in this era. In the film version Topol was cast rather than Mostel, and his more defiant, dignified Tevye fit 1971, when events in Israel were continuing to affect American Jewish self-conceptions.

The 1971 Jewison film offers a more direct confrontation with the Holocaust. The passage of time, new artists involved, and filmic format make this acknowledgment unsurprising. Wolitz points out that Jewison used the technique of reanimating photographs of shtetl life taken before the Holocaust, thus setting up parallels to later Holocaust photographs echoed in the conclusion, when all the Jews of Anatevka are forced to emigrate. In its ability to bring actual locations to life, the film also allowed further Holocaust resonances. Hodel sings "Far From the Home I Love" to her father in a small train station, on her way to join Perchik in Siberia. But the film was able to show the visceral Holocaust inspired imagery of a cattle car and huddled masses of Jews on a train. This choice cannot be coincidental. Wolitz argues that the film allows the melancholy of historical events to color its message. He points out that the later date, 1971 as opposed to 1964, might have an influence, but doesn't make a detailed argument. In fact this passage of time is crucial to the acceptance and encouragement of Holocaust imagery. As time passed, so did attitudes towards and knowledge of the Holocaust. By the 2004 Broadway revival, critics were far more direct about *Fiddler*'s resonances. Alisa Solomon, in the *Village Voice* offers a historical perspective: "Responding to a dawning post–Holocaust consciousness, *Fiddler* was the first big work of popular culture to call forth the Old Country with affection, evoking the richness of a vanished world" (2).

The revival's critics acknowledged the connection between the terror of the pogrom and the Holocaust. In 2004, Ruth Franklin in the *New York Times*, offers, "It is now impossible to look back at the villagers of Anatevka without the knowledge that their world was about to be destroyed, and by a force more powerful than modern love or the disintegration of tradition"(5). Because of this knowledge, we are now forced to directly confront the pain and destruction of the Holocaust. *Fiddler*'s substitution of the events of Russian exile and pogroms acts as a form of sublimation, as we saw in *Milk and*

Honey's restorative nostalgia. Parallels to another violent time are more approachable, while the shear unimaginable scope of the Holocaust is simply too much to process. *Fiddler* scales down the pain in order to acknowledge the larger tragedy below the surface. In the face of this disavowal or sublimation we find nostalgia.

Nostalgia

The type of nostalgia *Fiddler* produces has changed and will continue to change as audiences evolve, and as American culture continues to transform. The production of nostalgia exists in the space between the object and the audience, and in the moment between performance and reception. Sheldon Harnick puts it best in the statement at the top of this chapter, "[*Fiddler on the Roof* is] not really an accurate depiction of the *shtetl*, it's more like having false memories of a longing for community" (quoted in Rosenbaum 6). Here Harnick incorporates several phrases key to this study. "False memories" acknowledges the accusations that the musical presents a mythic world that never existed in actuality, and "longing for community," in view of the events of the Holocaust, remains a potent source of *Fiddler's* power.

SOURCE MATERIAL

Sholem Aleichem's "Tevye the Dairyman" stories, even upon their first writing, were a nostalgic exercise (Kalmar). The author was from Kiev, an educated, Russian-speaking urbanite who wrote about people he met on his travels through the countryside. *Fiddler's* authors, following the general understanding, viewed Sholem Aleichem through a nostalgic lens. Sheldon Harnick stated, "Sholem Aleichem was so at one with those people, had such a depth of understanding, was so emotionally moved himself to say what he said, that the stories proved to be intensely universal" (quoted in Stone 28). But the writer was not "at one" with shtetl inhabitants, he came from outside their world. Scholar David Roskies explains the urge to nostalgically alter Sholem Aleichem, arguing:

> By Aleichem's time [...] Yiddish writers were deliberately striving to revive the declining rabbinical tradition by means of an invented culture that combined old and new elements. Paradoxically, the invention was so successful that later generations accepted it as the real thing [quoted in Franklin 3].

As early as 1943, concerns in the Jewish community over the loss of remembered Eastern European culture and history led Maurice Samuel to write *The World of Sholem Aleichem*. According to scholar Seth Wolitz, this work "was not history but a readable defense and illustration of Jewish life in Tsarist Russia using Sholem Aleichem's creations as examples" (523). A 1939 film of the Tevye stories, directed by Maurice Schwartz, emphasized the manner in which Tevye's troubles paralleled the current plight of European Jews. According to Wolitz, in the Schwartz film, "The rhetoric of nostalgia cloaked Tevye in the stylized role of the archetypal folk Jew who maintains his customs in the face of adversity" (520). Post-Holocaust, extensive efforts were made to remember the shtetl world that had disappeared in that catastrophe. Memory books (collections of photos and stories from former shtetl residents) were created, and accessible translations of Sholem Aleichem were published, making use of the material as a form of living memory. In the 1950s and beyond artists continued to co-opt the Tevye stories in the same manner, including in a new form: on the stage. The Arnold Perl production of *Tevye and his Daughters* in the 1950s according to Wolitz, was an "exercise in nostalgia" (524). By the time Sholem Aleichem's stories were translated into the American musical *Fiddler on the Roof*, Tevye's character had made important shifts from the source material, but maintained its nostalgic connections.

DESIGN

Boris Aronson's set design for the original production acted as a nostalgic cue. According to scholar Raymond Knapp, Aronson's visual inspiration, painter Marc Chagall's work (which also inspired the title of the musical) offered a potent source of nostalgia, "[The creators] were able to tap successfully into two of the richest veins of nostalgic remembrance of shtetl life: the stories of Sholom Aleichem and the paintings of Marc Chagall" (216). The set, as with Chagall, depicted shtetl world details, but in a misty, hazy, impressionist manner more conducive to memory than strict realism. Faithful pictorial representations of houses and shops could not offer the same emotional connection to memory; Aronson's design allowed more distant audiences to grasp the expressionist *sense* of the place rather than its details. The designer's hazy Chagall-like backdrops combined with his play on the scale of buildings offered a more emotional connection to memory. Norman Jewison's film however, which offers the reality of an actual Yugoslavian village in which it was shot, problematized this intimate memory connection, complicating its reception in the process. Knapp also connects the stage design's evocative power to the Holocaust:

> To a large extent, [awareness that the Holocaust destroyed the shtetl world] has been the collective Jewish response to Sholom Aleichem's stories and Marc Chagall's images, and *Fiddler on the Roof* has been widely accepted as an extension of those remembrances [216].

Fiddler, by making use of the resonances from both these potent sources, doubles nostalgia. Audiences who already associate Chagall's work with nostalgia for an erased world, through the visual cues of the setting, add this power to their theatrical experience.

SCORE

Music as an art form carries an evocative power, intimately tied to memory, making it an excellent nostalgic tool. Knapp tells us, "*Fiddler on the Roof* creates a distinctive, persuasive, and haunting musical profile for its ethnic minority" (216). Apparently however, Jerry Bock did not feel the need to research the musical world of his score. As he states:

> I felt a sense of quiet confidence in being able to write this score [...] because I was able to draw on my own background, my own memories of music I grew up with. I never felt the urge to research the score; I felt it was inside me. And I was delighted to have the opportunity for the first time to express this kind of ethnic music I'd always had a friendship with [quoted in Altman 35].

He certainly convinced the critics. Howard Taubman reverently declared, "'Sabbath Prayer' is as hushed as a community at its devotions. 'Sunrise, Sunset' is in the spirit of a traditional wedding under a canopy" (217), while Linda Winer said in 2004, "Jerry Bock's music, with its stirring suggestions of ancient modalities [...] still linger[s] in the cultural psyche with the inevitability of myth" (2). However, music scholar Mark Slobin points out that Bock does not grant the Fiddler character definable Jewish melody types. Instead the composer's melody flirts with an American sound rather than a genuine Eastern European Jewish one. Scholar Seth Wolitz argues therefore that the score does not belong authentically to the world it depicts, instead underscoring the mélange of cultures that *Fiddler* encompasses, "the Fiddler's "Broadway" melody, which begins and ends the musical with its slight "exotica" *is* the message of the musical: Jewish community exists through accommodation and acculturation" (530, orig. emphasis).

According to his stated intentions, Jerry Bock wanted to capture the musical sound of the Old Country. A portion of *Fiddler*'s audience would have klezmer melody types authentically part of their memory, but perhaps still more audience members would have a secondary connection to that music, as did its composer. As Bock felt that the music was "inside him" so too could a second or third generation Jewish audience. In fact the Jewish community have claimed the *Fiddler* score as their own, and of course the songs feature prominently on the Hebrew National CD, "Music That Answers to a Higher Power," which we encountered in the last chapter. But as this audience may have grown up with Klezmer music, so too would they have been surrounded

by American and Broadway music archetypes. Non-Jewish audiences may or may not have had any level of exposure to the sound of Jewish music. Therefore *Fiddler*'s mixed audiences had a potentially wide range of reactions to its semi-authentic and varied score. Some level of nostalgia would nonetheless be part of many of those responses.

RITUAL

Fiddler makes use of staged ritual as a tool of particular nostalgic power. The musical includes various ritualized daily practices, such as kissing the mezuzah on entering and leaving buildings, spitting to keep out the evil eye, covering heads and wearing tallis (prayer shawls). The musical also, more importantly, depicts a traditional Sabbath meal and blessing: "Sabbath Prayer," and a Jewish wedding: "Sunrise, Sunset." An early draft, dated November 1961, also tried to incorporate further Jewish ritual — this time by incorporating the Jewish harvest holiday Sukkoth. This draft placed Tevye and Hodel's goodbye scene under the sukkah (a temporary building where meals are taken during the holiday). Both the songs that remained in the musical offer particularly potent nostalgic cues. After the lighting of the Sabbath candles, Harnick's lyrics to "Sabbath Prayer" comparatively literally translate the Hebrew parental blessing given every Friday at sunset over the Sabbath meal. In Jerry Bock's notes from the early drafting period at the New York Public Library, we find the actual translation from the Hebrew:

> May God make you like Sarah and Rebecca, Rachel and Leah.
> May the Lord bless you and protect you; May the Lord countenance you and be gracious to you; May the Lord favor you and grant you peace [Bock Collection NYPL n. pag.].

As the song progresses, we see families surrounding additional points of candlelight, performing their own Sabbath ritual. In the second ritual, Tzeitel and Motel's wedding, the bride is led to the Chuppah (wedding tent) and, with her mother and future mother-in-law, led in circles around the groom. The Rabbi and the couple enact the wedding ceremony while the community sings "Sunrise, Sunset" around them. This famous song by itself encompasses nostalgia for lost childhood and the fleeting nature of time. The ceremony includes traditions of a Jewish wedding, including the drinking of wine, and the stomping of the glass. An early draft included dialogue intended to further solemnize the ritual. Golde tells Tzeitel, "You will be beautiful as only a Jewish

OPPOSITE: *Fiddler on the Roof* (1964–1972 Broadway). Music by Jerry Bock, lyrics by Sheldon Harnick, book by Joseph Stein, directed by Jerome Robbins. Shown fourth from left: Maria Karnilova as Golde; third from left: Zero Mostel as Tevye.

bride can be beautiful… as only a daughter of Israel can be beautiful…" (Bock Collection NYPL n. pag.).

In all their detail, these ritualized scenes are intimately tied to nostalgia. Bock's handwritten notes during the drafting period offer a clue to the incorporation of ritual: "I think a big Sabbath meal could be fascinating for its ceremony, warmth and uniqueness on stage as well as providing a background that's part of the fabric of our show" (Bock Collection NYPL n. pag.). The team thought staged ritual provided "warmth and uniqueness," and would "fascinate" audiences. These words argue for double coding, for non–Jews might be more likely to be fascinated by ritual, while Jewish audiences fed by nostalgia might be likely to find warmth in remembered ritual. These scenes can be argued to create an ersatz religious power, power which functions on different levels for different audiences. The scenes offer solemn versions of these rituals, versions separated only by a sometimes-thin layer of theatre. For Jews familiar with these celebrations they may evoke associations of real rituals, and all their attendant sacred feelings or implications. For an audience less intimately familiar, including secularized Jews, these rituals could offer a sense of community, of spirituality perhaps only partially experienced in their own lives.

At the top of this chapter, Harnick surmised the show provides "false memory of a longing for community." These ritualized scenes, both of which highlight community, could activate this yearning. All the Jews of Anatevka share celebration of the Sabbath, in their own family units, and gather all together to celebrate Tzeitel's wedding. *Fiddler* takes care to demonstrate this sense of kinship throughout the musical, but particularly in these scenes. Ritual helps to bind or define community. Perhaps this underscoring of its comforts offered the most potent source of nostalgia in an age where fears of the disintegration of Jewish community prevailed.

The Shtetl We've Never Had

Walter Kerr, in his original review of *Fiddler on the Roof* argued, "I think it might be an altogether charming musical if only the people of Anatevka did not pause every now and again to give their regards to Broadway, with remembrances to Herald Square" (216). Other critics have voiced the same argument with varied levels of forcefulness. Nostalgia and postmemory help to create this concern. If *Fiddler* engenders nostalgia, in view of the unimaginable tragedy of the Holocaust, audiences wish it to be lived history, not channeled through "Broadway" or commercialized theatre. Even though *Fiddler* takes the form of a musical, perhaps the least documentary theatrical form that exists, critics or audiences still paradoxically crave realism, want the veil of memory to be untouched by "show business." The shtetl culture depicted in the musical had disappeared by 1964, and those remembering it, as Jewish author and scholar Cynthia Ozick argue, were operating out of desperation. As she states, in the 1960s, "the more intrinsic themes of Jewish conceptual life came to be understood only feebly, vestigially, at a time when they were either substantially diluted by the new culture or were disappearing altogether" (103). For Jewish audiences, large scale public recognition and embrace of the shtetl world through *Fiddler* both affirmed their culture and reminded them of the danger of steadily disintegrating tradition. Scholar Mark Raphael agrees that for Jewish audiences the fear of vanishing culture operates and controls nostalgia in *Fiddler*:

> Behind the façade of affluence and assimilations there is the unassimilated hard core of an all-but-forgotten past. [...] Tevye and his shtetl were the part of them which they had carefully stored away from conscious memory. Here it was, suddenly, so clean and bright and respectable [72].

How accurate is *Fiddler*'s shtetl? As Irving Howe famously put it, in a blistering attack written in 1964 after the show opened, "Anatevka in *Fiddler on the Roof* is the cutest *shtetl* we've never had. Irresistible bait for the nostalgia-smitten audience, this charming little *shtetl* [...] all bursts with quaintness and local color, and the condescension that usually goes along" (74). Howe was highly angered by what he saw as the damaging and false nostalgia for the shtetl world created by the show. In inflammatory language he also attacked, "the spiritual anemia of Broadway and of the middle-class Jewish world which by now seems firmly linked to Broadway" (73).

The staged ritual angered Howe still further. He called "Sabbath Prayer" a "Shabbos at Radio City Music Hall" (74) and was particularly upset by the portrayal of Anatevka's Rabbi, who frequently plays for comedy, including mistakenly dancing with a young girl in the wedding scene. He concluded by arguing that, "In Sholem Aleichem's stories, God is a presence to whom Jews can turn in moments of need and urgency; in *Fiddler on the Roof* He ends up as Zero Mostel's straight man" (Howe 74). Howe makes a strong argument for labeling *Fiddler*'s nostalgia false:

> American Jews suffer these days from a feeling of guilt because they have lost touch with the past from which they derive, and often they compound this guilt by indulging themselves in an unearned nostalgia.

He believes that *Fiddler* serves as an easy way for those not truly educated about the shtetl world to claim kinship with it nonetheless, and that in fact, the less true knowledge possessed, the more embraced and celebrated easy targets like *Fiddler* are. In the thrill and thankfulness that Jewish heritage and history are being shared publicly, standards of accuracy are put aside, "One understands the anxiety prompting such nostalgia, the nostalgia prompting a lack of critical standards, and the lack of critical standards prompting a surrender of dignity. But it is unworthy" (75).

The passage of time only multiplies what Howe sees as the loss of Jewish culture. By now concerns have only increased, as first and second-generation immigrants die, intermarriage continues and memories fade. By the 2004 Broadway revival of *Fiddler* the nostalgic functions of the show had become both clearer and somehow more powerful. Ruth Franklin argues in the *New York Times*, "The farther removed we are from the Old World, the more we long to recapture it. But what is surprising is that the pseudo-klezmer tunes and schmaltz-laden accents in *Fiddler* were ever assumed to be the real thing" (2). Despite what sounds like a dismissal of the musical, Franklin responds to Howe's 1964 attack on the show with the retort: "The idea that Jews don't even care whether a musical purporting to be about their culture is based on the real thing, or are too ignorant to tell the difference anyway, is almost as condescending as *Fiddler* itself" (4). She argues that the klezmer revival and the appearance of Jewish and Yiddish studies departments demonstrate a counter trend. However, the facts argue that Tevye and his world will always remain in the realm of myth and altered memory. As with any historical portrayal, the musical's creators did not live in the world they portrayed and had to rely on photographs, second hand accounts and artistic reactions such as Chagall's, which inspired the design. They could not perform ethnographic research because the whole world of the Eastern European shtetl had been wiped off the map by Russian and Nazi violence. The horrible truth of this violence likely engenders the extra anger felt by Howe and others at what they consider false nostalgia. It's easier somehow to remember the sweet, comic, even cute version of the shtetl than the flawed reality. Hazy nostalgia is easier, less painful, especially in view of tragedy. How one feels about giving in to that nostalgia depends on one's attitude towards dealing with trauma. Is it better to face head on the gray shades of truth, or to remember celebratory vagaries? Is taking the "easy" route understandable, or deplorable? These questions continue to circulate and arose in new form with concerns over the Jewishness of the revival.*

Americanization

In America, and on Broadway, nostalgia and Holocaust resonances interconnect in very particular fashion. Franklin argues:

*See Hillman, Jessica. "Goyim on the Roof: Embodying Authenticity in Leveaux's *Fiddler on the Roof.*" *Studies in Musical Theatre* 1:1 (2007): 25–39.

The creators of *Fiddler* chose to return the audience to a happier time — a time of poverty and hard labor, but before the terrible loss of innocence that World War II brought. Such escapism may not be authentic, but it is pure Broadway [5].

The dissonance of the pogrom argues against Franklin's point. In fact *Fiddler* treads a very fine line between Broadway musical comedy and tragedy, between 42nd Street and the shtetl. Certainly *Fiddler* offers escapism, but it also endeavors to address deeper themes than usually included in the musical theatre. However, distinctly American perceptions of the Holocaust, as opposed to European, are central to the approach taken to this material.

The scholarly field, "Americanization of the Holocaust" describes a process whereby an event that occurred across the ocean on another continent, during which Americans remained willingly ignorant, became embraced as an American tragedy. *Fiddler* implies that America can heal the devastation of that event, or at least provide an escape. In his Tevye stories, Sholem Aleichem does not present America as an effective alternative to persecution. In the source material, according to Wolitz, "America does not appear as a particularly desirable solutions for the Russian-Jewish condition, but as a place of exile" (519). Tevye does not immigrate to New York in the stories. Instead he stays in Europe and tragedies continue to befall him. In contrast, *Fiddler* offers America as a way out. The musical assures the audience that Tevye and at least some of his immediate family will be safe in New York City by the 1930s, that his descendents will be seeing Broadway musicals, not appearing on the lists of Auschwitz dead. The "universality" of *Fiddler* and its acceptance as a Broadway hit also emerge from this embrace of America as an escape. America accepts Jews, and allows them to prosper. The narrative of American-Jews has been a success story, enough so to universalize a story of their suffering through a Jewish created, but "All-American" art form: the Broadway musical.

Tevye's choice to immigrate to America held vast implications for all of *Fiddler*'s audiences, however his voyage was not the only depiction of America on stage. American ideas and ideals were also central to the shtetl world as depicted by Stein. Wolitz argues:

> A gigantic substitution occurred in the musical. American ideals of individual rights, progress and freedom of association are assimilated into the Judaic tradition, which is presented as a cultural tradition parallel to the American [527].

American concerns of the 1960s, particularly feminism and the generational divide of conservatism versus progress, are put into shtetl terms, and Tevye as the central character learns to grow, change and embrace increasingly progressive American ideas. The Russian anti–Semitic presence in the show stands counter to these values. Addressing American values of freedom and justice through their absence reiterates the fact that the Holocaust did not occur here, that America instead offers a tolerant and egalitarian tradition where Jews and non–Jews alike can prosper. America cast itself as the hero of World War II, however much that role was simplified in the service of ideology, and thus the blending of American values into a postmemory project was particularly successful in *Fiddler on the Roof.*

An early draft makes this connection to American values quite evident, and aims at yet another source of nostalgia, the American immigrant experience. In this long scene, later cut, Tevye reads a letter from his relative in New York City aloud to the whole shtetl community. The draft includes a several paragraph long, highly detailed letter, describing the usual highlights of immigrant nostalgia, including tenement living, and struggle for education and success. But significantly it also takes care to point out the potential of life in America:

> I have now been here in America for almost a year, and I am beginning to get used to American ways, which are very different from our own. [...] There are no pogroms, for it is against the law, and there is no danger of someone burning your house down, which is also against the law. [...] Our life is hard here, dear sister, but in some ways it is good. [...] The proof is, every week more and more come, but with all our troubles, no one goes back [Bock Collection NYPL n. pag.].

By cutting this scene, *Fiddler*'s authors apparently felt that this spelling out of the promise of the American dream was not necessary, and that the knowledge Tevye and his family were heading to America at the end of the musical was sufficient to call upon the same associations. Their original inclusion, however, points to the creators' intentions and belief in America's promise.

Robbins was briefly considered to direct the filmic *Fiddler*, and apparently wanted to drop the script altogether and start afresh. Actor Barry Primus told Robbins' biographer, "He had this idea which was to start with an album of pictures and then go backwards, an album of people, let's say on West End Avenue, and they go back in time" (quoted in Lawrence 350). Robbins' idea illuminates and makes obvious the connection already established between American ideals, nostalgic appeals and the shtetl world of *Fiddler on the Roof.* West End Avenue is on the Upper West Side of Manhattan, where many successful Jews lived after leaving the poorer neighborhood of the Lower East Side. Living on West End Avenue was a sign of success for second-generation Jews. By wanting the start the film there, and move back to the ancestors of these Jews, Robbins acknowledges pride in American success as a central theme of *Fiddler* and strengthens the contrast between Holocaust loss and American achievement. A draft of lyrics for a cut song called "Where Poppa Came From," found in Bock's papers, seem to come from the same impulse, starting the musical from a modern perspective and pointing to the not-too-distant ancestors who people *Fiddler*:

> The little town / Where poppa came from / A little town / I'd like to see
> The way of life / Where poppa came from / A way of life / that's part of me
> Was it a good way... a bad way? / It's not for me to answer yes or no
> It was the one way / Where poppa came from / Not so long ago
>   [Bock Collection NYPL n. pag.].

Although both these devices did not make their way into the final products, stage or screen, they make clear what is only slightly subtler in the productions we do see. In *Fiddler* successful New York Jews could remember where they came from, but more importantly where they managed to arrive. Success affords nostalgia.

Conclusion

Fiddler continues to shift and evolve as a site for emotional and nostalgic connections. Nostalgia operates on several levels in *Fiddler on the Roof*, for a "pastoral" life in the Old Country, and also, more complicatedly, in response to how that world was destroyed. Although Russian ignorance and bureaucratic policy destroys the Jewish community of Anatevka, the Holocaust destroyed *Fiddler*'s world with finality. Thus *Fiddler* intimately ties nostalgia to memory in a post–Holocaust context. In specific terms *Fiddler* examines strength in the face of oppression. It depicts hard times (Russian pogroms) in view of impossible times (Holocaust) from the place of good times (America). *Fiddler on the Roof* sublimates Holocaust pain into a more manageable realm of Russian oppression, and then offers a solution to that reduced difficulty through the shining promise of America.

CHAPTER V

Cabaret

"If you could see her through my eyes / She wouldn't look Jewish at all" [93].

Cabaret (1966) revolutionized the Broadway musical stage in numerous ways, not least through its daring subject matter. Kander and Ebb's musical representation of encroaching Nazism in the late Weimar Republic emerges from the American decade in which it was first produced. The tumultuous 1960s were a time of contrast, combining increasing acceptance of Holocaust discussion with an ambiguous attitude towards the moral implications of Nazi crimes. The link between Nazism and the Holocaust, so accepted today, was beginning to be established. The Eichmann trial had occurred early in the decade, and awareness of the troubled racial situation in America underlined frightening new parallels to root causes of the Holocaust. We can see reflections of both this new awareness and the moral confusion it evoked in *Cabaret*. Incarnations of the musical have changed along with the times, proving that *Cabaret* has radical potential, even fifty years after it was written. The weighty themes it grapples with in an uncompromising, unflinching and sometimes even comic way, defy traditional scholarly expectations of the limitations of musical theatre and of the "Americanization of the Holocaust."

Background, History and Productions

Cabaret is based on the stories of Christopher Isherwood, a young British author who wrote of his experiences living in Berlin at the end of the Weimar Republic. His two novels of Berlin life, *Goodbye to Berlin* (1939) and *Mr.*

90

Norris Changes Trains (1935) were combined in one volume and published in America as *Berlin Stories* in 1945. John van Druten dramatized some of the stories, focusing on the novella "Sally Bowles," in his 1951 Broadway play, *I Am a Camera*. The hit production, starring Julie Harris, was adapted into a film, also starring Harris, in 1955. Various producers became interested in musicalizing van Druten's play. Producer David Black first procured the rights to the material, and Sandy Wilson, author of *The Boyfriend* (1954), wrote a score with Julie Andrews in mind. When Andrews suggested prolific Broadway producer/director Harold Prince as a director or producer he made an appointment to listen to the Wilson score. Prince felt Wilson had too cheery a take on the material, but became interested in the project when he realized the parallels between the declining society of 1920s and 30s Berlin and the racial hatred and violence of 1960s America. Eventually, through much negotiation, Prince secured the rights from David Black, and Wilson was let go. Prince hired Joe Masteroff, with whom he had collaborated on *She Loves Me* (1963), to write the libretto, and John Kander and Fred Ebb, with whom he had worked on *Flora the Red Menace* (1965), to write the score. Prince directed the show himself, and Ronald Field was hired to choreograph. *Cabaret* had a long gestation period. From the summer of 1963 when the first draft was completed, until November 1966, when the production opened, numerous changes and shifts in focus were made. Kander and Ebb wrote about 47 songs, 15 ultimately ended up in the musical. Prince, trying to underscore the timeliness of the material, even ended one version with film of the Selma and Little Rock race riots, but later stated, "that was a godawful idea, and I came to my senses" (quoted in Ilson 137).

The creative team attempted to distance themselves from the van Druten play, which they felt missed the weightier themes present in Isherwood novels. Eventually they hit upon the metaphor and staging device that would make *Cabaret* so unique and successful. Prince recalled his experience in a nightclub near Stuttgart in 1951:

> There was a dwarf MC, hair parted in the middle, and lacquered down with brilliantine, his mouth made into a bright red cupid's bow, who wore heavy false eyelashes and sang, danced, goosed, tickled, and pawed four lumpen Valkyres waving diaphanous butterfly wings [quoted in Ilson 140].

This image stayed with Prince and became the central metaphor of the musical: the cabaret and it's Emcee as the microcosm of a decadent and decaying society. *Cabaret*'s structure was altered to enable numbers in the Kit Kat Klub to reflect the scene work which preceded them, allowing the club to reflect the insidious creep of Nazism. Many musical theatre scholars credit this staging conceit with pioneering a new trend in musical theatre structure: the "concept musical," where staging or a metaphor hold a show together, rather than the linear plot of an integrated musical. Boris Aronson's set was an integral part of the "concept" of this musical. The large tilted mirror he designed reflected the audience as it entered the theatre and at key moments in the show, underscoring the theme that, "it could happen here." Other set pieces included a large staircase where ensemble members watched the book scenes. Jean Rosenthal's lighting design also underscored the concept. It divided the stage into two areas, one for the realistic book scenes and the "real world" and another that stood for the "mind," which Prince termed "limbo." Several of the Emcee's numbers took place in the "real world" while others were placed in limbo.

Cabaret tells the story of Cliff Bradshaw, an Englishman living in the pre–Nazi Berlin of the early thirties. The decadence and decay of the city and German culture at large are expressed through the Kit Kat Klub, the cabaret of the title, where increasingly raw show numbers foreshadow the imminent Nazi regime and all its horrors. The vastly different treatments this material has received necessitate a plot synopsis of the original Broadway musical production in order to point out subsequent changes. Masteroff's adaptation opens in the Kit Kat Klub, where the ever present, ambiguous and troubling figure of the Emcee welcomes the audience ("Wilkommen"). The narrative then shifts to Cliff Bradshaw, an American writer, arriving in Berlin on the train. In his compartment he meets Ernst Ludwig, who uses Cliff to smuggle a suitcase in from Paris. Grateful for Cliff's help Ernst gives him the name of a rooming house, tells him of the Kit Kat Klub and agrees to be his first English pupil. Cliff goes to the boarding house and meets the landlady, Fräulein Schneider, who rents him a room for fifty marks, although she claims it is worth one hundred ("Who Cares"). Cliff meets other tenants, including Herr Schultz, owner of a fruit shop and admirer of Fräulein Schneider, and Fräulein Kost, a prostitute. Cliff tries to work but feels beckoned by the allure of the Kit Kat Klub and goes there to celebrate New Year's Eve. At the club the Emcee announces Sally Bowles, a singer from England ("Don't Tell Mamma"). After her number Sally makes advances towards Cliff, and the club's patrons celebrates New Year's 1930 with frenzied attempts to find a mate for the night ("The Telephone Song"). After Ernst's English lesson the next day, Sally, who has been fired from the club by her ex-lover, moves in with Cliff, winning him over despite his objections ("Perfectly Marvelous"). Back at the Kit Kat Klub the Emcee echoes this scene by singing of the sexual joys of cohabitation ("Two Ladies"). Meanwhile Kost and Schneider continue to bicker over Kost's oldest living profession, and Herr Schultz brings Fräulein Schneider a gift of an exotic pineapple ("It Couldn't Please Me More"). We cut back to the club, where a group of waiters sing a patriotic German song ("Tomorrow Belongs to Me"). Sally and Cliff discuss the life of decadence

they are living ("Why Should I Wake Up"), but Sally reveals that she is pregnant. Cliff agrees to go to Paris on unidentified political errands for Ernst in
order to earn money to support his expectant family. The Emcee sings of the
joys of money, complete with showgirls taking the roles of the ruble, yen,
franc, buck and mark ("The Money Song"). Fräulein Kost catches Schultz
and Schneider in a compromising position and Herr Schultz defends Schneider's honor by saying they are engaged. He then proposes in earnest ("Married"). At the couple's engagement party Ernst enters with a swastika on his
coat and Cliff discovers whose errands he has been running. When Schultz
sings a Yiddish song to entertain the guests ("Meeskite"), Ernst angrily warns
Schneider not to marry a Jew. Kost stops Ernst from leaving the party by
starting a vigorous group reprise of what turns out to be a Nazi song ("Tomorrow Belongs to Me"). The curtain falls on a fanatical circle singing the anthem,
excluding Sally, Cliff, Schneider and Schultz, while the Emcee appears smiling
above the scene.

Act II opens on a club number, a kick line that turns into a goose-stepping Nazi satire. Schneider tells Schultz she cannot marry him for fear the
Nazis will come to power. In another parallel between the club and the real
world, the Emcee sings of his forbidden love for a gorilla ("If You Could See
Her"). Cliff decides that he and Sally need to get out of Berlin, despite her
desire to return to the club. Schneider comes to tell them the wedding has
been called off and asks ("What Would You Do?"). Sally returns to the club,
contrary to Cliff's wishes, and when he goes to find her he gets into a fistfight
with Ernst and a group of Nazi thugs. Sally performs the eponymous paean
to the unthinking decadent life ("Cabaret"). The next morning she returns
to the flat to tell Cliff she has had an abortion and he decides to leave for Paris
without her. At the train station the club appears in limbo, now full of Nazi
patrons, and we hear key moments reprised from the show ("Finale"). The
club disappears and we are left with the tilted mirror, streetlamps and the
glowing Cabaret sign.

Cabaret opened at the Broadhurst Theatre on November 20, 1966, and
was an immediate box office hit. It starred Joel Grey as the Emcee, Jill Haworth
as Sally, revered comedian Jack Gilford as Schultz and Kurt Weill's widow,
theatre legend Lotte Lenya, as Schneider. It won eight Tonys, including Best
Musical, Best Composer and Lyricist, and Best Director. A national tour was
launched during the Broadway run, lasting several years. Productions were
mounted all over the world, and the Broadway company played 1,166 performances, closing on September 6, 1969. Critics were overall quite positive,
but the new conceptual territory broached by the show left some confused.
Critic Martin Gottfried, in a considered and prescient review, accused *Cabaret*
of having a split personality. The book scenes outside the club, including tra-

ditional musical theatre numbers, kept to the structure of the integrated musical, while the cabaret numbers struck out into new territory. Gottfried stated:

> *Cabaret* is two musicals and one of them is enormously striking and magnificently executed. However that marvelous part of it is a style, a sense, an attitude, rather than a complete scheme for musical theatre, and apparently at a loss to fulfill it, writer Joe Masteroff was forced into conventional Broadway musical plotting to fill out the evening [241].

Gottfried comments on the extreme gulf between the cabaret and "plot" halves of the show, proclaiming the book scenes to be uninteresting and flat, and the cabaret world to be revolutionary. Other critics confined their comments to casting and matters smaller in scope. Critics generally loved Joel Grey as the Emcee and hated Jill Haworth in the role of Sally Bowles. When Walter Kerr, in *The New York Times* proclaimed that, "*Cabaret* is a stunning musical with one wild wrong note" (242), the note he referred to was Haworth. Sally had been the central character in van Druten's play, as well as the most commented on character in Isherwood's stories. Contrastingly, Sally was simply not the star of *Cabaret* the musical. *Cabaret*'s Sally was not meant to be a strong singer, instead a deluded young girl with a fundamentally misguided wish for the decadent life. Haworth was not a singer, and her portrayal of Sally as a frail kewpie doll struck many critics as too weak, when compared to Julie Harris' star making performance in *I Am a Camera*. Haworth's performance, when later contrasted to the Sallys of other incarnations, most particularly Liza Minnelli's in the film, demonstrates the conflicting conceptions of Sally Bowles as a character. Minnelli was rejected as a candidate for Sally in the original production because she was considered too talented, too charismatic. These readings of Sally Bowles affect the show as a whole, underscoring the extent to which Sally lives as an outsider in Berlin society, and how much her willful ignorance of the Nazi threat acts as a contagious, appealing state. Other critics commented on Harold Prince's skill and the inventiveness of the score, and were generally quite positive about the show as a whole.

    Cabaret's reviews were much freer in their discussion of the Nazi element of the show than were reviews for *The Sound of Music*. Admittedly, the Nazi plot line takes a more central role in *Cabaret* than in Rodgers and Hammerstein's work. However, the critical reaction makes it quite clear that in 1966 Americans felt freer to delve into the events and implications of the Nazi era. Critic Richard Watts, displaying a typical regard for the gravity of *Cabaret*'s subject matter, noted, "From the first there is that rising undercurrent of decadence and vulgarity that was preparing the way for the ease with which a brutal racial insanity was able to take over a country" (240). Watts' choice to focus attention on *racial* insanity shows that the Holocaust was beginning to be foremost in American minds when considering the Nazi era. However, the link between Nazism and the Holocaust had not yet been fully established. For despite this new attention, a certain lightness and unconcern in critics' description of Nazis also demonstrates that the 1960s were a period of slow change in American attitudes. For instance, John Chapman rather quaintly described the period of the show as one when "the Nazis were beginning to feel their oats" (241). He then remarks rather disappointedly that, "*Cabaret* ends on a down beat — out of necessity" (241). One can't quite imagine this response from a modern critic, our collective attitude towards Nazism and the Holocaust has changed too much; the link has become unbreakable. Indeed, when we explore later critical reaction, we will find that attitudes towards the Nazism in *Cabaret* have indeed shifted.

Just before *Cabaret*'s original production left for tryouts in Boston, Jerome Robbins watched a run through, and encouraged the artistic team to make a stronger conceptual choice by cutting all the dancing except in the cabaret numbers. Prince decided to ignore this advice. It would take Bob Fosse's 1972 film version to move all the way towards a fully conceptual choice. This film was perhaps the most divergent from its original source of any major cinematic Broadway musical. Fosse returned yet again to the original Isherwood stories, and included several new characters, cutting others and radically altering those he kept. Cliff becomes the British Brian, now bisexual, a step closer to Isherwood's actual sexual preference. Fosse turns Sally Bowles into a brash American, famously played by Liza Minelli. Her portrayal radically changed the conception of the character, for her very talent meant the film's Sally was not the deluded, untalented girl, singing in a dive, described by Isherwood, but instead a vastly charismatic, shining talent, thereby increasing the glamour factor of the club. Ernst, Kost, Schultz and Schneider are dropped altogether in favor of the storyline of the young Jewish heiress Natalia who refuses to marry her admirer Fritz until he admits that he too is Jewish. The film also introduces the wealthy and aristocratic Maximilian von Heune, with whom both Sally and Brian have affairs. The most radical change however, was Fosse's choice to confine the music only to the club, with the exception of "Tomorrow Belongs to Me," also realistically sung by patrons at a Beer Garden. In addition to cutting all the non-club songs, several original numbers were replaced by new Kander and Ebb songs. For instance Sally's first song "Don't Tell Mamma" was replaced with "Mein Herr," and "The Money Song" was replaced with "Money Makes the World Go Around." One song was added for Sally, "Maybe This Time." By limiting the musical side of the film to diegetic song, or "realistically" sung numbers, Fosse helped not only to surmount the difficulty of suspension of disbelief inherent to the movie musical, but also thereby to strengthen the dramatic impact of that music and the film as a whole. Fosse cut between the club and outside events demonstrating encroaching Nazism, for example, between Nazi thugs beating a man in the street to a violent mock German dance number in the club. He retained Aronson's mirror concept and the final image of the club overrun by Nazi patrons from the stage production. *Cabaret* won eight Oscars in 1972, including Best Actress for Minnelli, Supporting Actor for Joel Grey, and Director for Fosse, but has the dubious distinction of being the only film in history to win eight Oscars without winning Best Picture, which went to *The Godfather* that year.

Prince restaged *Cabaret* on Broadway in 1987, with Joel Grey reprising his role as the Emcee. Prince felt that improvements could be made from his original production. Most changes were made to the score. "Why Should I Wake Up" was cut and replaced with a new song, "Sally Stay." Kander and Ebb's "I Don't Care Much," which had been cut from the original production, was replaced, sung by the Emcee in the second act. "Meeskite" was also cut, according to Prince because, "Meeskite was written pure and simply for Jack Gilford. Without Jack Gilford it didn't seem to belong in the show" (quoted in Ilson 340). Textual changes were made as well, including recognizing Cliff's bi-sexuality. Prince states, "We didn't deal with [Cliff's sexuality] originally... . We did this time" (quoted in Ilson 339). Additionally the original final line to "If You Could See Her" was replaced in this production, back to "She wouldn't look Jewish at all." It had been changed in the original production due to outside pressure. The critics, who were primarily positive about the revival, or more accurately, revisal, noticed this change. Clive Barnes in *The New York Post* noticed that, "The Nazis anti–Semitism is more pointed, particularly in the savage punch-line of Grey's duet with a gorilla" (quoted in Ilson 340). The original set by Boris Aronson was to be recreated for the revival, but the demands of the national tour, which was to precede and follow the Broadway run, forced a trimming of many of the elements. As a result, Frank Rich accused the producers of cutting financial corners in his *New York Times* review. Although other than Rich's anger the critics offered positive reviews, the Broadway production ran less than a year.

A more radical retelling of *Cabaret*, which transferred to Broadway in 1998, has most memorably been described by Ethan Mordden as creating a "drugagonzo Nazisexo inferno" (*Open a New Window* 159). The production, which originated at London's Donmar Warehouse in 1993, directed by Sam Mendes and starring Alan Cummings and Jane Horrocks, took five years to transfer to Broadway, primarily because Mendes was searching for the correct theatre environment. Mendes' concept was to complete the metaphor begun in the text, to make the cabaret the environment for the entire theatre-going experience. He wanted the cabaret:

> to operate as a metaphor for Germany. In the early 1930s you were in a club having a great time. By the mid–30s, the door was being locked from the out-

side, and by 1939 you couldn't get out. It's a physical metaphor; you're not an observer; you're part of it; you're there [quoted in Wolf 2].

Ultimately the show found a home in the Henry Miller Theatre — originally a theatre, then a series of run down clubs, and finally a theatre once again. The site was renamed the Kit Kat Klub, and patrons sat at cocktail tables and were able to buy drinks and food. Programs were not given out until after the show had ended, in order to facilitate the club atmosphere. The production later transferred to Studio 54, where the echoes of 1970s disco escapism and the mad party atmosphere associated with that club found parallels to 1930s Berlin. Mendes has said that the original production was "the embryo of a dangerous show that was wrapped in conventional Broadway wrapping" (quoted in Mordden *Open a New Window* 159). Mendes argued that he was less concerned "than Hal Prince had to be, really, in providing a sort of value-for-money night out on Broadway — big production numbers that ultimately don't say anything" (quoted in Wolf 3). Accordingly, the 1998 production was much rougher and more sexualized than the 1966 original. Mendes brought in emerging Broadway choreographer Rob Marshall to co-direct and choreograph. The production starred Alan Cummings, repeating his role as the Emcee from the Donmar Warehouse production; Natasha Richardson as Sally, Ron Rifkin as Schultz, Mary Louise Wilson as Schneider and John Benjamin Hickey as Cliff filled out the cast. The production kept much of the film score, while also reinstating songs cut from the original production. Sally sang both "Don't Tell Mamma" and "Mein Herr," and the Emcee sang "I Don't Care." Both "Meeskite" and "Why Should I Wake Up" remained absent. The film's "Money Make the World Go Around" was kept in favor of "The Money Song." The production won three Tonys for performance — Cummings, Richardson and Rifkin — and the Tony for Best Revival of a Musical.

Grim Realism

Close readings of the texts, both written and performative, of three iterations: the original Broadway incarnation, the film, and Mendes' revival, are necessary to fully explore the implications of the staged Nazi and Holocaust references in *Cabaret*. Combining the three analyses makes a trend towards grim realism very evident in the case of *Cabaret*. The linear nature of this development as described implies that the original production of *Cabaret* somehow glossed over the more difficult issues inherent to the subject matter. However, the extent to which the original production addressed challenging topics without flinching in 1966 is especially surprising within the context of the American musical, which had not been given full credit for depth of thematic material before the heyday of the concept musical which *Cabaret* inaugurated.

Cabaret's cast of characters and their reactions to the oncoming Nazi threat present an illuminating comparison to characters in *The Sound of Music*. Both musicals present the full spectrum of possible reactions to Nazism. There are characters who have fully subscribed to the movement, such as Herr Zeller in *The Sound of Music* and Ernst in *Cabaret*; those who go over to the Nazis within the span of the show, such as Rolf in *The Sound of Music* and Kost in *Cabaret* (the Emcee in the original production could also be placed in this category); characters who choose either to ignore or gloss over the coming storm, Max and Elsa in *The Sound of Music*, Sally, Schultz and briefly Cliff in *Cabaret*; and finally, characters who stand firmly against Nazi hatred, the Captain in *The Sound of Music* and eventually, Cliff in *Cabaret*. However, these similarities stop short of moral clarity. *The Sound of Music* maintains a much simpler worldview, underscoring the Captain's moral stance, while *Cabaret* undercuts Cliff's attempted stand. Although in both cases the characters exit the realm into which the Nazis encroach, the Captain does so with his family as part of a strong political statement, refusing to join the forces of the Third Reich, while Cliff slinks away after being beaten by Nazi thugs and after Sally aborts his baby, leaving her alone to face the ensuing storm. Cliff spouts the morally correct sentiments, "Sally can't you see — if you're not against all this, you're for it — or you might as well be" (95), but his weakness as a character undercuts his proper American viewpoint. Cliff begins his character's journey far more similarly to Sally's trademark willful blindness, reading *Mein Kampf* but performing Ernst's errands without asking, indeed refusing to hear, who they are for. His song, "Why Should I Wake Up," acts as a paean to blissful political ignorance, as does Sally's more famous "Cabaret." Directly after the first real indication of encroaching Nazism, "Tomorrow Belongs to Me," Cliff argues, "I said it was *possible* I was sleepwalking. And — if I am — who cares? What's the point in opening my eyes" (57)? The lyrics of the song then embrace the joy of dreaming and sleep, disconnected from any difficult realities. Despite this willful ignorance, the Nazi threat wakes Cliff up in the final scene of Act I.

Nazism creeps into *Cabaret* in the same manner in which National Socialism insidiously worked its way into political power in Germany. The encroachment of the Nazis builds to its first climax at the end of Act I. Although in the first narrative scene Cliff meets Ernst, smuggling his suitcase, we do not know for what purpose. In scene five Sally mentions that Ernst works for a political party, but she does not know or care which one. In that same scene Sally mistakes *Mein Kampf* for Cliff's novel, when he retorts that he is reading it because, "I thought I should know something about German politics," Sally blithely answers, "Why? You're an American" (37). This mention of Adolf Hitler's book stands as the first Nazi specific reference in the text. In scene eight a group of waiters from the club, described as "handsome, well-scrubbed, idealistic" (55), appear on the spiral staircase. They sing an unidentified patriotic anthem, "Tomorrow Belongs to Me." This song has become identified with the Nazis by the end of the act, but at this moment its meanings are left open, although the Emcee's presence establishes an aura of foreboding, underlined by the final image of the scene, "the waiters disappear upstage, leaving a leering Emcee alone as the lights dim" (55). Additionally the song itself embraces liminality, encompassing images from the pastoral to the martial. By the final stanza, the song's political implications become apparent, including the usage of the meaning-laden phrase "Fatherland." But the menace has still not been named.

It takes several scenes until *Cabaret* fully exposes the Nazi threat. The reveal occurs in the Act I finale, through powerful visual means. Ernst enters with a swastika armband on his overcoat, the first time this symbol has appeared. As we can see from the example of *The Sound of Music*, the swastika had not yet reached the level of convention it has attained today, and thus very likely still held a vast power to shock when *Cabaret* opened on Broadway in 1966. Cliff's reaction to discovering he has been smuggling for the Nazis quickly underscores the jolt of the swastika:

CLIFF: I've been reading your leader's book...
ERNST: Ah yes. *Mein Kampf*
CLIFF: Have you read it?
ERNST: Certainly
CLIFF: Then I don't understand. I mean — that man is out of his mind. It's right there on every page... [77].

Adolf Hitler remains unnamed throughout the show, despite several references. Glancing allusions and symbols are enough; America by 1966 knows exactly what those references and symbols stand for. And in 1966, they now stand for anti–Semitism, a connection not clearly established just seven years before.

Whereas *The Sound of Music* has a dedicated absence of Judaism, *Cabaret* approaches the issue head-on. Masteroff's book establishes Herr Schultz's religion almost as soon as it introduces him. Directly after meeting Cliff, Schultz offers:

SCHULTZ: I want to wish you mazel in the New Year.
CLIFF: Mazel?
SCHULTZ: Jewish. It means luck! [16].

Cabaret underlines Schultz's Judaism to a more ominous purpose in the final scene of Act I. An intoxicated Schultz, at the engagement party he has thrown for himself and Schneider, decides to entertain the guests with a song. He introduces the number by stating, "Now — the only word you have to know in order to understand my little song is the Yiddish word: 'meeskite.' 'Meeskite' means ugly, funny-looking" (79). Schultz then launches into a song that tells the tale of two ugly people who unite and produce a gorgeous child. Throughout the song he interjects Yiddish words and defines them. This song, sung amongst an audience of conspicuous non–Jews, including one avowed Nazi, firmly marks Schultz as the Other. *Cabaret* portrays Schultz as alone in his Judaism at the party, indeed, alone in the context of the show as a whole. Singing this song marginalizes him further. The text sets Schultz's joyful innocence against the seething hatred of the Nazi Ernst who watches "Meeskite" in ominous silence. Schultz exhorts his audience at the party to join him in his song, and specifically tries to get Ernst to sing along: "Sing with me, somebody? Fräulein Schneider? Herr Ludwig — we make a duet?" (80). Finally the oblivious Sally joins him in song. Schultz's naming of Ernst calls attention to the song's purpose in the show. Although critics at the time and even today have dismissed the song as merely a light comedy number tailored to the talents of Jack Gilford, the song powerfully underlined the central connection beginning to become apparent in America, the linking of Nazism with what would become its defining element, anti–Semitism. At the end of the song, the stage directions read, "(*all applaud except Ernst, who puts on his coat*)" (81). Ernst then proceeds to warn Schneider against marriage with Schultz:

> ERNST: Think what you are doing. This marriage is not advisable. I cannot put it too strongly. For your own welfare.
> CLIFF: What about Herr Schultz's welfare?
> ERNST: He is not a German.
> SCHNEIDER: But he was born here!
> ERNST: He is not a German. Good evening [82].

To stop Ernst from leaving, the prostitute Fräulein Kost, demonstrating how far Nazism has impinged on the population, begins to sing the anthem earlier sung by the waiters and now identified with the Nazi party, "Tomorrow Belongs to Me." Kost starts the song alone, and then the guests begin to join in, passing around swastika armbands as they sing:

> *Ernst, wearing the coat with the swastika armband, goes to her side. The guests form a circle around them, as if magnetically attracted. The guests join in the singing — their voices growing louder and louder, even rather frightening. [...] the Emcee appears at the top of the spiral stairs [...] he takes in the scene, Fräulein Schneider and Cliff watching the singers with great concern — Herr Schultz and Sally laughing, unaware of what is happening. [...] The people on stage freeze against a black background. The Emcee slowly crosses the stage, looking at everyone. Then he turns to the audience. He shrugs, he smiles and exits. Blackout [84].*

Cabaret (1966–1969 Broadway). Music by John Kander Lyrics by Fred Ebb Book by Joe Masteroff Directed by Harold Prince. Shown foreground: Edward Winter as Ernst Ludwig.

This potent image, where the two worlds of *Cabaret*—the cabaret and the real world—have collided for the first time in the piece, demonstrates with simple precision the nature and scope of the threat which has invaded Germany.

In Act II, Nazism finally takes center stage in *Cabaret*. The act opens with a kick line which turns into a satirical goose-stepping number and continues into a scene where Schneider tells Schultz she cannot marry him. Significantly, this scene presents the first use of the word Nazi in the text. Schultz comprehends Schneider's reasoning, but refuses to put any stock in her fears, for as demonstrated in the last stage direction, the original production portrays Schultz as an innocent, not comprehending, either through a simple nature or willful blindness, the personal danger provided by the Nazis:

> SCHNEIDER: I saw that one can no longer dismiss the Nazis. Because suddenly they are my friends and neighbors. And how many others? And—if so—is it possible they will come to power?
> SCHULTZ: And you will be married to a Jew.
> SCHNEIDER: *(frightened)* I need my license to rent my rooms! If they take it away...
> SCHULTZ: They will take nothing away. I promise you [89].

He almost has her convinced, stating, "Governments come. Governments go. How much longer can we wait?" (90), and singing a reprise of their love song, "Married," but the song crashes to a halt when a brick hurtles through Schultz's shop window:

> SCHNEIDER: You see? You see!
> SCHULTZ: It is nothing. Children on their way to school! Mischievous children! Nothing more! I assure you! *(Herr Schultz runs out. We see him outside the broken window, looking for the culprit and questioning the onlookers. No one seems to have seen anything.)* [90–1].

This scene serves to marginalize Schultz even more strongly. The presence of passers-by outside the window, complicit in the act of hatred which has just occurred, underlines Schultz's increasing Otherness, especially when placed in context of the song which immediately follows, the Emcee's love song to a gorilla, read as a Jew, "If You Could See Her."

Although from this discussion it is clear that *Cabaret* was able to approach sensitive political issues much more directly than *The Sound of Music* from its vantage point just seven years later, certain artistic choices were still deemed too sensitive and therefore off-limits. It is illuminating to note however, which elements were considered inappropriate in 1959, versus in 1966. In 1959 swastikas and staged Nazis were at issue, in 1966 comments perceived as anti–Semitic were the concern. "If You Could See Her," the Emcee's love song to a gorilla, caused extensive controversy upon the initial production. Fred Ebb wrote the lyrics to end with the line, "If you could see her through my eyes, She's wouldn't look Jewish at all" (87). The song was meant to evoke a complicated response, with an initial laugh caught by an audience who sees themselves in the overhanging mirror, then coming to an ashamed silence or embarrassed applause.

Fred Ebb states, "I'm very proud of that reaction, and it's exactly what the mirror concept means in *Cabaret*— that we're all capable of this" (quoted in Steyn 87). Apparently the audience in 1966 was not ready for the daring nature of this line. Near the end of the Boston try-out, the creative team started to receive angry letters, including one from a Rabbi. There were threats of major parties canceling their bookings if the line was not changed. And so Prince decided not to take the risk. Ebb was required to change the line, and came up with "She isn't a Meeskite at all," a reference to the former song. But he was unhappy with the change:

> I was doing it for what I felt were the wrong reasons. But I knew it had to be done anyway. [...] I wish Prince had held firm [...] but I can now understand and have great compassion for his not wanting to blow it for something as seemingly mild as one line in a song [quoted in Ilson 147–8].

John Kander spoke of the central confusion that underlay the response to the line:

> The song was to end that way [...] to make you the audience realize how easily you could fall into a trap of prejudice. And the Jewish members of the audience, my family included, all insisted that the song was really saying that Jews looked like gorillas. It's a puzzle that has never been solved [quoted in Ilson 148].

The rest of Act II's original text continues to underline the increasing threat and eventual takeover of the Nazis. A group of Nazi thugs at the cabaret beat Cliff when he goes to retrieve Sally. Schultz makes it clear that he will not leave Germany, and eventually Cliff gives up and leaves the country and its inhabitants to their doom. The finale presents a complete lack of any kind of compromising "happy ending" so seemingly integral to the musical form. Instead the final number is a nightmare-like montage of previous key scenes and lines replayed in a dissonant key. The Emcee reappears and re-introduces the Cabaret orchestra as he did in the first number, and the characters appear in limbo to restate key lines:

> *(But this time the picture and the mood are much different. The girls are not as pretty, German uniforms and swastika armbands are apparent [...] Dissonant strains of "Wilkommen" are heard. Then from among the moving people, we see Herr Schultz)*
> SCHULTZ: Just children. Mischievous children on their way to school. You understand.
> SCHNEIDER: I understand. One does what one must.
> SALLY: It'll all work out. It's only politics, and what's that got to do with us?
> SCHNEIDER: I must be sensible. If the Nazis come — what other choice have I?
> SCHULTZ: I know I am right — because I understand the Germans. After all, what am I? A German [114].

Sally reprises "Cabaret" one more time and the Emcee appears to wish us farewell, and then disappears. All that is left in the darkness is the flashing cabaret sign.

This work focuses on staged interpretations of the Nazi and the Holocaust, so an comprehensive analysis of the filmic *Cabaret*— examined extensively by film scholars — would be misplaced here. However, we should briefly note the aesthetic and structural changes made to the original material, which further demonstrates the changing times and shifting American attitudes towards Nazism. Cliff / Brian's sexuality and nationality are changed, rendering earlier attempts at having an upstanding young American as a foil to the degeneracy of Germany, null and void. Fosse's *Cabaret* was able to complicate these issues through a more ambiguous sexuality — still a daring move in 1972. Additionally, although Fosse cuts the named Nazi characters out of the film, particularly Ernst, his ability to edit film in order to juxtapose Nazi brutality with the gaiety inside the club serves to ameliorate this absence. By definition however, the phenomenological impact of the Nazi ascent to power is lost in the translation between stage and film. The most chilling scene in the film corresponds to the end of Act I. Instead of the party scene, we see an outdoor beer garden in the idyllic countryside where a young Aryan boy begins singing "Tomorrow Belongs to Me." After the first verse the camera pans down to his sleeve and pauses at his swastika armband. One by one the people join the song, and suddenly two more Nazi uniforms and armbands pop into the frame. No dramatic reveal of the swastika is necessary; the symbol appears from very the beginning of the film on armbands and scrawled on posters.

Finally, in the film, Fosse replaces Schultz as the sole Jewish character with a beautiful young woman and her suitor. The altered attitude this implies towards Judaism corresponds with the continued changing attitudes in America, and the growing strength of the perceived link of Nazism with anti–Semitism and the Holocaust. Jews can now be attractive, sensitive and young, as opposed to older and comic, making their foreshadowed victimization all the more tragic. The re-instatement of the original ending to "If You Could See Her" also reflects the film's renewed emphasis on anti–Semitism. John Kander notes however, that in the film the line, "She wouldn't look Jewish at all" is said in absolute silence, so that Fosse would have been able to dub over the line without complication, should negative reactions ensue. All subsequent stage productions have utilized this original line.

Sam Mendes' radical retelling of *Cabaret* emphasizes the sexual elements of the text, as allowed by our more permissive modern society, illuminating the trend towards grim realism quite clearly. In the original production the only reference to homosexuality was when Schultz stops the dancing at his engagement party because he sees two men dancing together. The show also exhibited a transgender moment in the brief cross-dressing of the Emcee in the kick-line that opened Act II. Critics at the time lumped the transgender and homosexual references together disparagingly. Norman Nadel, of the *World Journal Tribune* was rather disturbed by the original production's "world of brassy women, mincing homosexuals and raucous sound" (242). Mendes, however, sexualized the text to a great extent, often in a sado-masochistic manner. The Kit Kat girls are dressed in ratty old underwear, the runs in their stockings evident, the track marks from drugs and bruises from sexual encounters emblazoned on their bodies. Additional scenes written by Masteroff highlight Cliff's bisexuality, presented as closer to homosexuality in this production. Mendes also chose to re-evaluate Ernst's sexuality; his relationship with Cliff made the more complex because of an evident crush, including a kiss rebuffed. This revival portrays a pan-sexual Emcee who gropes both girls and boys alike. The finale of Act I offers one telling instance of how the sex-ualized nature of this production entwined with a more intense reaction to Nazism. In Mendes' production the Emcee lurks slowly upstage and at the final frenzied moment, bares his buttocks to the audience, where a small black swastika has been painted. The Emcee's action has been accused of being merely a shock tactic of Mendes's part. According to this argument, the swastika by itself has lost some of its power to shock through overuse, and therefore the director sought a new method of surprising an audience already numbingly familiar with the symbol. However, this moment has implications far beyond shock value. A swastika on someone's body, and a "forbidden" part of the body specifically, has an entirely different set of significations from a swastika on a flag. Mendes's conception implies superiority over and disrespect for the symbol. We are given the ability to belittle the swastika by combining it with the school boyish act of "mooning." The act, as a sick joke, demon-strates a violently sexual power. The homosexual overtones would have been especially repellent to the Nazi ethos, compounding this act of disrespect towards the Nazis and their symbol. Roger Copeland explains the implications of Mendes's choice in his article in *American Theatre:* "Mendes's production is about life in an entertainment state, where anything and everything — including the symbols and accoutrements of the Third Reich — can be reduced to a form of amusement" (28).

Ben Brantley remarked in *The New York Times* that the Kit Kat Girls in Mendes' production, "even bring to mind — intentionally, one presumes — images of the skeletal inmates of the concentration camps to come" (249). Mendes chose to cast bone thin chorus girls who appeared sickly in his pro-duction, rather than the "round Germanic" Kit Kat Girls of the original pro-duction. Mendes' choice, noticed by Brantley, highlights the link between Nazism and the Holocaust that has become so inextricable in our own time. Reviews of the original production make no mention of concentration camps; indeed it would have been shocking to do so. In the 1990s, the mention is entirely unremarkable and expected. The Kit Kat girls' appearances are not the only explicit Holocaust reference in Mendes' production. Mendes chose to make the unspoken link between Nazism and the Holocaust, one that was not necessarily fully established when *Cabaret* was first written, overt and obvious in a time where that link has become accepted as self-evident. The finale of the piece, instead of presenting a nightmarish Nazi filled Cabaret, as in the original text, now takes us to a apocalyptic Holocaust vision. The number begins with Cliff leaving Berlin at the train station. The Emcee appears, as before, and Sally, Schneider and Schultz silently enter. The Emcee announces the band, but the bandstand is empty, although the music con-tinues:

(Schneider, Schultz, Kost and Ernst come down the stairs and form a line [...] As they turn and walk US the door wall, and brick wall behind the band, fly out to reveal the Company. The set disappears. We are in a white space)[...] (The Emcee slowly takes off his coat. He is wearing the clothes of a concentration camp prisoner. Drum roll. Cymbal crash. Blackout.) [99].

This vision radically re-interprets the role of the Emcee from the original production.

In 1966, as played by Joel Grey, the Emcee became complicit with the Nazis. Although he started the show as a metaphor for the desperation of the German people, Carol Ilson states that, "the MC, through the eight numbers he eventually did, became the metaphor for Germany [according to Prince] "in an ascending curve energetically and descending curve morally" (140). Mendes took a different perspective. As Joe Masteroff states, "The master of ceremonies is now a figure of doom. There was always something impishly charming about Joel Grey that worked very well for the show is a more benign era" (quoted in Rothstein 3). With this benign era unquestionably over, Mendes casts the Emcee as the surprise victim.

Mendes' Emcee's prison stripes carried the insignia of two of the victim groups of the Holocaust, the yellow Star of David, and the pink triangle of the homosexual. Aside from directly stating the previously implied connection to the Holocaust, the imagery of this moment unites the thematic concerns of this production, and indeed of *Cabaret* as a whole: sexuality and fascism, demonstrating how these concerns are vastly more intertwined than might immediately be acknowledged. The pervasive sexuality in this production, a sexuality that was less overt in all previous productions of *Cabaret*, serves a deeper purpose than the shock value that some critics attributed it to. Mendes shows us the connection between the erotic turn-ons that seem omnipresent in the 1990s, the leather, the fraying "heroin chic" look which pervaded commercial culture, and fascist aesthetics. As Roger Copeland states in *American Theatre*:

> [Mendes] is showing us that much of what our current popular culture finds erotically appealing has its roots in German fascism. Yes, it's our look, our fashion statement, but the thematics and the metaphysics of these trends — and the instincts that they manipulate — take us deep into the heart of Nazi aesthetics [3].

The aesthetic appeal of a leader's total dominance over a massive crowd, seen in fascist propaganda films such as Leni Riefenstahl's *Triumph of the Will* (1934), implies a sexually tense atmosphere. As Copeland states, "The relationship is both erotically charged and highly regressive. Total dominance implies total submission. Hitler offers his masses the promise of instant gratification — and that requires a return to a state of childlike dependency" (4).

We will return to this connection when we discuss *The Producers*; however it is important to note that within this context Mendes' imagery of sado-masochism, dominance, regression and sexuality also returns us to the consideration of Nazism and its horrific results. With the chilling final concentration camp imagery we are suddenly reminded of the role of the emcee throughout the production. As Copeland argues, "He's someone who thinks that he can appropriate the icons of Nazism into fashion statements and turn-ons. And the dark joke, of course (if we dare to call it that), is on him" (5).

Comedy

Scholars often cite *Cabaret* as the show that marks the transition between musical theatre as "musical comedy," and the newer concept musical. *Cabaret* incorporates serious material within what was still in some aspects straightforward musical comedy. This transition, still in its beginning stages, offers some fascinating sites of ambiguity, especially concerning Nazi related humor.

Some straightforward uses of humor in *Cabaret* are of the type more frequently seen against Nazi subjects. These can be placed in the tradition of "comedy of tyranny," explored by scholar Daniel Gerould. This type of humor's theoretical basis corresponds with Mel Brooks' (author of *The Producers*) statement, "If you can laugh at your enemy, you've won." The laughter it evokes comes from a place of triumph. The kick-line that turns into a goose step that opens Act II can be placed in this category, slyly making fun of the connection between Nazism and show business. "If You Could See Her," while causing much controversy, belongs in this category of humor as well, making fun the enemy through belittling their own belief system. However, the seemingly straightforward anti-fascist humor in *Cabaret* renders the audience complicit in the same manner as the song's final line. This complication comes through the compromised figure of the Emcee, who in the original production was ultimately allied with the Nazis. Even Mendes, who revealed the Emcee as a victim rather than an aggressor, staged the character ambiguously for much of the show. We do not know entirely where his sympathies lie, and he confounds straightforward readings as a victim, thus complicating the clear-cut anti–Hitler humor.

Another source of humor in *Cabaret* presents a startling contrast to *The Sound of Music*. While in *The Sound of Music* Nazis are non-singing, not humorous characters, the Nazi figures in *Cabaret* not only are initially amusing, but have co-opted the moral power of singing. "Tomorrow Belongs To Me," initially staged as a beautiful pastoral anthem, becomes debased by its association with Nazism. The song, fervently sung by guests at the party, arguably presents the most powerful and frightening moment in the show. Group singing, portrayed as the essence of freedom and beauty in *The Sound of Music,* has been tarnished by its association with the warped values of Nazism. Nazis have also invaded the sacrosanct realm of comic characters. *Cabaret* presents Ernst in particular as a humorous figure, with his mala-propisms from learning English, and his amusing appreciation of Cliff's wom-anizing powers, "Such a to-do! I will see you Friday for the next lesson. But I am telling you something: I think I am taking from you the wrong kind of lessons!" (34). The libretto also presents Fräulein Kost in a comedic light dur-ing her contest with Schneider over her morals and profession, and later reveals her as a Nazi sympathizer when she begins singing "Tomorrow Belongs to Me."

    Cabaret broke through musical theatre barriers because it approached this kind of recent tragic material within a traditionally light form. However, although much about *Cabaret* was revolutionary, including the use of humor in the piece, vestiges were left from musical comedy days. Critics understood Herr Schultz, played by famous stage comedian Jack Gilford in the original production, as one of those remnants. His songs, including "It Couldn't Please Me More" and "Meeskite," were interpreted as straight comedy numbers. *The Wall Street Journal*'s reviewer Richard P. Cooke states, "Before the evening is over, Miss Lenya and Jack Gilford, produce some first rate comedy, including a ludicrous and affecting song about such a humble matter as the gift of a pineapple" (243). "Meeskite," despite the previously discussed conditions that undercut the humor in the song, was also understood by critics of the time as a traditional piece of musical theatre comedy. Cooke described the song as "an excellent comedy number entitled 'Meeskite,' about homely people" (243), and Walter Kerr called it "A rapid-fire comic turn [...] one of the treasures of the occasion" (243). The implications of this number, staged under the glaring eye of Nazism, seem not to have impacted the original audience — or at least 1966 critics. These audiences were not fully conditioned, as we have been, to immediately connect impending horror and doom to a Nazi's hatred of a Jew. However, Gilford was famous as a very Jewish comedian, and asso-ciated with left-wing liberal causes. He was named by Jerome Robbins to the House Un-American Activities Committee and made his way back onto the stage with, among other roles, Mr. Dussel in the original production of *The Diary of Anne Frank* in 1955. For Broadway audiences, the associations of Gilford's two roles would have been striking, as a Holocaust victim in *Anne Frank* and then a character destined for that fate in *Cabaret.*

    Schultz's number has been cut from all major revivals, perhaps due to the dissonance evoked by a light musical comedy song sung in the face of intense anti–Semitism. The character himself presents a difficult conflict between sweet comedy, low vaudeville type humor — including cracks about fruit giving him gas — and the reality of his ultimate doom. In his final scene, Schultz comes to tell Cliff that he will leave the boarding house. When Cliff tells him that he is returning to America, Schultz replies:

SCHULTZ: America! I have sometimes thought of going there —
CLIFF: Why don't you? The way things look here —
SCHULTZ: But it will pass — I promise you!
CLIFF: I hope you're right.
SCHULTZ: I know I am right! Because I understand the Germans... After all, what am I? A German [108].

Schultz's attitude makes it clear he will not leave Germany and will therefore be caught in the whirlwind of hatred and murder that was to come. Therefore he presents the most glaring conflict with theories of Holocaust comedy, specifically to film scholar Sander Gilman's proposition that in Holocaust related humor "the victim must be in a position to win or to at least survive the world of the Nazis" (286). Schultz, a stock comic type, will not survive. The Emcee in Mendes' production offers the same paradox; he presents much of the humor in the piece, and yet, in a stunning turn-about becomes a victim, not "winning" at all. Perhaps the phenomenologically and aesthetically rich and complex field of musical theatre, ignored by Holocaust scholars, allows this conflict where other forms would not

There are no heroes in *Cabaret*, only flawed characters. Although Cliff disapproves of the encroaching evil, he makes no valiant gestures and slinks out of the country, defeated. His passivity, underlined and enforced by his role as Isherwood's "camera," undercuts any heroism his moral stance might evoke. *Cabaret's* unabated grim ending stands in opposition to scholars who have pointed out a trend of "Americanization of the Holocaust" where Americans demand "happy endings" to their Holocaust stories. We saw this trend in early American treatments of *The Diary of Anne Frank*; we see it in the film *Schindler's List* which focuses on a Christian savior and those who survived rather than the millions who died, as well as in Arthur Miller's *Incident at Vichy*, which also offers a Christian sacrifice as a hopeful ending. *Cabaret*, however, an early work addressing Holocaust themes, does not grant the audience their "happy" ending. Sally will self destruct, Schultz will no doubt end up in a concentration camp, and the rest of the characters will be caught in the unstoppable destruction of World War II. Although productions of *Cabaret* have increasingly embraced this unadulterated pessimism, it exists in the original text, making *Cabaret* a unique work of the Holocaust and musical theatre canons.

CHAPTER VI

The Rothschilds

"This Moses wants to see the Promised Land / in my own Lifetime"
(II-4-33)

The Rothschilds, Bock and Harnick's final collaboration, opened on Broadway in October, 1970, six years after their incredibly successful *Fiddler on the Roof*. While the events of the musical take place in the late 18th and early 19th centuries (1772 to 1818), the musical also speaks to modern American Jews, through potent nostalgia for the familial unit. Simultaneously, the Holocaust resonates perhaps more strongly in this piece than in any of the others we have discussed, complicating nostalgic readings. There are sites invoking memory in the musical, but they don't function here the same way; they are complicated, dissonant, and angrier, reflecting the musical's emergence from the more cynical 1970s. *The Rothschilds* thus presents one of the most complex Jewish themed works of American musical theatre.

History

The Rothschilds takes as its source the history of the banking dynasty begun by Mayer Rothschild in 18th century Germany. A brief account of the fortunes of the real family serves to historically ground a discussion of the musical. We know that ancestors of the Rothschild dynasty, registered as traders and moneychangers, lived in Frankfurt, Germany, by the 16th century. Mayer Amschel Rothschild was born in 1743 or 1744. He was sent to Yeshiva, but when his parents died he joined the family business, and married Gutele Schnapper, who brought with her a large dowry. He worked as a rare coin and medal dealer, and sold much of his stock to Prince Wilhelm of Hesse, who appointed Mayer as court agent in 1769. Mayer expanded his business by helping the Prince finance the English in the Revolutionary War. War against Napoleon's France helped to expand Mayer's fortunes through his agreement to supply the Austrian army. When his five sons were grown Mayer dispersed them across Europe in order to collect monies for Prince Wilhelm. When Wilhelm was forced into exile after Napoleon annexed his kingdom, the Rothschilds continued to work for the Prince, including Mayer's son Nathan Rothschild, who invested in England. The Rothschilds revolutionized their business by ensuring fast communication using messengers and carrier pigeons. Because of the strength of their family ties across Europe they were able to amass great wealth, status and power. Mayer died in 1812, but his sons magnified the empire he had begun. The brothers were made nobles in 1817 and nominated as barons in 1822, a particularly surprising honor for Jews in the period. The musical's plot ends at this point, but the Rothschild dynasty has enjoyed fame to the modern day. In 1970, when Bock and Harnick's musical opened, a current Rothschild family member had been appointed to a high position in the English government. Rothschilds are still powerful today as a banking dynasty across Europe.

Several theatrical depictions of the Rothschild family were written before the musical, including a play called *The Five Frankfurters*, which played London's Lyric Theatre in 1912 and New York in 1913. The most noteworthy portrayal of the family for our purposes here was 20th Century Pictures' *House of Rothschilds* (1934), starring George Arliss. Bankers as protagonists were touchy enough subjects in the middle of the Great Depression. But the Anti-Defamation League was particularly worried about potential backlash of a film about *Jewish* bankers. The ADL tried to stop film production all the way through 1933. They were worried that the characterization of the Rothschilds fit stereotypes of greedy Jewish bankers, despite the film's attempts to portray the Rothschilds as using their power and influence for good. The ADL remained worried, and after they failed to block the film entirely, they lobbied to change its content. When those efforts largely failed, the ADL decided to warn their representatives across the nation with a confidential memo. It seems their worries were largely unfounded; the movie was well received as an anti–Nazi piece. *House of Rothschilds* was nominated for Academy Award, and in the wake of its success the Jewish community seemed to agree that the ADL had been too cautious about a potentially negative interpretation. The magazine *American Hebrew* put an image from the film on its 1934 Passover cover headed by a quotation of Mayer's dialogue, "neither business nor power nor all the gold in Europe will bring you happiness until our people have equality, respect, dignity — until we can trade with dignity — until we can live with dignity — until we can walk the world with dignity!" (quoted in Herman 73).

Framed copies of the magazine cover were in great demand. Clearly sensitivity to stereotypes complicated the film's reception. Similar issues will shape consideration of Bock and Harnick's musical.

The Musical's History

In the early 1960s, producer Hilliard Elkins had an idea to base a musical on Frederic Morton's bestselling biography *The Rothschilds* (1961). As early as 1963 Elkins approached Bock and Harnick to write the score, but they were not pleased with an early libretto by Wolf Mankiewicz. They were also busy writing *Fiddler on the Roof* at the time. Elkins continued to pursue the matter and went through at least four librettists in four years, finally settling on playwright and TV writer Sherman Yellen's treatment. This was Yellen's first musical libretto, although he later went on to write a skit in *Oh! Calcutta!* (1969) and the libretto for Richard Rodgers' *Rex* (1976). Yellen's original script used an auction as a non-realistic framing device, offering for sale various plot elements or characters. Although Bock and Harnick were worried about taking on the musical because of its many similarities to *Fiddler*, Yellen's take on the material persuaded the authors to join the project. Diverse actors such as Roddy McDowell and Gene Hackman were considered for the role of Mayer (Bock Collection NYPL n. pag.), but the young and unknown Hal Linden won the role. Paul Hecht was hired to play his son Nathan, and Jill Clayburgh to play Hannah, Nathan's romantic interest. The production process was stormy, and a dispute over the firing of director Derek Goldby caused a rift between Bock and Harnick, making *The Rothschilds* their last collaboration to date (excepting a new song written for David Leveaux's *Fiddler* revival). Michael Kidd took over for original choreographer Eliot Feld, and during tryouts in Detroit, for British director Goldby. Harnick states, "I think to this day Jerry feels that Derek was quite capable and we didn't give him a chance" (quoted in Mandelbaum 9). Various songs were cut during tryouts. The creative team also changed the libretto's structure. Whereas at first Mayer had died at the end of Act I, they now changed history to keep him alive through most of Act II. They also added a stirring eleven o'clock number for Mayer entitled, "In My Own Lifetime." The auction framing device was lost along the way.

While *The Rothschilds* was announced to open every year after 1962, it eventually made its way to Broadway on October 19, 1970, at the Lunt-Fontanne Theatre, with orchestrations by Don Walker, sets and costumes by John Bury, and directed and choreographed by Michael Kidd. The musical received nine Tony nominations, but only two wins, including Linden. The rest were largely lost to Sondheim's *Company*. *The Rothschilds* ran for 507 performances, and did not make a profit. In fact the musical only returned twenty-five percent of its investments, perhaps due to the fact that it was at that point the most expensive musical ever produced on Broadway. The musical transferred to San Francisco after closing on Broadway, and there Bock and Harnick trimmed the libretto, which they hadn't had time to do on the road. According to Harnick, "When we opened in California it was a better show; it was a tighter show, and we were a big hit there" (quoted in Bryer 92).

Reviews were mixed. Most praised Hal Linden's performance; in the *New York Post* Barnes called it, "one of the best musical performances now on Broadway" (184). However, critics pointed out problems in Act II, and had difficulties with the financial subject matter. As Walter Kerr argues in the *New York Times*, "Bonds don't dance, dollars don't sing" (181). Kerr also disapproved of the general tone of the evening, "It is probable that *The Rothschilds* has succeeded in becoming exactly what it meant to be: an unhappy musical comedy" (181). Martin Gottfried in *Women's Wear Daily* hated the musical, for reasons we will shortly discuss. He called it a, "morass of vulgarity, expense and exasperating, misguided and archaic Broadwayism" (185). Many critics pointed out the difficulty of making a piece of theatre about historical events that may or may not have dramatic weight or structure. Douglas Watt in the *Daily News* called it a, "undeniably placid success story [...] the Rothschilds are too unfailingly triumphant for the best interests of dramatic suspense. They don't even experience any problems over love" (185). Harold Clurman in *The Nation* adds, "The evening never mounts to a boil of pleasure. [...] It is more documentary than drama" (506). Because so many years were covered, critics argued that the book tried to fit in too much, too fast. According to Gottfried, "the result is a patchwork of storytelling snippets, thirty seconds per chapter" (185).

Few theatres attempted to produce *The Rothschilds* after the Broadway run ended, until the American Jewish Theatre revived the musical, opening on February 25, 1990. Lonny Price, who had played a child in the national tour of the original, directed. The hit production transferred to Off Broadway's Circle in the Square on April 27, 1990. There it ran fourteen months, and according to Harnick gave the show, "a new lease on life" (quoted in Bryer 93). Director Price vastly scaled down the show and used only a very small cast. With doubling, the cast went from forty to fifteen. Critics hailed the more spare production. Stephen Holden in *New York Times* argued, "Seen in intimate close-up with the glitz pared away, the pageantry is subsumed into the show's exploration of family psychology, ethnic self-assertion, and the politics of oppression" (16). Due to conflicts with the Off Broadway production, a simultaneous production at New Jersey's Forum Theatre was not allowed to extend. Price remarked on the renewed interest, "No one was touching the show for a long, long time. [...] Now people see it as being about larger issues — the breaking down of the walls of oppression" (quoted in Klein "Conflict Develops" 18). AJT marketed the show by appealing to modern sensibilities with their tag line, "They were young — Jewish — and upwardly mobile" (Bock Collection NYPL n. pag.). The revival pointed out strengths of the musical that many had not seen in its original production. As Hap Erstein states in the *Washington Times*, "If the material is not of the first rank, it certainly did not deserve to be ignored for two decades. If, unlike the Rothschilds' treasury, *The Rothschilds* is not pure gold, there is still plenty there that glitters" (E3). A production translated into Yiddish opened in Jerusalem in 2001, but otherwise the rejuvenation forecasted by the 1990 production has not occurred.

Synopsis

The Rothschilds opens in 1772 in an opulent drawing room, where Prince William of Hesse and his court sing of their life of leisure ("Pleasure and Privilege"). Contrasting with the splendor, the song shifts to ominous bells, underscoring the Town Crier closing the Frankfurt Jewish ghetto for the night. Mayer Rothschild arrives home after a year, just in time for the closing. The guard and three urchins taunt him and demand a bribe, and that as a Jew he, "do his duty," and bow to the children. Finally let into the ghetto, Mayer meets with Gutele, his intended wife, and tells her of his dreams for prosperity through a rare coin dealership and currency exchange. She protests that she only wants a simple life ("One Room") but Mayer wants more. He travels to the fairgrounds to peddle his coins, exaggerating their historical value ("He Tossed a Coin"). Prince William arrives at the fair and Mayer sells him a coin cheaply, in order to solicit a marriage permit (only a certain amount of Jews per year were allowed to marry). The plan works, and Mayer forges an alliance with Budurus, the Prince's secretary. At court his current bankers displease Prince William, who instead approves of Mayer. The bankers hire Mayer as their go-between. Mayer sings of his need for progeny to build his empire ("Sons"), and as the song continues, his wife grants his wish, five times. Years continue to pass and the children are trained to work in the shop. Peasants riot in a pogrom, and the family hide their goods and retreat to the cellar. When they emerge, sixteen years have past, and pogroms have continued to be a fact of life. The grown boys, angry at the restrictions under which they live, tell their mother of their aspirations ("Everything"). Mayer and his sons go to court to convince Prince William to allow them to handle an important banking deal with Denmark. When they finally prevail they jubilantly sing of their new financial firm ("Rothschild and Sons"). Napoleon's French Grenadiers approach ("Allons"), forcing Prince William to flee. The Rothschilds triumphantly return from Denmark ("Reprise: Rothschilds and Sons") to find the Prince gone. They decide to take it upon themselves to collect his debts across Europe during his exile. Mayer assigns his sons to countries spanning Europe, and sends Nathan to London to invest the collected sums. Gutele worries and mourns, but her sons slip out of the ghetto to make their fortunes as Act I ends ("Finale to Act I: Sons Reprise"). Mayer's final words to Nathan reinvent the urchins' taunts from the opening: "Jew, do your duty!"

Act II opens in London, where John Herries, Chancellor of the Exchequer, leads the banker / brokers in a hymn against potential French invasion ("Act II Opening (Part 1): Give England Strength"). Nathan, just arrived, joyously sings of the glories of the city ("This Amazing London Town"). The family sets up a complicated special messenger system so they can receive important political information first ("Messenger Ballet"). Nathan's reputation has quickly grown and the bankers speculate on his methods enviously ("They Say"). The heiress Hannah Cohen comes to Nathan to ask him to contribute to various charities and he instantly falls for her ("I'm in Love! I'm in Love!"). She does not initially share his feelings. He offers to fund the British army in its fight against Napoleon if England convinces its allies Austria and Germany to lift its restrictions on the Jews. Hannah exasperatedly agrees to marry him ("Reprise: I'm in Love! I'm in Love!"). Metternich gives his pledge to lift the Jewish restrictions. The Napoleonic wars over, Mayer resolves to attend the peace congress at Aix-la Chapelle and sings of his hopes that fighting and oppression will end ("In My Own Lifetime"). In Aix-la Chapelle ("Have You Ever Seen a Prettier Little Congress?"), Metternich leads the chorus in an ominous song explaining the kind of government he will enforce ("Stability"). He then rescinds his promise to end Jewish oppression. Angry and defeated, the Rothschilds return home. Mayer dies and his sons read his will aloud while mourning. The brothers hatch a plan to undersell government bonds to force Metternich to capitulate. Although it will risk their considerable fortune, Nathan convinces the family to take the challenge. They put their plan into action ("Bonds"), and its success forces Metternich to enter the ghetto to talk terms. He gives the brothers a Declaration of Rights for the Jews and promises to hereafter use only the House of Rothschild for his state bonds. Metternich tells Gutele that success will change her sons, but when Gutele tells Nathan to "never forget who you are," he ends the musical by asking "Do you think they will ever let us?" (II-8-55).

Nostalgia of Family

The Rothschilds offers several categories of nostalgia, perhaps the most potent for the Jewish familial unit. "Nostalgia of Family" offers one of Ben Furnish's three categories for modern Jewish nostalgia. He argues, "The nostalgia of family offers the reassurance of continuity amid sweeping change — *l'dor-v'-dor* (from generation to generation), whether the story is a simple parent-child relationship or, […] a generational saga" (135). *The Rothschilds* offers a clear example of this kind of nostalgia, as the anecdotal evidence of a letter to the producers, kept in Bock's papers at the New York Public Library, demonstrates. A Mrs. Mildred Kahn wrote, on February 6, 1971:

> Gentlemen: Thank you for producing *The Rothschilds*. My daughter had been dating a young man on and off for more than four years and he had told her that he did not want to get married. Being a Jewish mother and she an only child, I was anxious to see her settle down. A few months ago after he had taken her to see *The Rothschilds* he proposed to her. The legend of home (he never had one) and family (especially of having sons) seemed to appeal to him. Tonight the knot will be tied. I hope to be able to purchase tickets soon to see *The Rothschilds* and find out what really inspired my future son-in-law to take the big step. Again, thank you. Sincerely, (Mrs.) Mildred Kahn (Bock collection, NYPL)

Mrs. Kahn seemed to believe that the family presented in the musical was compelling enough to convince some audience members to create their own Jewish families. According to Furnish, "nostalgia for relationships: the bonds of "family," whether personal, spiritual, or linguistic, as well as certainty for knowing one's place within that sphere" (2), offers one of the most important categories of Jewish nostalgia.

Indeed, *The Rothschilds* seems to purposefully tug at powerful memory strings, creating nostalgia for the loss of stable Jewish community, and for the associated personal love of Jewish family. As we have seen, fears about increasing intermarriage and loss of community were beginning to be discussed in earnest in the mid 1960s, and at the start of a new decade in 1970 *The Rothschilds* was primed to react to those concerns. As with *Fiddler*, Bock and Harnick again took a large and close Jewish family as their subject. Elie Wiesel, in an article entitled, "Treasured Family is the Secret Wealth of *The Rothschilds*" in the *New York Times*, argued the musical to be successful because it praised the Jewish family, "The most moving aspect of this play comes when we realize that we have been present at a true celebration of the family, any family, irrespective of its ethnic origins" (n. pag.). Wiesel believed that due to the power of theatre, this portrayal of family, "stirs up ancient, forgotten yearning" (n. pag.). Wiesel's phrase, "ancient yearning," points towards nostalgia, and here he connects that yearning to familial love. The production emphasized the strength of the family unit through casting as well. Each of the family members was as carefully developed and individualized as possible, while each of their enemies, in four major characters, were played by the same actor, Keene Curtis. In this way the musical placed the warmth of family in opposition to an abstraction.

Furnish argues that generational stories present one of the categories of Jewish nostalgia of family. A powerful nostalgic yen to pass values from parents to children can be seen in *The Rothschilds*. Fathers' love for sons, and vice versa, offers the central theme of the musical. In an extended musical number entitled "Sons," time passes while Mayer and Gutele have five boys and Mayer exults on the power of progeny to help realize dreams and conquer the world. Mayer creates an empire through family; sons will continue what he has begun, and will carry his legacy. The modern audience has the knowledge that this dynasty will survive and prosper until modern times, proving Mayer's argument. In *The Rothschilds*, family allows Jewish continuity and the continued struggle against oppression. In his will, Mayer offers this benediction, "May God bless you, my Princes. And may you know the greatest joy a man can know — SONS!" (II-5-40, original emphasis). The brothers do in fact experience that joy, creating their own families. In the second act, when the Rothschilds have been scattered, the libretto brings us back to the theme of fighting for family:

> JACOB: My sons are not going to suffer the humiliations I endured when I started out in Paris.
> NATHAN: And they will be no stronger than the weakest child in this ghetto. We cannot buy them dignity. We must battle for it [II-6-43].

Critic John Chapman titled his review, "*The Rothschilds'* Tells of a Dad and His Boys" (185), and indeed the show's creators realized this was the strength of their show, perhaps too late. Harnick recalls:

> It wasn't until after we had opened that Jerry Bock and I were in a taxicab with Jerry's twelve-year-old son and he said, "You guys really blew it." We said, "What do you mean?" He said, "The love story is about the father and the five sons, not about Nathan and Hannah." And he was right [quoted in Bryer 92].

Almost unanimously the critics pointed out that Act II weakens when the libretto separates the family.

Furnish's "Nostalgia of Family" also emerges from that font of stereotypes, the Jewish mother. Early drafts of the musical offer a fuller picture of Gutele and her sons' love for her, and yet still contained humorous Jewish mother tropes. When the brothers are set to leave home, a draft of the libretto, dated September 1969, offered this exchange:

SOLOMON: I'll miss Momma's cooking.
BOYS: (*altogether*) Momma's cooking?
SOLOMON: Where in England will I ever get that kind of heartburn? Why
    you can't find a kosher home in all Europe with a cook like momma [Bock
    Collection NYPL n. pag.].

Another draft of the libretto written before the score was composed points out
a moment where nostalgia might be emphasized, "Possible song here between
Nathan and Gutele. She is the eternal, rationalizing Jewish mother, he the dis-
contented son" (Bock Collection NYPL n.d. 1–22). Although stereotypical jokes
at Gutele's expense were included, a more poignant warmth and love were also
important in drafts. Songs including, "Momma, Come Stay With Me," sung
by all the sons, telling about their success and their love for their mother, and
"Just a Map," sung by Gutele, mourning her sons leaving her, were cut from the
final score. While the drafts clearly grant Gutele status as a strong but complex
Jewish mother figure, the musical that opened on Broadway had essentially
cut her role down to a one-note joke about her need, like Mrs. Mildred Kahn,
to have her children married. In Act II, with Nathan in London making the
family's fortune and reporting to Mayer, Gutele chimes in periodically:

GUTELE: And Nathan…
NATHAN: Yes, momma?
GUTELE: Your brothers are all engaged.
NATHAN: I'll try, Momma [II-1-6].

Nevertheless, some of Gutele's strength seems to have remained, at least for
Elie Wiesel, who argues her to be central to the success of the musical. This
warmth and love displayed towards the Jewish mother, combined with the
strong love between generations of sons and fathers, together demonstrate the
potent sources of nostalgia for the Jewish family in *The Rothschilds*.

Restorative Nostalgia and Israel

As in *Milk and Honey*, *The Rothschilds* makes use of many Old Testament
biblical references. For instance Mayer shows Gutele an, "ancient Judean coin.
That's King Solomon's temple. And on the obverse side, the Lion of Judah.
[…] [T]his one is my favorite" (I-2-8). When Prince William says the boys
are too young for the business, Rothschild says, "They are five thousand years
old" (I-8-56). Mayer and the boys repeatedly refer to breaking down walls,
stating that they are, "another Joshua!" (I-8-60). Gutele refers to their enemies
in biblical terms: "Mayer, you are breaking up our family, and for what? To
serve that Pharaoh in Prague?" (I-9-71). Nathan turns his love for money into
a biblical reference, "I've a remarkable memory for numbers. Why even as a

boy in Hebrew School I would tally up the angels in Jacob's dream — multiply the sheep in Laban's flock — compound the interest on the gold that Solomon got from Sheba — It's my natural resource" (II-3-19). And in a draft of a song later cut, entitled "Starting Over," Mayer makes use of yet another biblical allusion, "I feel like David / Facing Goliath / With a handful of gravel / And a second hand sling" (Bock Collection, NYPL, n. pag.). The importance of the actual Rothschilds to the history of Israel offers a real-world explanation for these biblical references. According to Greer Fay Cashman in *The Jerusalem Post*, "The Rothschilds underwrote large segments of the Zionist dream, turning them into reality, and amongst their many, many contributions to the State of Israel are the Knesset and Supreme Court buildings" (12). These contributions seem to underscore the characters' "right" to make biblical references. Although faint, the calls to restorative nostalgia, as seen in *Milk and Honey*, are nonetheless present in *The Rothschilds*. These emerge from an era where an increasingly embattled Israel was becoming more central to American Jewish identity. Thomas Disch in *The Nation* argued that the central ballad, "In My Own Lifetime," with lyrics including, "In my own lifetime / I want to see the fighting cease. / [...] I want to see my sons enjoy / the fruits of peace. [...] This Moses wants to see / the Promised Land / in my own lifetime!" (II-4-33), resonated with historical events of the 1970s: "one can't help but hear Sheldon Harnick's lyrics and Jerry Bock's soaring melody as the unofficial anthem of the Camp David accords" (30). Although the accords (signed between Egypt and Israel and brokered by Jimmy Carter) were not signed until 1978, it is significant that Disch ties Israel's multiplicity of meaning, most especially hope for peace and stability, to *The Rothschilds*. Restorative nostalgia does not take a central place in the musical, however the biblical references that are included aim to harness the emotional power of nostalgia for the ancient homeland of Israel.

Europe

Furnish includes "Nostalgia of Place" as a major category of Jewish memory. In the next chapter we will examine the Lower East Side of New York City as a potent site of nostalgia for American Jews. If this neighborhood offers specific associations and memories for Jews of Eastern European decent, how might old Europe, specifically Germany, function as a Jewish nostalgic site? The history of German Jews in America offers a much different narrative than their Eastern European brethren. Although scholars are continually challenging the boundaries between waves of Jewish immigration and Jewish immigrant identities, most have agreed that the "German Jewish period" of immigration to America occurred 1820s–1870s. Many of these Jews became highly successful and were well established by the time waves of Eastern European began to arrive at Ellis Island. German Jews were often more educated and sophisticated than later shtetl Jews, some of the most famous families establishing department store lines like Macys, Bloomingdales, Levi and Strauss, and more. German Jews established organizations to help later Eastern European waves of immigrants, most famously B'nai B'rith. German Jewish identifications changed throughout the 20th century. World War I, and later the Nazi regime, caused many German Jews' to replace sympathies to the German homeland with loyalty to America and the Jewish community. It's unclear how much perceived boundaries between American Jews based on their place of origin persisted in 1970. However we can see possible references to this relationship in a parallel between Nathan, child of the Frankfurt ghetto, and his love interest, Hannah, whose family had been established and successful in England for years. This exchange, cut from the final libretto, hints at that level of reference:

> COHEN: Hannah, he's not our kind. Our people have been in England for over 300 years. He's scarcely here for three. Now do you understand?
> HANNAH: Yes, Papa. He's a Jew and we're Israelites [Bock Collection, NYPL II-9].

In a reversal, here Nathan, the German Jew, stands in for the Eastern European shtetl Jew, and the English Hannah for the more successful German Jew.

The German ghetto doesn't allow nostalgia for Jews of German decent, in the way that the shtetl functions in works such as *Fiddler*. Bock and Harnick instead attempt to translate their ghetto locale into wider known, Eastern European terms. Scholar Ronald Sanders calls the Frankfurt ghetto a, "hoped-for mythic equivalent of Anatevka" (29). He argues that the ghetto locale cannot easily connect to an American Jewish sensibility, "It is quite noticeable that, whenever *The Rothschilds* seeks to explore the vein of Jewish-ironic that the play implicitly needs so badly [...] out comes some gesture or piece of folklore from the shtetl" (29). Sanders cites Mayer's anachronistic use of the Yiddish word *chutzpah*. German Jews did not speak Yiddish, and thus Mayer's use of the word points to efforts to create Eastern European shtetl resonances, as in *Fiddler*, that more American Jews could recognize.

The Rothschilds includes a more complex relationship with Europe than pure nostalgic longing. Raymond Knapp, in a fascinating exploration of American musical theatre's post-war relationship to Europe, argues that the war redefined Americans' relationship with "the continent." If Europe offered our spiritual land of descent, Knapp argues that Rodgers and Hammerstein's *Sound of Music* presents a version of ancestors we wish for, and Kander and Ebb's *Cabaret* a branch of ancestry, "spinning out of control, seducing us if we are not careful" (229). Knapp argues that Americans needed to find the proper response to Nazism's take-over of Europe:

> If [evil] were not an aberration, then [U.S. citizens] had to convince themselves that Americans, conceived to be the spiritual, cultural and even biological descendants of Europe, had become a fundamentally different people from them [228].

We will examine this relationship more fully when discussing the Holocaust resonances of the musical, but here we should note that, like *Cabaret*, *The Rothschilds* distances itself from the majority of citizens of old Europe, instead drawing a parallel between Americans and the oppressed Jewish minority confined in their ghetto. The Jewish heroes explicitly fight an old and evil European establishment. For instance, the opening number of the musical, "Pleasure and Privilege," presents a lovely scene of untroubled wealth, only hinting at the oppression hidden behind the façade. The scene swiftly changes to the ghetto and the music shifts into a minor, dissonant and frightening key when the Town Crier shuts the Jews in for the evening. The musical shift underscores the disparity between Old Europe and those it oppresses. In a later number, "Have You Ever Seen a Prettier Little Congress?" we again see a representative image of old Europe, "*as the music starts, four dancing couples dance a cool, stately, minuet-type dance*" (II-5-34), followed by the song "Stability," which spells out the price of such imagery, where the upper classes discuss the secret police crackdown on dissent, then (*dance wildly and insanely, [...] They all stop suddenly, gesture front and walk menacingly downstage and stop)*" (II-5-35-6, 38). These representatives of the ruling classes then point out that "alien religions" are a perfect target upon which angry mobs can focus their anger and thereby ensure the "stability" of the song title. The musical demonstrates the price of "Stability" and the manner in which Europe can spin out of control. Instead of offering nostalgia for the "homeland" of Europe, the musical instead displays its failings, only one of the ways in which *The Rothschilds* rejects easy nostalgia.

Score

The Rothschilds' score paints the duality of Europe's outward beauty countered by its dark within. While both Jewish music and operetta — both encompassed in the score — might provoke wistful memory, *The Rothschilds'* complicates any resultant nostalgia. Stanley Green tells us that Bock and Harnick chose to write the show because they wanted to move away from their most famous hit: "The texture of the score would be more akin to eighteenth and nineteenth century European music than it would be to the traditional Hebraic and Russian themes of *Fiddler*" (303). The creators took pains to explain why and how the score for *The Rothschilds* was different from *Fiddler on the Roof.* Harnick elaborates:

> In *Fiddler* the entire score (with the exception of perhaps three or four songs) could be described as "Hebraic" (or Russian or Slavic) in character. For *The Rothschilds*, the entire score (with the exception of perhaps three or four songs) is *not* Hebraic or ethnic in character. Jerry painted a much wider musical canvas than for *Fiddler* [quoted in Mandelbaum 10; orig. emphasis].

This canvas included a classical sound. In order to emulate 18th and 19th century music, Bock and his orchestrator changed the make-up of a typical Broadway orchestra pit, using 28 rather than 20 players, and adding a baroque trumpet for Act I. In Act II, which reached for a romantic 19th century sound, they included two trumpets, three French horns, a trombone, added strings, and excluded saxophones.

Critics found overtones of operetta in Bock's score, often in a negative context. Martin Gottfried scoffs, "With *The Rothschilds* [Bock and Harnick] have gone all the way back to the operetta. [...] It is ludicrously expensive, naïve and misled" (185). Jerry Bock sought an operatic sound in the musical's opening section, as we see in his original notes to orchestrator Don Walker: "1st 25 minutes [should consist of] opera? Operetta [...] set up *duality* right away" (Bock Collection NYPL n. pag.; original emphasis). Bock's concept of duality explains the real purpose of the classical / operetta score influences. The opening number "Pleasure and Privilege," which begins with a basic operetta sound and structure, ends on an eerie minor key, introducing the ghetto, and the more "Hebraic" portion of the score. The score's duality aims to paint the world of European prosperity in contrast to the difficulties of life for a ghettoized minority. This opening moment demonstrates the disparity between social groups, and also lays out the score's two different musical genres. Bock's notes to his orchestrator explain his intent for mixing musical forms, and are worth quoting at length:

> The first act is late 18th century classic [...] the sound should be Haydn-Mozart and a forecast of Beethoven [...] within this outline is a Semitic strain — not in terms of *Fiddler* but buried under the graces of the outline — with the potential to pour out suddenly, privately, impulsively [...] and ultimately affecting all the "classic" layers with streaks of obliqueness, persevering, anger [...] In the second act the layers become thicker [...] and these 19th century sounds are fuller — richer — but no less haunting — except that it takes more to push through to haunt than it did before [Bock Collection NYPL n. pag.].

Although it seems that with Jewish melodies the creators may have been trying to encourage nostalgic identification (the way their music functioned in *Fiddler*), darker aims clearly circulate in *The Rothschilds'* score. As scholar Ronald Sanders points out, the show's musical world doesn't have the same nostalgic possibilities as *Fiddler*, "The German ghetto is at an enormous musical disadvantage alongside the Russian shtetl [...] who knows what — with the possible exception of some liturgical fragments — the Frankfurt Ghetto really sounded like?" (29).

Despite the authors' pains to point out the scarcity of Jewish melodies in *The Rothschilds*, or the inherent difficulties of incorporating them into the European ghetto world of the show, "Hebraic" music nonetheless infuses the score. For example, "Sons" utilizes a continual switch from minor to major, from a Jewish minor melody when praying for male offspring, and joy in a major key upon the receipt of such children. In "They Say," sung by anti–Semitic British bankers impressed with Nathan's financial acumen, the bankers take on a pseudo Russian Jewish tune. This adoption of Nathan's "Hebraic" music indicates that Nathan has obtained the upper hand.

"Everything" offers the most clearly "Jewish" sounding piece in the entirety of the score. Bock and Harnick intended the song to encapsulate the Rothschilds' strength and wish to take on the difficult fight for equality. Bock describes the song in his notes as:

> the first wrench from tradition — the open, instinctive, Yiddish sound turned into a militant dedicated purpose. These are the Jewish Maccabees — not the Jewish *victims*, this is the kibbutz, not the shtetl. [...] [T]he Semitic turns are subtle, a kind of filigree weaving in and out but never masking the bare bones [Bock collection NYPL n. pag.; orig. emphasis].

While the song possesses the strength its authors work towards, it also encompasses dissonant undertones. A flatted "Hebraic" seventh tone occurs on the first syllable of the word "Everything." This simple musical choice underscores the manner in which the song can be read as an ode to greed. The brothers sing of their need for the "everything" of the title, arguing that if others are entitled, so are they. The lyrics also compare their want to a sickness. Given the dangerous relationship of anti-Semitism with the perception of Jewish greed, the insistent power of the driving "Jewish" music asking for "Everything" — an everything the Rothschilds ultimately receive financially — allows this song to be read in a manner entirely different from the way Bock and Harnick intended. We will shortly examine these dissonances more closely.

Ritual

Most of the musicals we have examined thus far stage Jewish rituals. In the final produced version of *The Rothschilds* a ritualized moment occurs when

Mayer recites his will in a voiceover from the grave; his sons, clad in prayer shawls, mourn him by completing the reading of the document. The staging implies a kind of truncated funeral. But despite its emotional heft, we have to look to the early drafting and preview periods to find numerous examples of more specific rituals in *The Rothschilds*.

In one of the earliest libretto drafts, Mayer's parents have died in a pogrom. When his brother (later cut from the musical) asks Mayer the reason for their death, Mayer quotes famous rabbis and then, "*covers his face as he struggles against his emotions. He converts his sobs into the Kaddish prayer for the dead*" (Bock Collection NYPL Draft n.d. 11). We will see another example of the staged Kaddish, the Jewish prayer for the dead, in the next chapter. Later drafts of *The Rothschilds* included various attempts to integrate the Jewish harvest holiday of Sukkoth into the text. In one version, during a scene leading into the pogrom, "[on roof of the shop] *Gutele and her daughters* [also cut from the final production] *now begin to erect the Sukkos tent out of branches. They beat the branches and weave them into roof of tent. This is a choreographed movement*" (31). Telescoping of time occurs, as in the final production, and the sons emerge from the cellar years later:

> *The SONS ASCEND TO TERRACE where they look in admiration at the festive Sukkoth tent— set up under the starry night sky)*
> SALOMON: It's a miracle — they didn't touch it.
> NATHAN: *(scoffing)* What miracle? This year Momma used branches with thorns [Bock Collection NYPL n.d., n. pag.].

These drafts also encompass an outdoor Sukkoth celebration with neighbors from the ghetto. During the celebration Mayer prays, in a more or less literal translation of Deuteronomy Chapter 16. The Town Crier's warning that the ghetto will soon close ends the celebration. Significantly, each of these staged religious ritual examples are accompanied by evidence of prejudice and hatred against Jews.

The musical also included an onstage wedding, here between Nathan and Hannah. Unlike *Milk and Honey* and *Fiddler on the Roof*, this wedding did not make the final production. Stage directions in a draft read, "[Nathan] *signals and the entrance to* [Hannah's] *house sprouts a wedding canopy— a rabbi, chanting the wedding prayer, walks into view. Cohen appears— the wedding is rushed through, Nathan breaks the glass and whisks Hannah into the coach*" (Bock Collection NYPL n.d. 11–25). Finally, Michael Kidd, after he had assumed directorship of the show, considered adding yet another example of staged ritual. In notes after a dress rehearsal dated August 11, 1970, Kidd suggests incorporating a Passover scene after Aix-La-Chapelle:

> Rock through window during it — the four questions — this Jewish exodus compared with the biblical one. [...] There is no safe plateau for the Jews. Too

many are waiting to push us down to the bottom again. Only by placing ourselves on an equal footing with those in high positions can the Jews attain any
feeling of security [Bock Collection NYPL n. pag.].

Notes from a meeting two days later read:

> The idea of having a Passover dinner might exploit religious sentiment — it
> might be dangerous, but it can be worked against by not highlighting the cere-
> mony itself, but use it as a tool — it must be used as environment. [...] We must
> be careful not to overemphasis the Jewishness of the family. The Seder can be
> done in a crisp — real — unsentimental manner [Bock Collection NYPL n. pag.].

Why were these examples of staged ritual omitted from the final libretto? Certainly the creative team seemed torn between an urge to include ritual with
its attendant nostalgic, emotional and theatrical force, but were also nervous
about potential side effects. They did not want to be "too Jewish" for the gentile audience, and also worried about offending religious Jews. They tried to
find the delicate balance between these two audiences, carefully "double coding" their libretto. Perhaps these rituals were struck from *The Rothschilds*
because of its darkness, making sentimental nostalgic rituals seem out of place.
When we examine the numerous Holocaust resonances in *The Rothschilds*
shortly, we will see a potential clash of emotional style that may have made
staged ritual ineffective.

Double Coding

The authors' indecision about including ritual demonstrates their continuing concern with universality. How might *The Rothschilds* be "double
coded" according to Bial's theory? In other words, how did the musical attempt
to appeal to both Jewish and gentile audiences? The creative team, consistent
with their experience on *Fiddler*, valued universal appeal. In notes from a
meeting during previews on August 13, 1970, they discussed:

> Although we are a Jewish show, we should not play to Jews only in our solu-
> tions to problems. What we need to be is a Jewish show that translates itself
> into universals. So that anyone can identify with it. We must take in that we
> don't only speak to our own kind. It is a matter of selection so that most people
> can identify with it. Not to eliminate everything and make it smooth and bland
> and round [Bock Collection NYPL n. pag.].

Despite the universal intent, *The Rothschilds* contains much Jewish specificity
and a dark, sometimes aggressively angry tone that even the creators found
troublesome. Notes from that same day continue, "It must be established that
Mayer's anger is not with Christianity but with the power structure. [...] Cut

as much woefulness of Mayer's past — don't emphasize the past miseries. Take out the militancy tones" (Bock Collection NYPL n. pag.). The musical can certainly encourage an "us vs. them" mentality, as when the Rothschild sons bemoan the oppression and unfairness they endure:

> NATHAN: They rob us — and then they lock *us* in like thieves. [...]
> JACOB: They don't even let us walk in public gardens. [...]
> AMSHEL: And what about the extra taxes we have to pay?
> GUTELE: You forget the Bible says: Render unto Caesar that which is Caesar's.
> SOLOMON: Momma — that's the New Testament!
> GUTELE: So — they can't always be wrong, can they? [I-7-44; orig. emphasis].

Although saved with a knowing joke at the end, this exchange, including the humor, delineates sides, and aligns itself with only one. Another example of playing to a specific audience by pointing to Jewish oppression occurs in the next scene, when Rothschild tries to convince Prince William to hire the family as bankers:

> WILLIAM: (*amazed*) What nerve!
> MAYER: Beg pardon, Serenity. We call it *chutzpah*.
> WILLIAM: More Danish words?
> MAYER: No. This one is Yiddish. It means a special kind of courage that makes triumph of disaster.
> WILLIAM: And your people teach it to their sons?
> MAYER: No, Serenity. *Your* people teach it to my sons [I-8-53-4; orig. emphasis].

Bock and Harnick wanted to avoid all instance of Yiddish in *Fiddler*, but here they use a Yiddish word — anachronistically — to underline pride in the face of oppression. They appeal to a Jewish audience that may have personal knowledge of oppression, or awareness that they too, in another place and time, could have encountered these obstacles. Jacob Rothschild dreams, "I would love to walk in a public garden or go to a theatre. Just once in my life I'd like to waste something as precious as time" (I-9-71), also encouraging audience identification. A Jewish audience member at *The Rothschilds* might be reminded by this line that they themselves are currently enjoying the privilege of attending theatre, one denied to fellow Jews in the past.

For the rest of the audience, *The Rothschilds* acts universally by appealing to the great American success story, mythologized as attainable for any and all ethnic groups. In the face of oppression, *The Rothschilds* tells a success story of overcoming subjugation by amassing wealth and power. Although the Rothschilds' actually lived this success story in 18th century Europe, within the context of the musical theatre form, their triumph bends it's meaning to the more relatable myth of the American dream. Mayer tells Gutele in the first scene, "I can make a better life for us here" (I-2-8), and his rags to riches tale emerges from an American ethos, not a European one. Bock and Harnick actively encouraged the contemporary relevance of an American struggle for civil rights and success. As Ken Mandelbaum tells us, "Bock and Harnick also saw a distinct relevance to 1970 in the Rothschilds' fight for human rights and the younger Rothschilds' determination to have a better life than that of their parents" (8). When speaking of the historical Rothschilds in December 1970, Harnick speaks in the language of the American Dream, "Our interest has been to show how they got started, how people with no more resources than their wits, chutzpah, ambition and courage could rise out of their situation" (quoted in BMI: "The Many Worlds of Music," Bock Collection NYPL n. pag.).

By escaping the ghetto the Rothschilds are able to fight anti–Semitism and experience their dreams of success. On a small scale, the family encompasses the already attained American Jewish success story. Since Jews lived their American Dream in large numbers by 1970, telling of the Rothschilds' achievement encourages nostalgic identification.

Intertextual Nostalgia

When *The Rothschilds* opened on Broadway in 1970, Bock and Harnick's more successful musical, *Fiddler on the Roof* was still running a few blocks away. That would seem to negate the possibility that *The Rothschilds* would nostalgically appeal to the greater hit. However, persistent critical comparisons and textual similarities argue that memories of *Fiddler* circulated within the piece. The creators continued to insistently deny similarities. Bock stated, "It was a whole new ball game. *Fiddler* had been produced and we knew there were risks of comparison, of repetition. And yet, we would not have undertaken [*The Rothschilds*] had we felt the similarities outweighed the differences" (17). Critics argued the opposite, and scholar Stanley Green concurs, "*The Rothschilds* could not help but be perceived as Tevye's wealthy relatives" (303). While much of the comparison rested merely on the fact that both shows concerned Jewish families with five children, *The Rothschilds* also contained more specific attempts to replicate *Fiddler*'s nostalgic power. Critics pointed out one particular similarity to *Fiddler* in the script. When pursuit of fortune separates the family in Act II, a theatrical conceit, where Nathan steps out of a scene and reads letters to Mayer, connects him to his father. Tevye famously speaks to God; Nathan speaks to Mayer. One other moment aims for the sort of humor *Fiddler* employed successfully. Whereas Tevye continually quotes his own personal renditions of proverbs, in a scene with Prince William, Solomon Rothschild argues:

SOLOMON: There is a well know proverb: To win a race, the horse and his rider must finish together.

WILLIAM: I never heard such a proverb.

SOLOMON: *(Sheepishly)* You're right, Serenity. I just made it up [I-8-57].

By the American Jewish Theatre revival in 1990, the creators were tired of the constant comparisons to *Fiddler*. After publicity stunts such as the *New York Post* Page Six appearance from December 15, 1990, "The five young men who play brothers in *The Rothschilds* at Circle in the Square downtown have invited the five actresses who play sisters in [the revival of] *Fiddler on the Roof* at the Gershwin to their show and dinner afterwards" (Bock Collection NYPL n. pag.), Bock finally wrote a letter to the artistic director and producers of the AJT revival:

> Don't you all think, after nineteen years, that it's about time *The Rothschilds* stood on its own two feet, sang in its own particular voice, and was sent out to soar on its own as well? Isn't this a remarkable opportunity to get out from under the omnipresent shadow of *Fiddler* and begin to celebrate *The Rothschilds* in its new shining light? [Bock Collection, NYPL n. pag.].

Despite Bock's plea, *Fiddler's* nostalgic power was so strong that merely by evoking it, *The Rothschilds* inherits power by association. Distinction between the two musicals was very important to their creators. Harnick argues one difference, significant to our purposes here:

> Tevye's people were resigned to their poverty. The Rothschilds were determined to break out of theirs. And, although shtetl […] life was meager and circumscribed, there was a warmth that people do look back on with a kind of nostalgia. There never was any nostalgia for the austere, restricted life that pervaded the walled-in ghettos of Frankfurt and elsewhere [Bock Collection NYPL n. pag.].

If the ghetto world discourages nostalgia, what might it evoke instead?

Postmemory

Harnick makes a strong argument for *The Rothschilds'* anti-nostalgic world. Whereas *Milk and Honey* and *Fiddler on the Roof* hint at the Holocaust in order to strengthen the nostalgic world they pose in counter to it, *The Rothschilds* takes a much harsher and more direct look at the implications of the Shoah, in line with the era from which it emerged. By the late 1960s and early 70s musical comedy was beginning to be eclipsed by musical theatre with darker, more complex themes like those in *Cabaret*. Sondheim's groundbreaking *Company* opened the same year as *The Rothschilds*, for instance. The 1970s were also a time of budding interest in the history and implications of the Holocaust. In Chapter I we found that the period of silence regarding the Holocaust immediately following World War II had begun to come to an end by the early 1960s. As we have also seen, in 1967, the Six-Day War in Israel contributed to the changing understanding of the Holocaust. Plays and movies about the Holocaust had appeared throughout the sixties, and although a full explosion of Holocaust related material happened a bit later, in the 1980s and 1990s, direct references to the Holocaust would certainly be recognized as more acceptable in 1970 than in the past. At times *The Rothschilds'* references to modern history were quite explicit. Enough so in fact, that a critic, for the first time, acknowledged the Holocaust in a published response. Walter Kerr, bemoaning the darkness of the musical, discusses Metternich's refusal to follow through on promises to lift Jewish oppression, "Will [the promises] ever be kept? As if our own heads weren't filled with enough history to give a dour answer to that question, the libretto insists on answering it for us" (182). While Kerr does not explicitly name the Holocaust here, his references to "dour history" make the reference clear. In a postmemory generation, oppression against Jews cannot help but be linked to the single most horrific anti–Semitic example in history, the Holocaust.

Drafts of *The Rothschilds* make references to the Holocaust and to extreme anti–Semitism that were later deleted or toned down. A draft from September 1969 contains this exchange:

METTERNICH: Rothschilds —*the Jewish question* is too complicated —
NATHAN: But the Christian answer isn't! Change it [Bock Collection NYPL II-51; emphasis. mine].

And in a later draft from a year later in September 1970 we find:

NATHAN: Do you have our copy of the declaration of rights?
AMSHEL: No. It's being studied by experts on the *Jewish question* [Bock Collection NYPL n. pag.; emphasis mine].

The term "Jewish question," while having been used in an anti–Semitic context throughout the ages, also has very specific and memorable Holocaust overtones, as in the "Final Solution of the Jewish Question." Its use here cannot be accidental. Clearly Nazis and the Holocaust were on the creators' minds during the writing process. As Harnick states:

It's possible that the Holocaust more directly affected some of the lyrics in *The Rothschilds*. [...] My research into the period [...] resulted in my putting certain words in the mouth of Prince Metternich but I suspect that those words were colored by my feelings about what had transpired in World War II [personal communication].

In an early, undated draft, Mayer has studied at Nuremberg. Handwritten marginal notes on the draft include the following:

Dare we go off in time to describe an aborted ironic history of *Nurnberg* [Nuremberg]
1933 — Hitler's annual Sept. convention
1935 — Nurnberg laws divided Germany into three classes
    1. Aryans
    2. Jews with 2 or more Jewish grandparents
    3. Hybrids —1 or 2 Jewish [grandparents] but who were not of faith or married to Jew [Bock Collection NYPL n. pag.].

Additionally, Bock's notes for the orchestrator concerning the cut song "William's Fine Troops," make clear that Nazi imagery was on the minds of the creators, "this could sound subtle — Nazi — a toy soldier goose step" (Bock Collection NYPL n. pag.).

Although these moments were cut, considerable Holocaust related material still remained in the show that opened in 1970. Yellow Star of David armbands served as perhaps the most potent reminder of the Holocaust. While from ancient times Jews have been forced in various periods to wear identifying armbands, after World War II this image has been inescapably identified with Nazi persecution. Mayer Rothschild, upon his first entrance, appears, "dressed in traditional clothes of a rabbinical student. [...] He wears an armband with a yellow Star of David around the upper sleeve of his long, black overcoat" (I-1-3). In a later scene Rothschild and Budurus tell the Christian bankers, as a trick, that Prince William wants them to wear Star of David armbands in the Prince's presence. To avoid this fate, they let Rothschild act as their go-between (I-4-21). The creative team even added additional armbands after a dress rehearsal, as evidenced by notes from August 11, 1970: "Boys — yellow stars on right arm for Palace scene" (Bock Collection NYPL n. pag.). There were still more Star of David references in the original drafts. In a song later cut, Nathan sings of his love of London, "Still I'm excited by the / sights I have not seen here! / No guard by the ghetto / with chains on the gate. / No bright yellow armbands / to hate" (Bock Collection NYPL n.d. 2). Most tellingly, in a July 1970 draft Nathan tells Hannah the reason Jews must stick together:

> NATHAN: Miss Cohen — my people are your people. Your great grandfather may have escaped his ghetto two hundred years ago — but when ignorance becomes a blood sport again — we are all Jews together.
> HANNAH: Sir — misery does not have to wear a yellow star to exist. I cannot share your provincial view of the world [Bock Collection NYPL 2-3-23].

Someone has crossed out Hannah's line on this draft. Clearly the creators were deliberating on how many Holocaust references to include. But Nathan's warning of "ignorance becom[ing] a blood sport" quite clearly indicates the creators' mindset.

The Rothschilds largely takes place in the Frankfurt ghetto, and the constant reminders of being locked in and a palpable sense of danger highlight potent overtones of World War II ghettos, Warsaw in particular. The brothers escape through a tunnel leading outside the ghetto from their house, also recalling Holocaust stories. The pogroms that frequently sweep through the ghetto also point to the Holocaust in their evocation of Kristallnacht, and of anti–Jewish violence as a whole. As in *Fiddler* we find firsthand evidence of violence against our Jewish central characters. From a post–Holocaust perspective, this violence cannot fail to resonate. The telescoping of time, where the brothers go into the cellar to escape a pogrom and emerge sixteen years later after another violent episode, effectively demonstrates the scope of anti–Jewish violence. In the first pogrom scene the boys and Mayer rush to hide their goods, and Nathan declares:

NATHAN: (*bitterly*) Poppa — I hate them.
MAYER: Don't ever say that.
NATHAN: But they hate us.
MAYER: What's that got to do with us? They're a mob. We're a family. Hatred
  comes cheap to a mob. A family buys it dear. [...]
In the very dim light, darkly clad PEOPLE run through the ghetto and into the
shop where they break the counter fronts, chairs, strew the shop contents about, dump
drawers and generally go through it like a blitz. [...] A woman screams and two last
peasants dash through the ghetto. The Pogrom ends [I-6-39, 40].

Walter Kerr reacted quite tellingly to the pogrom scene: "The ghetto is regularly visited by marauders, [...] who are only too happy to [...] knock down what little the Jews beyond the barbed wire fences have succeeded in putting up" (181). Barbed wire was not invented until the late 19th century. Therefore, either Kerr or the scenic designer John Bury made the leap from early 18th and 19th century European ghettos to images from World War II, including concentration camps. Although we cannot ascertain details of the set design for certain, barbed wire imagery tells us that Holocaust connections were being made, either visually or critically. Finally, revered Holocaust survivor Elie Wiesel wrote an article about *The Rothschilds* for the *New York Times*, reprinted as a flyer for publicity purposes. The resonances of Wiesel, a famous and respected survivor, being used to promote the musical cannot be underestimated. Wiesel states, "The danger is not corruption of morals and traditions by money, but rather isolation, oppression and death. For [the Rothschilds], evil lies not within the family, but outside it" (Bock collection NYPL n. pag.). The phrase "evil [...] outside the family" holds deeper reverberations when coming from the author of *Night* (1958), and demonstrate that the time was right for direct Holocaust references, even within the ostensibly light musical theatre form.

The Rothschilds (1970–1972 Broadway). Music by
Jerry Bock Lyrics by Sheldon Harnick Book by Sher-
man Yellen. Directed & Choreographed by Michael
Kidd. Shown: Hal Linden (as Mayer Rothschild).

Anti-Semitism

Holocaust references
in *The Rothschilds* occur
both directly and more
implicitly. While we have
seen many clear references
above, there are many further examples of indirect
echoes. In modern mem-
ory, virulent anti–Semitism
in any context, the stereotypes feeding it and the
means to fight it, all lead to
thoughts of the ultimate
realization of that horrific
hatred, the Holocaust. Evidence of anti–Semitism in
the text therefore necessitates examination.

Early drafts of the
libretto show us the most
virulent examples of anti–
Semitic hatred, many of
which were later cut. In
one draft an angry peasant
throws a rock through the

window of Gutele's house. The criminal has attached to the rock a caricature
of the brothers beating a cross with moneybags. A cut song for Mayer in the
opening scene entitled, "I Will Bow," offers an examination of the effect of
anti–Semitism on personal pride:

> When will I learn / resistance is useless / anger is pointless / pride... will get me
> nowhere [...] I will bow, I will bend, I'll abase myself. / I will stand hat in hand
> and efface myself [Bock Collection NYPL n. pag.].

In later drafts we find another cut song offering the most virulent examples of
anti–Semitism encountered in the many versions of *The Rothschilds*, in fact, in
any of the musicals examined in this work. In "Jew, Do Your Duty," the guard
takes Mayer's prayer shawl and gives it to a whore, and then the Urchins sing:

> Bow to your better! / That's your Jewish duty! / Bow, Jew, and lick my shoe! /
> Come and kiss my beauty! [They take away his hat and sit on it] [...] (*swaying*

derisively) This is the way / Jews have to pray / inside their Jewish church! [...]
(*they sway and moan, a parody of Jewish chanting; they laugh at each other's antics.
Then:*) You'll go to hell Jew! [...] To the lowest level [...] None of your cunning
will keep you from the devil! [Bock Collection NYPL n. pag.].

A dance section where they pull Mayer's beard, shout obscenities and remove
his armband, using it to stand for the tail of the Devil, follows these lyrics.

In *The Rothschilds'* final libretto this scene has been reduced to a brief
exchange where Mayer must bow to the urchins, but the musical as produced
on Broadway still contains extensive anti–Semitic incidents. The scene and
song "Everything"—with its Jewish melody as discussed—encapsulates the
Rothschilds' anger at their oppression:

> GUTELE: Everything! It costs nothing for a man to be a Jew! Who needs more?
> NATHAN: We do. Momma, it's expensive for a Jew to be a man. (I-7-46-8)

Nathan then sings of the injustice of wanting the same thing as other men
but being kept in the ghetto by hatred. At the end of this song we again hear
the Crier's warning of the ghetto's closing and Nathan tells us, "Momma, it'll
take a fortune to kill that lullaby!" (I-7-49).

Jews and Money

The Rothschilds intensifies its portrayal of anti–Semitism by engaging the
endlessly complicated stereotypes regarding Jews and money. As scholar Gerald
Krefetz tells us, "Jewish money — its purported influence and power — is one
of the oldest canards of anti–Semitism" (3). And of course, Nazi hatred and
propaganda based itself on and exploited these stereotypes. As we have seen,
concern over stereotypes of Jewish greed and financial power caused the Anti
Defamation League to try and block the 1934 film version of the Rothschilds'
lives. Similar difficulties plagued the musical. And yet, money, by necessity,
takes a central role in Bock and Harnick's *The Rothschilds*. Mayer runs a money
changing business in the first Act, like that famously hated Jew: Shylock.
Krefetz continues, "The idea of the Jews as moneychanger, pawnbroker, or
banker became indelibly etched into the popular psyche — often in the most
pejorative and contemptible terms" (6). In fact, Jews needed to attain financial
success in order to survive. As Krefetz argues, "Whenever Jews were not eco-
nomically successful and financially indispensable, they were dismissed,
expelled, or murdered. It has been incumbent upon them to succeed" (5–6).
This kind of anti–Semitism cannot be confined to distant historical periods.
It exists still, often concerning the same issues. Modern American anti–Semitism often concerns stereotypes about money and power.

Scholar Ronald Sanders points out that the musical's source material — Morton's biography *The Rothschilds* (1961) — came out of an general era of prosperity and an American-Jewish renaissance of the 1950s and 60s:

> It was above all at that moment, and in this country, that a popular-style book describing with unequivocal glee the financial conquest and lordly lifestyles of [the Rothschilds] could have been received by Jews entirely without nervousness and by the public at large without any apparent hostility [23].

Although acceptance of Jewish-Americans was certainly widely prevalent by 1970 when the musical opened, the material, as with the 1934 film discussed earlier, still created uneasiness. Critics, having to address the immense wealth of the Rothschilds dynasty, tread the confusing line between prejudice and admiration in their descriptions of the family. Stephen Holden, responding to the 1990 revival, uses particular buzzwords from conspiracy theories that circulate around the Rothschilds. Though clearly not meant as anti–Semitic, his reaction to the lead performance still circulates within an uneasy set of boundaries: "Conducting business [Mayer Rothschild] flashes obsequious crocodile smiles, and you can almost feel the gears whir behind his glinting eyes as he calculates his odds" (16). Earlier critics pointed to the issue more directly. They felt that money as a topic for musical theatre presented difficulties. Martin Gottfried had the most dramatic reaction to the topic:

> Put bluntly, *The Rothschilds* is a musical about Jews and money. Either would be an excellent subject for any kind of theatre [...] But *The Rothschilds* does not explore these subjects — it is about them. [...] This lead footed and overstuffed musical, [...] only represents the vulgarity of money and the vulgarization of Jewishness [184–5].

Gottfried's reaction does not surprise, when we examine the virulence of stereotypes regarding Jews and money, in particular relating to the historical Rothschilds. When you search the name Rothschild on the internet, the vast majority of sites revealed are devoted to conspiracy theory, relating both to the Illuminati — of recent *The Da Vinci Code* fame — and to the "Protocols of the Elders of Zion," a forgery purporting to be a secret book written by Jews detailing their plans to rule the world. Reluctant to give such insane ramblings space here, but in order to demonstrate the kind of hysteria the Rothschilds evoke, I quote Henry Makow "PhD" on his own website:

> I'm afraid *Protocols* may be genuine. [...] M[a]yer Amschel Rothschild played a key role in advancing this monstrous conspiracy. He was a follower of the occult Cabbalism (or Lucifer worship) that is the basis of Illuminism and Freemasonry. [...] Luciferians like Rothschild, Lenin and Hitler still control the planet and intend to enslave humanity [http://whale.to/b/makow1.html].

Fritz Backhaus describes some of the reasons the Rothschilds in particular might act as a lightning rod for anti–Semitism:

Their wealth was so immense and its sources for the most part so unfathomable, their ascent out of the ghetto so rapid, that they became the ideal screen onto which both hopes of social advancement and hatred of modernity could be projected. The Rothschilds were, particularly for those with anti–Jewish agendas, the perfect embodiment of all clichés [95].

The musical, by necessity, must confront some of these conspiracy theories, but it does so in a limited manner, and points out the economics behind the phenomenon. Nathan asks his brothers if they have seen pamphlets entitled:

JACOB: "The International Conspiracy of the Rothschilds." Why should I waste my time on the spewing of ignorant peasants?

NATHAN: You know damn well they are printed by the very aristocrats who borrow money from us. We finance our own destruction! [II-6-44].

Through this brief mention the authors acknowledge then belittle conspiracy theories. *The Rothschilds* attempts to destroy the anti–Semitic rumors around their subjects by constructing sympathetic and fully embodied characters. The creators also felt the need to deal with the implications of the Rothschild wealth quite carefully.

In the face of the stereotypes' strength, the creators of *The Rothschilds* fought valiantly to clarify how money functions in this musical: not for greed, but for a purpose, as a weapon against hatred and a means to fight for equality. Elie Wiesel points to money as one of the strengths of the musical, but he does so by impressing upon us that financial success functions only as a method for fighting oppression and hatred. Stanley Green, not surprisingly, describes the musical through a comparison with *Fiddler*. His wording is instructive, however, "But unlike the impoverished, powerless Jews of *Fiddler*, the family Rothschild was able to triumph over its oppressors through the weapon of money" (303). Throughout the drafting process, the authors took pains to prove that the Rothschilds were not greedy, but instead use money for other ends. In the earliest draft the authors' marginal notes prove instructive, Mayer tells a secret to Gutele:

I don't like being poor. [...] The secret is — I'm going to be rich!

Marginal notes: Isn't it necessary to find a more substantial reason — more meaningful — historic, etc. This seems a bit arbitrary — a bit frivolous — *dig deeper* [Bock Collection NYPL n. pag.; orig. emphasis].

Perhaps in answer to this note, another early draft explicates Mayer's reasoning further:

MAYER: Gutele, it's the one battle cry the authorities allow! They live for it! They die for it! And they don't care much who shouts it — so long as it serves their interest. Why, it's so powerful a force it can even cut through their hatred for us. And it can break down walls!

GUTELE: Mayer — what is it?
MAYER: Money. [...] Money! (*now, a firm shout as he wheels cart through disappearing shop, into set of Frankfort fair*) MONEY! MONEY! MONEEEEEEEE! [Bock Collection NYPL n. pag.; orig. emphasis].

Wealth, at least in the musical, gains equal rights for the Jews of Europe. The real Rothschilds did not start with such lofty goals in mind, according to Backhaus, who argues that only after they attained financial success did higher purposes of justice and equality become part of their reasoning for wealth acquisition. However, the real Rothschilds attained legendary status in the Jewish community for their generosity. According to Israeli critic Greer Fay Cashman, "The Rothschilds not only made money — they also gave it generously to numerous philanthropic causes and to beggars who came knocking at their doors" (12).

The musical effectively makes the most out of these positive legends of Rothschild generosity. Various moments in the show point up that generosity and use of financial success as a weapon. By Act I Scene 6 the Rothschild sons, though young, are already working in the business and adept with money. Nathan gives an old coat to a pauper, but charges him a nominal fee to allow him to keep his pride:

SOLOMON: Why couldn't you just give him the coat?
NATHAN: Because this way we made a sale... and we gave to charity... and we got rid of the old coat, all at the same time. [...] Solomon, he came in as a customer. You want him to leave as a pauper? (I-6-37)

This scene shows the combination of financial acuity and generosity that characterizes the Rothschilds throughout the musical. The aims of the creators seem to have paid off, and critics were convinced. For instance, Clive Barnes pointed out that the musical has "a certain moral force" (184).

The theatricalized Rothschilds also reclaim anti–Semitism for their own purposes, and make moral concerns their central goal in earning money. Mayer sends his boys off to financial success in Europe at the end of Act I by spurring them to action with the phrase the urchins taunted him with: "Jew, do your duty!" (I-9-17). Mayer acts as the moral center of the musical, and therefore we can read his last will and testament as the ultimate expression of the themes the authors attempt to underscore. In that document he advises, "Since Jewish wealth is like snow in March, I enjoin my sons to prevent the thaw. [...] There is no virtue in riches. But there is none in poverty either. Virtue can only be found in the acts of men — acting for mankind" (II-6-39). Mayer's wife also emphasizes the moral imperative incumbent on those of wealth and power. After Mayer's death, Gutele refuses to leave the ghetto, arguing, "Nathan, I have friends here who are not fortunate enough to be Rothschilds. I will leave the ghetto when there is no ghetto" (II-2-12). In a final pivotal scene the brothers decide to risk their entire fortune to force Metternich to grant Jewish equality. The boys are dejected at the beginning of the scene, expressing their disillusionment in biblical terms, "Amshel: We thought we were Moses leading our people out of slavery. We're not. We're only merchant bankers. We have no miracles at our disposal" (II-6-41). But their mother inspires them to fight:

> GUTELE: I see how our people look at you. You are the first men of this ghetto who are not victims of your world, but makers of it. If you leave now, defeated, you betray your father's hopes, and theirs.
> JACOB: Momma, what do you want?
> GUTELE: Me? I want everything! [II-6-45].

In this fashion the meaning of "Everything" transforms from money to equality, an uneasy alliance, but one underlined in the libretto. In this manner the text attempts to erase overtones of greed. Inspired, the brothers undersell Metternich's bonds in an exciting musical number, and force him to come to the ghetto and make terms with them. Not only do they get a "Declaration of Rights" for the Jews, but they also make Metternich guarantee that the Rothschilds will hereafter handle all state bonds. They therefore receive equality *and* money *and* Baronial titles, proving that, in musical theatre at least, risk for moral good always pays off.

Dissonance

The authors make the Rothschilds' struggle against persecution the central narrative strain of the musical. Despite their historical deeds however, fighting injustice was not as central in the real lives of the Rothschilds; the musical takes the most uplifting historical slant. This convenient narrative tells us more about American views in the 1970s than about Europe in the 18th and 19th century. Some critics were not convinced by rationalizations for economic gain. Reviewer Harold Flender in "The Stage Reporter," sums up the musical's attempted moral argument while airing some of the worries a Jewish audience might harbor:

> With all the troubles Jews are having [...] the very last thing we needed, I felt, was a play about millionaire "fiddlers on the roof." On the contrary [the musical] [...] shows that above everything else, the Rothschilds were concerned with human rights, particularly overcoming the denial of these rights for those forced to live in the ghetto [11].

Can this moral concern be quite so straightforward? Sanders tells us, "the authors strove desperately to impose the moral virtues of the ghetto upon the second half [of the musical] [...] the result is some rather severe tampering with the facts" (30). Despite the many legends and true tales of the Rothschilds' bounty and generosity, they were real men and not musical theatre heroes. According to source materials, the Rothschild brothers went to the conference at Aix-la-Chapelle in order to impress upon European leaders the extent of their financial power. They undersold Metternich's bonds, but history does not offer evidence that they did so for political purposes. The musical makes a dramatic arc out of these events in order to emphasize the fight for Jewish equality. The musical also keeps Mayer Rothschild alive longer than historical accuracy would permit, in order to allow him to attend the congress. While the authors have attributed this choice to dramatic necessity alone, Sanders argues that this choice was made in order to further underline a sentimental and "moral credit that the show so desperately needs at this point" (31). The creative team clearly sought moral authority for their characters throughout the production process. In a note on August 18, 1970, they emphasized, "The Rothschilds' first concern must always be 'lift the restrictions'" (Bock Collection NYPL n. pag.). A day later they write, "It sounds like the Rothschilds are willing to bribe everyone for the loan too — we shouldn't imply this even though it was true" (Bock Collection NYPL n. pag.). This last phrase clearly underlines the departures from history taken in order to impose a more virtuosic and heroic dramatic arc.

The historical Mayer and Gutele Rothschild had five daughters as well as five sons. But as in reality, where all Rothschild daughters and their husbands were excluded from the family business, women have been all but erased from the musical. The Rothschild women function as a foil to the men's financial aspirations. Their marginalization therefore impacts the musical's argument of wealth's moral force. Gutele often acts as a contrast to the men in her life when they strive for more. Her first song, "One Room" argues that all she needs to be happy is just one little room to share with her husband. In response to "Everything" she lists their blessings to her sons: their basic needs are met, and that they have each other and their faith. However, as we've seen, the authors cut many of Gutele's songs, and reduced many of her scenes, diminishing her moral power in the journey from the early drafts to the show's opening. Hannah Cohen, Nathan's love interest and the only other major female character, acts as a crusader for various charities, according to Nathan, "a Jewish Joan of Arc" (II-3-18). Through Hannah, the libretto characterizes charity as identifiably Jewish:

HANNAH: One does what one must do!
NATHAN: ...You're Jewish!
HANNAH: Ah, you know my father?
NATHAN: No, madam, just your conscience [II-2-14].

She argues, "There is no future for the rich in England. Don't think your contribution will hold back the revolution" (II-2-15). And yet Nathan's own brand of capitalism wins her over. He offers a bribe to finance the end of the war in Europe if she marries him, and ultimately, in dramaturgically unsatisfying manner, she consents. Although in the cut song "Hannah," Nathan sings, "She turned my pound and shilling world / to a world of milk and honey / She's more precious than music. / She's more beautiful than money" (Bock Collection NYPL n. pag.), clearly money holds quite an allure as well. These women's erasure hints at dissonance behind the musical's argument of money's moral power.

The final moment of *The Rothschilds* as it shifted through the drafting process demonstrates the conflicting messages at work during the process of making the musical. An early draft from September 1969 implies that the Rothschilds *become* the power they have been fighting:

> *The family enters the Grand Ballroom. The victory dance resumes [...] the music becomes faster—louder. The Jewish melody of the ghetto sequence is incorporated into the dance music—but as the dance continues and the Rothschilds mix with their partners in power—the melody looses its minor key character—it blends with the ball music—struggles for a moment to keep its identity as the Rothschilds become paler, more distant—finally merged with the great dance. The three ghetto urchins of the opening stand peering at the dancing figures. They do not notice Mayer Rothschild, who passes by them, ascending the podium. [...]* CURTAIN [Bock Collection NYPL n. pag.].

In a later draft Gutele warns Nathan not to let success change him:

GUTELE: Don't let them forget who you are.
NATHAN: If they do, Momma... I'll remind them [Bock Collection NYPL n. pag.].

In the final draft, which appeared on Broadway, Metternich tells Gutele that money will change her boys:

GUTELE: (*angry*) They will not change! Remember that! [...] Nathan?
NATHAN: Yes, Momma?
GUTELE: Never forget who you are.
NATHAN: Do you think they will ever let us? [II-8-55].

In these three versions the message changes from money's inescapable assimilatory force, to the necessity of valuing Jewish identity in the face of success, to recognition of continued inequality. In the same manner in which this message changed, so do the conflicting loyalties of *The Rothschilds* as a whole. While the musical celebrates Jewish success and financial acuity, fighting to prove the moral authority of money when used for good, it also treads dangerously near areas of intense stereotyped anti–Semitism, the kind that helped the Nazi regime justify the Holocaust. The musical tries to maintain a balance between the nostalgic celebratory possibilities of family and the American Dream, while also reminding us of the extraordinarily high price Jews have paid for their success. *The Rothschilds* simultaneously appeals to wistful memory, while angrily resonating with the Holocaust, and rejecting easy calls to nostalgia. The result is a highly complex text, largely overlooked until now.

CHAPTER VII

Rags and *Ragtime*

"Sometimes we don't love things, till we tell them goodbye / Oh my homeland / My homeland / Good-Bye" [*Rags* I-1-3]

"America is our home now. America is our shtetl." [*Ragtime* 12]

One third of the entire Eastern European Jewish population came to America between the ascension of Russian Czar Alexander III in 1881 and World War I's outbreak in 1914. A vast majority of those immigrants came to New York City and settled on the Lower East Side. These immigrant years — to which most American Jews can trace their heritage — offer a potent nostalgic source. Portrayals of immigrant Jews at the turn of the century span the arts, popular and otherwise. Television series, movies, novels and non-musical plays all tell immigrant tales. Musical theatre versions dip into popular narrative tropes and clichés that have emerged around the subject matter. Both Strouse, Schwartz and Stein's *Rags* (1986), and Ahrens, Flaherty and McNally's *Ragtime* (1998), through nostalgia for the Lower East Side and the immigrant era, share a sublimation of Holocaust reverberations into tales of American success.

Nostalgia of Place

By 1910 there were approximately 1.1 million Jews in New York City, as opposed to 70 thousand in 1870 (Howe *World of Our Fathers* xix). So while Jewish immigration to America was not limited to the turn of the century or to New York City, this time / space looms largest in Jewish collective memory. Scholar Beth Wenger argues, "The Lower East Side [is] a site continually in the forefront of American Jewish consciousness, as a place and an idea that has been reinvented in different ways to suit the cultural needs of various generations" (*Remembering the Lower East Side* 2). Because this neighborhood was significant to such a large group of American Jews, even Jews whose ancestors did not actually live there have adopted it as their own. As a place of such evocative power, nostalgia must surely be central to the region's consideration.

As we've seen, Furnish separates nostalgia into three categories: time, place and family. In immigrant tales, nostalgia for a place, New York City, as the largest point of entry for Jewish immigrants, as well as where many stayed and made their American lives, takes a central role. For example, there were more Jews in New York than in the state of Israel for its first 20 years of existence, and at one time nearly half of all American Jews lived in New York (Furnish). But after the peak years of immigration there has been a downward trend in the New York Jewish population. After Jews attained success and left New York City, the immigrant world of the Lower East Side that had been new, frightening and alien, could now act as a nostalgic source.

We can tease out a double layer of memory in artistic works that concern this era. Immigrant characters feel nostalgic for the homes they have lost, the shtetls they will never be able to return to. The same could be said for immigrants from the *immigrant community*. Audiences possess nostalgia for the immigrant era or neighborhood, which they in turn have left. They feel nostalgia for the immigrants' nostalgia. The new world replaces the old, and nostalgia doubles in size and emotional impact. The Lower East Side could stand in for the shtetl world, as it held the vestiges of that disappearing community — the sights, smells and sounds that came over from the old world to the new. But combined with Old World elements was the growth inherent to the immigrant era, the signposts of these Jewish immigrants' journeys to their new American lives. As Jews moved to suburbia or to wealthier New York City locations, memories of the neighborhood's troubles faded, replaced by a longing for community. As Furnish argues, "However much these individuals welcomed leaving the crowded, airless Lower East Side tenements, their move also led them out of the dynamic cultural and community life of the area" (72). Loss of that community created a nostalgic longing. Jonathan Boyarin further complicates immigrant nostalgia. He sees the Lower East Side as a place of *forgetting*, rather than remembering; of purposefully moving away from origins, resulting in loss of community. He points out that, "Mourning for lost common places is suppressed by the constantly reinforced shame of origins, which is complemented, not overcome, by sentimental nostalgia" (3). Nostalgia helps to sugarcoat those aspects of the "old neighborhood" which might be embarrassing. The Lower East Side, for those Jews who have moved away from the neighborhood and become prosperous, becomes a site of cleaned-up, simpler nostalgia.

Nostalgia for the immigrant years on the Lower East Side began as early as the 1920s and was in full force by the interwar years. Both remembering and distancing from the neighborhood was a pivotal part of constructing what it meant to be an American Jew. As Jewish Studies scholar Beth Wenger argues, nostalgia proved quite useful in this period to contextualize American Jews' increasing success. Nostalgia, as we have discussed, rather than concerning the period remembered, often has more relevance to the period being remembered *from*. Although Wenger's article focuses on the 1930s, her understanding of the uses of Jewish nostalgia extends to today, "Romantic recollections of the Lower East Side established an historical link with the past, fostered Jewish identity, and measured the accomplishments of a generation" (9).

The neighborhood attained a mythic status partially by becoming a commodified cultural product. As early as the 1930s the neighborhood could sell the experience of living on the Lower East Side to those who no longer did, with a busy tourist trade, museum exhibits, and products ranging from culinary to religious. Authors like Irving Howe with his award-winning book chronicling the neighborhood, *World of Our Fathers* (1976), and photographers like Jacob Riis and Lewis Hine also served up products that encouraged nostalgia for the neighborhood, even while they explored its darker sides. The arts offer commodified products as well. Many American movies and plays of the last few decades take a nostalgic point of view towards the Lower East Side, among them Herb Gardner's *Conversations with My Father* (1992) and Joan Micklin Silver's *Crossing Delancey* (1988) and *Hester Street* (1975). Broadway musicals also offer a nicely packaged piece of the Lower East Side, allowing a nostalgic trip to the old neighborhood without even having to take the train downtown.

Time's hazy effect on Lower East Side memory has not been universally applauded. For example, the increasing tourist trade in the neighborhood has raised questions regarding the salutary or harmful nature of nostalgia. Nostalgic memory, instead of offering a harmless personal connection, can erase unpleasant aspects of a place or time. Many prominent Jewish thinkers have criticized increasing nostalgia for the Lower East Side. In 1989, Martin Peretz, in his article, "Identity, History, Nostalgia" decried a trend of ethnic essentialism, "What is generally left of the immigrant cultures in the lives of their heirs is sparse. It's largely nostalgia for twice-removed memories, a few foul words, and a residual culinary preference" (2). In 1986, Irving Howe, whose angry reaction to *Fiddler* we have already witnessed, wrote angrily about what he called "Immigrant Chic:"

> What at times leaves me a little irritated, is the upsurge of nostalgia I detect among a good many young people for the immigrant world [...] which they barely know. They aren't nostalgic for anything they themselves experienced,

with either joy or anguish; they're nostalgic for the nostalgia of other people ["Immigrant Chic" 76].

He argues that life for the immigrant on the Lower East Side was often harsh, poor, raw and hugely difficult. Although Howe helped create this burgeoning interest in the immigrant world through his classic book *World of Our Fathers*, he continued to argue, "For I don't want the immigrant–Jewish milieu — it's my life you understand — to become "material" for the chic museum displays and cozy Yinglish musicals" (76). Howe argues persuasively, but the trend continues nonetheless. Here we examine why and how the "cozy Yinglish musicals" he might be referencing function to inscribe cultural memories.

Postmemory

By the 1980s and '90s, with Holocaust education practically universal in public schools, with a museum in Washington D.C. dedicated to the Shoah, and with pervasive popular culture representations of the Holocaust, we now understand the death of six million as the central event of the Nazi era. After Nazi imagery was connected with genocide in every American mind, after America had taken upon itself identification with the Holocaust as "an American tragedy," even a dramatic project most seemingly distant from the actual killing and horror of the Shoah could not escape from overtones of the genocide. These musicals must contend with this association.

We find Holocaust or postmemory resonances in both *Rags* and *Ragtime* from two contradictory sites. First, immigrant suffering stands in for the suffering of the Holocaust. Secondly, and contrastingly, the musicals suggest that immigrant trials can never compare to that ultimate suffering, and that in fact, the immigrant world offered an escape from the Holocaust. These conflicting ideas circulate simultaneously. Dorothy Seidman Bilik, in her book *Immigrant-Survivors* (1981), examines the new immigrant novel. She points out that as early as 1957, the Jewish immigrant became a character in novels again, in a way that that hadn't been seen since the 1930s:

> In essence the new immigrant novel is not a literature of assimilation. Instead, deeply concerned with the continuing importance of the Jewish experience, it can be thought of as a manifestation by Jewish American writers, of a delayed post–Holocaust consciousness [3].

She discusses Holocaust survivors as direct immigrant characters in these novels, but also extends her analysis further. For example, she discusses famous Jewish author Bernard Malamud, who writes immigrant characters who are not actual survivors, but who nevertheless, "are indirect embodiments of post–

Holocaust consciousness" (6). Bilik defines this consciousness as a focus on, "the preservation of cultural identity" (9). She argues, "Another expression of post–Holocaust sensibility was the renewed interest in the Jewish American immigrant past, a phenomenon of the late sixties and seventies" (13). Musical theatre, as a commercial and communal art, often comes late to socially circulating issues, so in this context, *Rags*, which premiered in the 1980s, could emerge from this renewed interest. Correspondingly, *Ragtime* came out of a period of even more exposure, the 1990s. To what extent do these immigrant characters in *Rags* and *Ragtime* emerge from this post–Holocaust consciousness? They are not survivors of the Holocaust, but they are indeed survivors. In this way their immigrant suffering could stand in for the suffering of the Holocaust, as in Malamud's work. In the opposite manner however, underscoring the pain and humiliation of the immigrant experience points out the fact that the immigrant characters in these musicals emerged from that pain, many triumphantly. Thus *Rags* and *Ragtime*, in a reassuring manner, point out that very shortly after the immigrant period American Jews were far luckier their European brethren. Their immigrant struggle allowed these Jews safety in America instead of death in the Holocaust. America offered a haven for its Jews in World War II. Allowing nostalgia for early suffering points out that it was part of "gentler" time, and calls up Holocaust associations in contrast to the relative "ease" of the immigrant period. Detailed examinations of these musicals will help to contextualize their nostalgia.

Rags

   Rags owes much of its fame to the fact that its original Broadway production closed after just four performances. Why devote time to a study of a show that lasted for such a short time? First, the pedigree of its authors demands that attention be paid to the musical. Charles Strouse had composed several notable Broadway successes, most famously, *Annie* (1977), and lyricist Stephen Schwartz had written *Pippin* (1972), *Godspell* (1976) and other hits when they wrote the score. Joseph Stein, librettist, was already famous for *Fiddler on the Roof.* Additionally, *Rags'* impact has not been limited to its Broadway production alone. Instead it has enjoyed cult status and continued production across the country at large regional and community theatres. Finally, *Rags'* subject matter is so redolent with nostalgia, so appropriate to our topic, it becomes necessary to examine reasons for its failure, the intentions of its creators, and the messages it imparts to audiences.

   The road to *Rags'* began when Joseph Stein sent a screenplay about Jewish immigrants to producer Lee Guber, who said, "you're crazy, this isn't a movie;

it's the book for a musical" (quoted in Klein 2). They approached composer Charles Strouse, who wanted to use his classical background to explore the immigrant era's musical sounds. At first Stein wrote a central role not far from his previous hit character Tevye, but worried about comparisons to *Fiddler*, he instead he chose a leading female character: Rebecca, an immigrant fleeing the pogroms of Eastern Europe with her son. The musical suffered a legendarily stormy production process. Before *Rags* opened, articles appeared in the *New York Times* declaring the show in trouble. The original director, Joan Micklin Silver — director of films of similar content, *Crossing Delancey* and *Hester Street* — left during rehearsals for non-disclosed reasons. The authors took charge of the musical out of town. *Rags* went through numerous directors and choreographers, and was significantly re-envisioned along the way. James Lapine and Jerome Robbins came to the show at the behest of the producers to consider directing, and there were rumors that Mike Nichols and Jerry Zaks were made offers to take over the helm. Gene Saks was eventually hired, but the revolving door process had done its harm. The opening night was postponed three times. Paula Kalustian, who began as an assistant director to Silver, was given the role of "creative production coordinator," keeping a measure of stability while the production was falling apart. She remembers "a lot of craziness," (quoted in Smith 24). Kalustian states that when Saks was finally hired, "to focus the scenes and tighten the production, I knew that most of the heart of *Rags* was lost as a result. [Schwartz's] original concept of the piece as an ensemble cast got caught in between twenty highly creative but different visions" (quoted in Smith 24). Kalustian lamented this move away from an ensemble cast. Instead, Teresa Stratas, famous Metropolitan Opera star, played Rebecca, and the authors altered the musical to accommodate her star status. The musical announced its closing shortly after its opening, though there were brief hopes that the show could re-open. After the Saturday matinee, cast member Lonny Price spoke to the audience at the curtain and led the actors and about one thousand members of the audience on a march to the half-priced TKTS line, chanting "Keep *Rags* Open." There they encouraged people on the line to buy tickets to that night's performance. They sold more than 750 tickets, prompting press coverage in the process. Josh Ellis, the production spokesperson, announced August 25th that the show would reopen in September if they could raise an additional $500,000 to $1,000,000 to produce a new television commercial and to keep the show running for at least a month to build public support. But three days later, the producers announced in the *New York Times* that the show would not re-open. Producers Guber, Martin Heinfling and Marvin A. Krauss stated:

> We had the cooperation of the unions, our star, Teresa Stratas, and our theater owner. [...] However we could not bring the weekly operating budget of *Rags* to

a sufficient level to sustain the operation of the show. [...] Do we want to keep *Rags* open? Yes. Can we keep *Rags* open? No [quoted in Kuchwara 1].

Kalustian argued that the critics did not allow the show to find its audience, "My relatives came off the boat at Ellis Island, and they told the same stories *Rags* did. *Rags* was a people's show, not a critic's show" (quoted in Smith 24). Significantly, in this statement Kalustian calls *Rags* a "people's show" because of her nostalgic connections to an ethnic past.

Rags has been through many incarnations, the plot shifting slightly each time. The changes necessitate a synopsis of the original production. The musical follows the experiences of a group of Jewish immigrants who arrive at Ellis Island in 1910 on a "rag ship" from Eastern European shtetls. Rebecca and her young son David, fleeing a pogrom in their village, come to New York to join her husband Nathan. Avram and his daughter Bella, who has befriended Rebecca, come to better their lives. Ben Levitowitz, in love with Bella, looks forward to making his fortune. At Ellis Island hucksters look to make use of the endless hordes of immigrants ("I Remember / Greenhorns"). When no one meets Rebecca, Avram and Bella vouch for her and take her into Avram's brother's home on the Lower East Side. Their first night in America, Rebecca and David sing of the potential of the world that lies outside their window ("Brand New World"). Rebecca remembers the horrors she has overcome during her flight from the pogroms ("Children of the Wind"). Rebecca finds work in a sweatshop, Bella's father forces her to stay home and take piecework, Avram becomes a peddler, and Ben works in a cigar factory. A klezmer band playing on the streets accompanies their work ("Penny a Tune"). At Rebecca's sweatshop she meets Saul, a revolutionary working to unionize the shops. Rebecca argues with Saul, who wants her to educate herself and her son ("Easy For You"). Rebecca and Saul grow closer, and after he takes the group to the Yiddish theatre, where they see a version of Hamlet ("Hard to Be a Prince"), she begins to fall in love with him ("Blame It on the Summer Night"). Ben has begun a new business selling gramophones. He finally finds Bella and shows her the wonders of this new machine ("For My Mary"). When Avram, who disapproves of Ben's business dreams, forbids Bella to see Ben anymore, she angrily lashes out at her father about the life she's forced to live in America ("Rags"). She runs uptown to gaze at the rich inhabitants, who snub her. She comes home angrily, refusing to leave her room. We finally see Nathan, Rebecca's husband, who has renamed himself Nat Harris and works with corrupt Tammany politicians ("What's Wrong with That"). He hears Rebecca and David are in New York and vows to find them. David gets beaten up by local youths when he tries to fight, as Saul taught him. Rebecca angrily breaks off her relationship with Saul ("Nothing Will Hurt Us Again"). Nathan finds his family as Act I closes.

Act Two opens at a cafe ("Cherry Street Café") where Nathan espouses his love of America ("Yankee Boy"). He tells Rebecca of his wish to rise above their immigrant world ("Uptown"). Rebecca, back with her husband, may not see Saul anymore, but still they express their feelings ("Wanting"). Rachel, a widow who has set her eyes on Avram, romances him by singing of the home they could share ("Three Sunny Rooms"). David helps Ben become a success in his gramophone business by marketing to mothers of all ethnicities who want to immortalize their son's voices ("The Sound of Love"). Bella, contrary to her father's wishes, has insisted on getting a job at a sweatshop. A tragic fire strikes, trapping the workers inside, and killing Bella. The men gather to sit Shiva (the Jewish method of mourning) and to sing the prayer for the dead ("Kaddish"). Awakened by her friend's death, Rebecca leads her sweatshop in a strike ("Bread and Freedom"), defying Nathan, who refuses to risk his future with Tammany. Rebecca has chosen to stay with Saul and fight injustice ("Dancing with the Fools"). She has finally become American, as another boat of immigrants arrive to begin the cycle again ("Finale").

The musical's critical reception in 1986 was, on the whole, negative. Reviewers almost uniformly praised Stratas' performance and Strouse's score, but their reaction to the book and to the show overall was scathing. The libretto tried too much, agreed the critics. Linda Winer, in *Newsday*, sums up reaction to the confused libretto:

> *Rags* [...] is ambitious, smart, beautiful and funny. Unfortunately, it's also clichéd, long, ludicrously inflated with crises and ultimately undramatic. [...] The creators, [...] seem unable to agree whether to go for poetic schmaltz, rollicking musical comedy or a dark, edgy message about the disillusionments of the immigrant experience [240].

One common reaction held that the show was too dark. Joel Siegel commented, "The immigrant experience was hard and humiliating, but every immigrant who came here, came with hope. And that is exactly the feeling you won't find in *Rags*, a cynical, mean-spirited musical" (241).

Rags' Broadway production lasted just four performances, but the musical has had a much more extensive life, due, most likely, to the appeal of its nostalgic subject matter. Although it was a financial failure, the musical attained cult status for musical theatre fans, allowing numerous productions since 1986. The creators did not freeze the musical, but instead chose to continue working. As Alvin Klein tells us, "The creators of *Rags* [...] have been struggling to get it right for 14 years. And that's if you don't count all the years of suffering it took to get it wrong in the first place" ("The Musical [...] that Refused to Die" n. pag.). There have been several major regional productions, including at American Jewish Theatre in New York City, American Musical Theatre in San Jose, Coconut Grove Playhouse in Miami, and the Paper Mill

Rags (1986 Broadway). **Music by Charles Strouse Lyrics by Stephen Schwartz Book by Joseph Stein. Directed by Gene Saks. Shown at center, from left: Josh Blake, Teresa Stratas.**

Playhouse in New Jersey. The last two productions cut the size of the cast, to eleven in Miami and to fifteen at the Paper Mill. As Charles Strouse stated hopefully after the Paper Mill production, "We've still got growing pains after all these years [...] but I think we've made the bad spots good and the good spots better" (quoted in Klein n. pag.). In this production, according to Strouse, songs were not removed or added, but "reshaped," and made, "more impressionistic" (n. pag.). Even after the 1999 New Jersey production, the quest to fix *Rags* was not complete. The authors continued to work on a major production in 2000 at Walnut Street Theatre in Philadelphia and for *Rags'* UK premiere in 2001 at the Bridewell Theatre in London. These productions were miniaturized, inexpensive and low-tech. By doubling characters, the cast size was reduced even further. Rodgers and Hammerstein Theatricals currently licenses a version of the script closer to these latest productions. It adds one song for Rebecca and Bella, "If We Never Meet Again," and cuts two. Rebecca's son David now narrates the show. It refocuses the musical on Rebecca's relationships with Bella and Saul, and Nathan's part correspondingly reduces in size. The new version also aims to make the show more producible, by reducing the cast size and the technical requirements. Although these altered versions of *Rags* received happier critical treatment — in England Rhoda Koenig in *The Independent* argued that, "this modest treatment reveals the show's modest virtues" (n. pag.) — the revamped *Rags* still did not enjoy critical acclaim. In England, at least, the relevance of the show suffered. According to Koenig, "You would never know from Joseph Stein's book that Jews have a reputation for being funny. [...] Indeed, after a while, the show's insistent drabness becomes absurdly self-righteous" (n. pag.).

Rags has worked quite well in community productions, particularly at Jewish Community Centers. Is this the perfect audience for the musical? Was this why the original production failed; because it was too specific? As Pittsburgh critic Christopher Rawson writes, "A flop in one arena can be just the ticket in another" (n. pag.). A production at the Pittsburg JCC in February 1994 brought about Rawson's thought-provoking response:

> [*Rags* is] perfectly at home in a community theater in the community whose story it partly tells. [...] *Rags* becomes a big, happy celebration of painful history converted to warm nostalgia. [...] Though *Rags* was written for Broadway, the JCC is the sort of home it was destined for from the start [n. pag.].

The musical's acceptance by such a specific audience raises the same issue of universality versus specificity we encountered in *Fiddler on the Roof*. Although *Fiddler* portrays a specific ethnic community, it was hailed as universal. *Rags* tried to attain this universality, and by extension commercial acceptance, by painting a broad portrait of an era. It tried to cover its bases, including the important immigrant tropes for all ethnic immigrant groups: oppression versus the American Dream; labor versus bosses; a sweatshop fire; Statue of Liberty imagery. Instead of honing in on a specific community, *Rags* tried to paint a larger canvas, hoping audiences would associate with at least one of the above immigrant narratives.

What audiences does *Rags* seek? Again Henry Bial's theory of double coding proves helpful, for the musical aims at both Jewish and larger audiences. An audience at the JCC is more likely to forgive the musical's flaws, to embrace the story of their forebears because of their nostalgic connection to the material. *Rags'* wide-ranging pageant structure functions well in this case because it covers significant ground, reaching more potential audience memories. At the same time the musical also aims at universality. While *Rags'* central characters are Jewish, the creators simultaneously refer to other immigrant groups, who lived in the neighborhood with the Jews and shared a similar story of overcoming oppression. Irish and Italian groups are included in "The Sound of Love," and Rebecca's sweatshop compatriots include these ethnicities as well. These references to other immigrant groups underscore the musical's attempts at universality, allowing a large percentage of the audience to connect to the musical. As Howard Kissel points out:

> *Rags* [...] begins in a place likely to have instant impact on 90 percent of the audience — Ellis Island in 1910. [...] Even if one's overall response is fragmented, *Rags* taps into feelings so deep inside us we can't help but surrender [239–240].

These feelings are often nostalgic and are not limited to a Jewish audience, though most of the sources we will now examine are particularly aimed at Jewish communal memory.

Nostalgia

Rags' very first words evoke doubled nostalgia. An immigrant coming to America sings hauntingly, "I remember summer evenings / sitting, you and I / While the cranes were calling / in the Eastern sky / Sometimes we don't love things / till we tell them goodbye / Oh my homeland / my homeland / good-bye" (I-1-1). While touching, the score undercuts this nostalgia when Rebecca sings, to the exact same melody, of her traumatic experience in that homeland hiding from the Russians, watching her village burn. This disparity marks *Rags'* complicated relationship with memory. We can read both levels of nostalgia in terms of Svetlana Boym's "mourning of displacement," discussed in her book, *The Future of Nostalgia* (2001). She describes a nostalgic desire to return home, complicated by the knowledge that "home" has forever gone. An urge to return to the "Old Country" was made impossible by the Holocaust, which wiped out Jewish shtetl life with utter finality. Therefore when that nameless immigrant opens *Rags* nostalgically saying goodbye to their homeland, we map our own bereavement, displacement, and knowledge of destruction onto the immigrants' mourning. Immigrants left the Old Country with no hope of return, for them, the goodbye was final. But the horrors of the Holocaust grant that finality a certain death knell.

As we have seen, New York City's Lower East Side has offered a site, both literally and figuratively, for nostalgia-laden narratives. Most critics agreed that the musical did not make the most out of its rich material, and instead included too many clichéd characters and plot points. Critics pointed out that the material seems, "secondhand" (Gussow 2), or "over-familiar" (Spencer 1), and in doing so they responded to the vast bulk of literature, arts and media that have trod the same steps as *Rags*. Nostalgia for a simple immigrant narrative — from tribulation and oppression to dawning success — simplified a complex and difficult era, essentializing the Lower East Side.

The Yiddish Theatre

The title *Rags* echoes a Yiddish play from the 1920s by H. Leivik called *Schmattes*, [rags], a Yiddish name for the garment industry (Furnish). For the audience member educated in the Yiddish theatre, this could have offered a nostalgic nudge. But for the rest of the audience, a more blatant look back at the Yiddish theatre was required. The Yiddish theatre was an integral part of Lower East Side culture, offering a potent source of nostalgia for a Jewish audience. In the 1960s, when *Milk and Honey* opened, the Yiddish theatre was a more recent memory. By 1986 the nostalgic source was more distant. *Rags* had no Molly Picon, but instead included a scene which took place directly in a Yiddish theatre. The distance of time allows a more general, stereotypical portrayal of this theatre genre. With *Rags* attempting to embrace all the tropes of an immigrant nostalgia piece, the inclusion of the Yiddish theatre was vital. Saul, Rebecca, David and Bella attend a Yiddish *Hamlet*, and this classic's makeover supplies stereotypical humor. To begin, Saul tells David one character is named Rosencrantz, which prompts Bella to ask:

> BELLA: Rosencrantz? He's Jewish?
> SAUL: Of course Jewish — they're all Jewish [I-9-39].

We then proceed into further stereotyped territory. For example, the famous soliloquy is "Judaified" thus, "Hamlet: To be or not to be — a terrible question. In other words, to live or to die.... Both bad! Living we know about — suffering without end — but dying is better?" (I-9-39). Jewish momma stereotypes are also included. The Yiddish Ophelia argues, "And Hamlet, you shouldn't say such mean things about your mother. Your mother is your best friend! (*Audience applauds*)" (I-10-40). The Yiddish troupe ends their play singing, "So make a smile and cheer up, Hamlet / Next year we're gonna be, gonna be / In Jerusalem!" (*The flag of Palestine is brought onstage, followed by the American flag. Audience cheers wildly*) (I-10-41). The scene concludes with the audience and the actors joyfully dancing and singing together. This finale briefly points out yet another source of nostalgia: for early Zionist sentiment of the type we see in *Milk and Honey*.

Score

Rags' musical influences are intensely nostalgic. As discussed, music connects us swiftly to memory, and "Jewish melodies," however wide that definition, can immediately lend the weakest of material emotional weight. Critics highly praised Strouse's score when the musical opened and his work continued to gain admirers in the years since. Strouse purposefully makes use of an evocative mix of the previously mentioned influences. For Strouse, whose ethnic heritage was German Jewish, writing *Rags* was an opportunity to combine musical theatre with music from his ethnic heritage. As he explains, "Nothing exists in a vacuum. I was consciously trying to relate the music of the klezmers — Jewish street musicians — to the more structured jazz that came later" (quoted in Smurthwaite 2). While the Broadway score may function nostalgically, it is the "ethnic" music that pulls the most weight. As Charles Spencer in *The Daily Telegraph* states, "The haunting Jewish melodies prove remarkably potent" (n. pag.). Certainly the Klezmer musicians onstage evoked Old World music in a one-to-one relationship, but Strouse professed a more complex aim. He wanted to demonstrate how musical forms influenced each other and created a new American music. The scoring of "A Penny A Tune" most dramatically reflects these strange harmonies, clashing and then resolving into new and evocative forms, creating new American music. Strouse's score thus allows nostalgia for traditional Jewish melodies and for the genres they influenced: ragtime, jazz, and most notably, Broadway.

Ritual

Staged ritual also connects to memory. We have seen Jewish rituals performed onstage in previous musicals considered, a Sabbath prayer in *Fiddler*, weddings in both *Fiddler* and *Milk and Honey*, and the many cut from drafts of *The Rothschilds*. *Rags* includes a more solemn ritual, making the connection to memory darker and more complex. After Bella dies in a sweatshop fire, the community gathers to sit Shiva and the men say the Kaddish, the Jewish prayer for the dead. Tony Kushner's *Angels in America* (1993) and Harvey Fierstein's *Torch Song Trilogy* (1982) also include the Kaddish or funerals — clearly this ritual holds proven stage power. As with all examples of staged ritual, this funeral invokes and privileges community. Neighbors and friends gather to support the mourners, and a powerful chorus of men sing the Kaddish in unison. However, perhaps the most interesting twist on this scene involves gender and Jewish law, and poses a challenge to the community's rigidity. David opens the scene (in the revised script) by stating, "I'm getting dressed to join the men in a prayer for the dead — for Bella. The women aren't allowed to do this prayer with the men — it's a law" (II-6-93). The men begin the song, with the women sitting separately. Rebecca adds echoes and descants, and then "(*Rebecca's grief, her love for Bella, her memories are too strong to control*)" (II-7-94), and she breaks in, singing a portion alone. She tries to join Avram, he rejects her, but they end the song together. Although Rebecca challenges the community, she also underscores its moral force by joining the ritual. By finishing the prayer together, she and Avram validate its power. What does the staged reciting of the prayer achieve? The ancient intensity of the words invokes a solemn sense of religious power. Strouse writes his own take on cantorial Jewish music, but does not use a traditional ritual melody, for the mourners Kaddish is usually spoken. This inauthentic, musicalized ritual makes use of the emotional weight of music to grant solemnity and a borrowed power to the moment. The use of the ancient Aramaic of the prayer could be seen as alienating, or as a call to memory or nostalgia, depending upon its audience.

The use of the Kaddish underscores the very finality and difficulty of the immigrant path to success. Many were sacrificed along the way. This ritual, given the universal aspirations of *Rags*, hopes to mourn for all of them. It can also mourn for the six million Jewish victims of the Holocaust — for the echoes of this very intensely scored scene cannot help but to resonate with the loss on a far larger scale that these immigrants stand in for. Bella dies in a fire, trapped in a small room with many other young immigrants, most of them Jewish. Echoes of concentration camp ovens should not be overlooked. Bilik's earlier mentioned theory of immigrant-survivors manifesting a post–Holocaust consciousness here expands beyond immigrants who survive — and instead encompasses immigrants who do *not* survive the violence and trauma of the American experience. Instead Bella's suffering and painful end acts as a substitution for millions of other deaths not immediately acknowledged in the text. The Kaddish therefore transcends its specific moment onstage and takes on a far larger meaning.

Radical Jewish Humanism

Yet despite the Holocaust evocations in this scene, *Rags* also contradictorily portrays the immigrant world as an escape and a solution — a place of opportunity for Jews. The freedom to fight for change as part of the labor movement offers a central example of this kind of opportunity. Therefore, the Lower East Side's association with the labor movement offers one reason why Jews might feel a strong sense of sentimental memory for the immigrant era. In *Rags*, the character of Saul evokes a nostalgic connection of particular interest. He takes the part of a crusading Jew, embodying the ideals of new social liberalism, and he eventually converts our heroine, Rebecca, to the cause. Saul even goes to see Emma Goldman, a character we will find in our other immigrant musical, *Ragtime*. This interest in social liberalism offers an important element of Jewish self-identification. Saul exemplifies Jewish belief in political liberalism, allowing nostalgia for social progressiveness uncomplicated by success.

The ideals of the labor movement emerge from radical Jewish humanism, as discussed in literary criticism. Regarding the work of E.L. Doctorow, author of the novel *Ragtime*, scholar John Clayton argues, "Identifying with the oppressed, the Jewish voice, [...] argues in defense; humor or pathos or both come out of the ironic tension between human beings expressing kindness, dignity, hope and a world expressing injustice" (109). This identification with the oppressed in the face of injustice can be seen in portrayals of the labor movement in the immigrant era as central to perceptions of the Lower East Side. Gerald Sorin, in a historical study of Jews in America, points out that radical Jewish organizers, "learned to explain socialism and class struggle in terms of social justice, the prophetic tradition, and the concept of *tikn olam*, an injunction, derived from Judaic religious culture, to repair or improve the world" (107).

Jewish belief in social justice flowered partly from ancient and biblical sources. It offers no surprise then that this belief has continued to be linked with Jewishness, even after much of the Jewish proletariat had ascended the class structure. Jews have continued to be associated with the labor movement, or with radical Jewish humanism. As Sorin argues, "Although the movement lasted little more than one generation, its accomplishments and progressive echoes continue to reverberate in the contemporary world and to inform Jewish American social and political values" (107). Jewish writers and artists privilege those progressive echoes by deciding what to remember, and what to forget. Scholar Hasia R. Diner points out:

> It is striking, for example, that we remember the many Lower East Side laborers, but very few of the entrepreneurs who turned a profit in the neighborhood. Lower East Side memory culture abounds with the poor, but not with those who succeeded economically [5].

In fact, many of the bosses laborers fought against were themselves Jewish. Nostalgic recollections of this era, including in *Rags*, tend to overlook this fact in favor of stirring memories of the immigrants who fought for equality and justice, portraying America as a land of opportunity where social justice is in fact a possibility.

In its opening number, *Rags* points out the capitalist system, with hucksters singing about how they will take advantage of the "greenhorns" they await at Ellis Island. Or, as Nathan points out, "There are Cossacks here, only here they wear nice suits and ties" (II-2-65). The push and pull between Rebecca and Saul embodies the forces of personal need against collective greed. Tragedy converts Rebecca to the cause of unionization and personal fulfillment through radicalism. "Bread and Freedom," the song where she embraces the labor cause, demonstrates the culmination of the central through-line of the piece: Rebecca's conversion to the correct cause. This stirring anthem shows her deciding her course of action. Rebecca chooses to remain with the strikers, prompting Nathan to ask:

> NATHAN: What happened to you, Rebecca?
> REBECCA: I don't know Nathan. I guess America... [...] I guess America happened to me [II-8-102].

Rebecca then reclaims her Jewish name and leaves her husband.*

By pointing out the corrupt system Jews ultimately triumphed over, and their ideals of strength and justice, *Rags* allows nostalgia for a period where Jews fought clearly on the side of the "right;" for an uncomplicated liberal cause, unlike the years that have followed. It also highlights America as a land where Jews could successfully fight injustice, as opposed to the Europe that was to come. Fighting from below against a corrupt hegemony presents a rosier picture of moral certitude than perhaps any era since, with the exception of perhaps the civil rights movement where Jews participated in large percentages. Certainly by the Reaganomics years of the 1980s, the early labor movement offered a powerful nostalgic site. While Jews are still involved in liberal causes today and were in the 80s when *Rags* premiered, as a whole they are not oppressed themselves, but are instead one of the more financially successful ethnic groups in America. And yet, in a 1988 *Los Angeles Times* survey, "54 percent of the persons interviewed answered that a commitment to social equality was most important to their Jewish identity" (Waxman 191). At the videotaped Broadway performance in *Rags*' original run, the audience broke into exuberant applause when Rebecca stands up to leave her oppressive shop, demonstrating the audience's emotional investment in her liberal political stance. And yet, as sociologist Waxman tells us, "Blue collar laborers and craftsmen were 80 percent of the adult male Jewish work force in 1900 but only 25 percent by 1948; they would eventually decline to less than 10 percent by 1980" (19). Jews were no longer struggling themselves, and yet that struggle was pivotal to Jewish identity. A sense of the kind of unity and community that liberal beliefs causes, encourage nostalgia in the wake of the loss of that community.

In addition, remembering or privileging the Jewish struggle for humane

---

*As this instance demonstrates, *Rags* ties immigrant labor issues to feminism. Interestingly, an unscientific look at recent books on Jewish immigration yield a large percentage about the female immigrant experience. Many were published around the same time *Rags* appeared on Broadway. Clearly there has been recent interest in female perspective of the immigration experience. The fight for personal actualization remains quite similar, whether fighting against ethnic or gender inequalities.

working conditions and equality creates a sense that in the immigrant period Jews fought on the side of truth and justice. This emphasis confronts Holocaust postmemory, as Jews in this movement were heroes instead of victims. As in *Milk and Honey*, Jews in the labor movement evoke strength and power in the face of the victim label engendered by events of the Holocaust. The labor movement was populated by active Jews, fighting for justice, the justice they could not get in Europe, a justice that neatly fits into the American success story.

Despite its inherent critique of turn-of-the-century America through the glorification of the socialist labor movement, *Rags* fundamentally demonstrates belief in the possibilities of the American dream, a dream which largely came true for American Jews — certainly by 1986 when the musical opened. Despite critical arguments that *Rags* was unrelentingly dark, its creators contend the musical offers a positive message of the possibilities of the American dream. As producer Lee Guber stated, "This isn't drum-beating or plastic patriotism. We see how tough and unforgiving things can be, but the people who came over here wearing rags had possibilities" (quoted in Klein, "Hoping to Turn *Rags* into Riches n. pag.). The libretto echoes his sentiments. When Avram, crushed by the death of his daughter, considers leaving America, Rebecca angrily argues, "Here they let you do anything. They don't make it easy for you, but they let you do it" (II-9-105)! David's generation offers the most possibility. He has already adapted to his surroundings early in the show, and in the last scene he uses the phrase "O.K.," explaining to his mother, "That's American, Mama" (II-10-106). In the closing sequence he and his mother sing triumphantly, that America now *belongs* to them. The authors don't seem to intend this collapsing of capitalistic ownership with Americanization satirically. Instead they uncritically celebrate a sense of personal destiny. Rebecca's dream, expressed in her anthem "Children of the Wind," to see generations of her family happily settled and grounded in one place, has come true. *Rags* presents an America that allows change, which treats immigrants harshly, but allows them eventually to prosper. The ultimate prosperity of American Jews allows this positivistic and nostalgic understanding of the immigrant era. The musical contrasts the promise of America with the desperate world the immigrants came from, and implicitly, with that world some 40 years later, the world of the Holocaust.

Rags brings to fruition what *Fiddler on the Roof* only implies. We find many intertextual echoes of *Fiddler on the Roof* in *Rags*. These resonances are not coincidental: Joseph Stein wrote both librettos, the second in response to the first. Stein resisted calls for a *Fiddler* sequel for over twenty years, but eventually, with *Rags*, he acquiesced. *Rags'* cannot help but recall *Fiddler*, echoing a process that occurs throughout the musical. Not only do we nostalgically recall the immigrant New York world through *Rags*, we also recall *Fiddler* and its own use of nostalgia. We feel nostalgia for our previous nostalgia. Alvin Klein, attending the Paper Mill production, witnessed the negative repercussions of this collapsing of *Rags* into *Fiddler*:

> To some observers, there is evidently no difference between Jews driven out of the shtetl and Jews unwelcome in a new land. Jews are Jews; oppression is oppression; a ghetto is a ghetto, and paradox is irrelevant ["After Anatevka" n. pag.].

Both musicals offer America as solution to oppression, even, paradoxically, oppression which *occurs* in America. By doing so, both offer an alternative narrative to Jews in a later era who could not escape oppression, and who did not make it to the American promised land.

Ragtime

Ragtime, which opened on Broadway in 1998, took a more commercially successful look at turn-of-the-century America. However, the musical considers immigration as only one among many themes. Both *Rags* and *Ragtime* share stories of the journey of Jewish immigrants to America, their encounters with the labor movement and the manner in which that movement intertwines with the myth or reality of the American Dream. *Ragtime* follows its Jewish immigrant character, Tateh, through a rags to riches story, from hope upon entering America, to desolation, and finally to financial success and acceptance into the larger American family. The musical evokes nostalgia of place less clearly than *Rags*, though a section does take place in the Lower East Side. *Ragtime* must therefore be examined in terms of its move away from its source material to a very particular political and cultural effect.

Ragtime is based on E.L. Doctorow's novel of the same name. Published in 1975, the book was highly acclaimed, winning the National Book Critics Circle Award, and becoming the bestselling novel of the year. The novel follows three groups of different races or ethnicities that come together into a small family, a microcosm of the blending nation. The novel's merger of fact and fiction presented its most unique aspect, with historical characters interacting with those created by Doctorow. Milos Forman's 1984 film version was a disappointment to many, including Doctorow, whose own screenplay Robert Altman was meant to film. The film reduced the vast panoply of characters that make up the Doctorow novel and focused more specifically on the story of Coalhouse Walker, an African-American musician turned revolutionary. The film ignored the narrative distance Doctorow employed in the novel. When it came time to write the musical's libretto in the 1990s, Terrence

McNally, the celebrated playwright hired to do the job, knew he needed to make use of this unique voice. He therefore incorporated direct address from individual characters to the audience, who spoke of themselves in third person and then entered their scenes. The creative team, with Garth Drabinsky, a particularly active producer, began working on a musicalization of Doctorow's novel in 1995, with the novelist's blessing. They went through the unique process of auditioning songwriting teams, asking for tapes of sample musical numbers emerging from McNally's early treatment. From this process, lyricist Lynn Ahrens and composer Stephen Flaherty were hired, whose previous hit, *Once on This Island*, opened in 1990. The musical had a long gestation period, including two public readings, a workshop, a CD released before the opening, a production in Toronto in December, 1996, and in L.A. in June, 1997. The publicity for *Ragtime* also included the building of a new Broadway theatre made of two older decaying houses, and re-christened the Ford Theatre after its sponsors — not-coincidentally portrayed in the musical. The musical opened in New York City in January 18, 1998, directed by Frank Galati, and musically staged by Graciela Danielle.

Synopsis

The musical opens with a little boy viewing his WASP community through a stereopticon. Groups of African-Americans and immigrants intrude on the placid scene. Each main character introduces themselves to the audience in the third person. Mother, Father, their son — The Little Boy — and Mother's Younger Brother are privileged white denizens of New Rochelle, New York; the musician Coalhouse Walker and Sarah, the mother of his child, are African American; and Tateh and his Little Girl are Jewish immigrants. Historical characters include Emma Goldman, Harry Houdini, Evelyn Nesbit, Booker T. Washington, Henry Ford, and J.P. Morgan. These groups physicalize their mutual distrust through musical staging ("Prologue"). Mother sends Father off on an expedition to the North Pole with Admiral Perry ("Goodbye My Love"). Leaving, he passes an immigrant rag ship coming to America with Tateh and his daughter on board ("Journey On"). We're introduced to the object of Younger Brother's lust, Evelyn Nesbit, in a vaudeville number. Her husband killed her lover in a shocking murder ("The Crime of the Century). While gardening in New Rochelle, Mother comes across an African American baby buried in the ground. When police apprehend the mother, Sarah, Mother takes responsibility for mother and child ("What Kind of Woman"). Tateh and his daughter arrive at Ellis Island, move to the Lower East Side, and are beaten down by poverty and destitution. Tateh resolves to leave the ghetto

and find his ideal America ("A Shtetl Iz Amereke" / "Success"). We meet Coalhouse Walker, a ragtime musician in love with Sarah. Although he treated her badly, he has repented and vows to find her ("Gettin' Ready Rag"). Henry Ford sings about the glorious assembly line process he invented, which turns every worker into a "cog in motion" ("Henry Ford"). Tateh encounters Mother on a train platform in New Rochelle, as he is heading out of the city. He is surprised to find her civil ("Nothing Like the City"). Sarah, alone in New Rochelle, sings to her baby ("Your Daddy's Son). Coalhouse, arriving in his new Model T Ford, finds Sarah. She refuses to see him, but he vows to continue visiting each week until she will ("The Courtship"). After weeks of visits, Mother invites Coalhouse inside, and he plays rag music on their piano, finally coaxing Sarah downstairs to see him. Father arrives home from the North Pole and is surprised how things have changed without him ("New Music"). Coalhouse takes Sarah on a picnic in his new car and they sing about the bright future they envision for their son ("Wheels of a Dream"). Emma Goldman narrates the horrifying conditions Tateh labors under in a mill in Lawrence, Massachusetts. Goldman's speech transforms Younger Brother at a rally in Union Square ("The Night that Goldman Spoke at Union Square"). Tateh, trying to send his daughter to the country to remove her from danger, jumps onto the train carrying her away at the last minute. To calm her down he shows he a picture book of silhouettes of an ice skater he has made for her ("Gliding"). Coalhouse and Sarah drive past a firehouse, and the racist firemen, led by Willie Conklin, trash his new Model T ("The Trashing of the Car"). Infuriated, Coalhouse vows not to marry Sarah until the wrong against him is righted ("Justice"). Sarah goes to see the Republican Vice-Presidential candidate speak, hoping to help Coalhouse receive his due, but when she tries to get the candidate's attention, the guards, nervous from the recent assassination of President McKinley, shoot her ("President"). Act I closes at Sarah's funeral where the community mourns and prays for a new day of justice ("Till We Reach That Day").

Act II opens with Coalhouse, distraught over Sarah's death, shooting firemen, and vowing to continue to do so until they restore his car and bring it back to him, along with Willie Conklin ("Coalhouse Demands"). Shocked over the news and worried about his family's involvement, Father attempts to regain normalcy by taking his son to a baseball game ("What a Game"). Events continuing to worsen, Father takes his family away ("Atlantic City"). There they meet Tateh, now calling himself the Baron Ashkenazy, whose entry

OPPOSITE: *Ragtime* (1998–2000 Broadway). Music by Stephen Flaherty Lyrics by Lynn Ahrens Book by Terrence McNally. Directed by Frank Galati. Shown center: Judy Kaye as Emma Goldman.

into the fledgling movie business has made him wealthy. He explains his success story and the name of his company ("Buffalo Nickel Photoplay Inc."). Mother and Tateh grow closer to each other while watching their children become friends ("Our Children"), and Tateh confesses his true immigrant identity to Mother. Younger Brother comes to Harlem looking for Coalhouse, who remembers the first day he met Sarah ("Sarah Brown Eyes"). Brought to Coalhouse, Younger Brother desperately wants to express his sense of kinship, but is able only to say, "I know how to blow things up" ("He Wanted to Say"). Mother and Father have grown apart, and she expresses the sense of her changing identity ("Back to Before"). Coalhouse and his men take over the J.P. Morgan Library, and with Younger Brother's help, threaten to blow it up if their demands are not met. The police bring Father in as a negotiator / hostage, and enlist Booker T. Washington to dissuade Coalhouse from his course ("Look What You've Done"). Convinced by Washington, Coalhouse agrees to leave the building, first instructing his men ("Make Them Hear You"). Against promises, the police shoot Coalhouse. In the final number each character again narrates their story. We hear that Father has died and Mother has married Tateh. Together they will raise Coalhouse and Sarah's baby. Their new blended family, combining each of the three major groups from the opening, walks off together into the American sunset ("Epilogue").

Although *Ragtime* was a modest hit, running 861 performances, the box office was not enough to pay back the investors (a scandal involving Drabinsky's falsification of financial statements and escape to Canada under charges of fraud were no help). Subsequent tours helped to redress the financial balance. The show was respected, although tepidly, by critics. Critic Vincent Canby's title in the *New York Times* sums up the general feeling: "Big and Beautiful, 'Ragtime' Never Quite Manages to Sing." Canby also states a recurring argument about Ahrens and Flaherty's music, "Towards the end of the show, the score has begun to sound like a non-stop series of personal epiphanies and gallant resolves to plug on to some better tomorrow" (207). Powerful *New York Times* critic Ben Brantley, while lauding the scope and ambitions of the project, asks why it feels "so utterly resistible," or, "has the aura of something assembled by corporate committee" (n. pag.). Critical response to Tateh's story also tended to the skeptical side. In an early review of the L.A. production, critic Steven Winn in the *San Francisco Chronicle* pointed out:

> Rubinstein's [the actor who played Tateh in San Francisco] scenes methodically click off his character's components. [...] His quirky success as a film director doesn't have a serendipitous kick; it's another line in his resume [n. pag].

Rick Simas in *Theatre Journal* points out that Tateh's transformation to the Baron and his marriage to Mother, "strains credibility" (542). Finally, of course, there were the inevitable comparisons to *Fiddler*. Brantley describes the Broadway performance of Peter Freidman who, "mostly resists the understandable temptation to play Tateh as Tevye in *Fiddler*" (n. pag.).

Source Material

Ragtime, unlike *Rags*, had a literary source to work from. It is therefore instructive to examine departures from that source. The musical smoothes over some of the novel's complexities, particularly the portrayal of Tateh and immigrant Jews. Critic Ben Brantley insightfully points out that the determined positivity of the Broadway show:

> is a far cry from a character's observation in the book that "the world composed and recomposed itself constantly in an endless process of dissatisfaction." Now dissatisfaction is not an emotion to make you sing and dance [n. pag.].

Audience expectations seem to be at the heart of the matter. As a vast generalization, musicals — with some exceptions, most obviously the Sondheim canon — tend not to blatantly question the political status quo or to forward anything other than a generally positive world-view. Audiences are taught not to expect to be challenged by a musical and instead hope to be uplifted, rather than "dissatisfied" by the form. *Ragtime* seems complicit with these expectations. Hischak argues, "The musical sometimes panders to a congenial public's desires. [...] The immigrants are usually as flawless as the WASP Americans are narrow and wrongheaded" (226). Hischak blames this on the fact that *Ragtime* "seems to have one eye on the box office at all times" (226), and in fact the heart of the musical's contentment with the status quo does seem to lie in financial and commercial concerns. Perhaps this was also due to the diverse American eras from which *Ragtime* emerged. 1975, the novel's cultural moment, allowed cynicism to dominate the American narrative. As Paul Levine states, "The concatenation of political events beginning with the Kennedy assassination and culminating in the Watergate scandal created a cultural climate more hospitable to a skeptical reading of the American past" (131). The climate was not as clear in 1998, requiring a more simplified reading of race relations and the immigrant past, at least in the realm of musical theatre. If the era when the novel was published allowed political cynicism, Levine argues, "McNally's musical play, produced in the Clinton era of centrist politics, is both politically correct and patriotically upbeat" (139). The Jewish characters clearly emerge from this upbeat, anthem-invoking outlook, allowing for easier, simpler immigrant nostalgia post–Holocaust.

Before we examine the central Jewish immigrant character Tateh, and his simplification from the novel, we should also acknowledge the presence of two other Jewish characters, the historical personages, Houdini and Emma Goldman. These characters stand for other aspects of the Jewish immigrant experience — show business and politics — and as with most historical characters in the piece they are also one-dimensional. Houdini, according to the libretto, " was one immigrant who made an art of escape" (I-4). Standing as the epitome of immigrant accomplishment, he comes to his fellow new Americans as they are crushed below a bridge carrying J.P. Morgan and other capitalist heavyweights in the musical number "Success," and encourages them to push the bridge up, by the strength of his example. Houdini's love for his stereotypically Jewish mother, whom we see speaking only in Yiddish, offers his most salient character trait. Meanwhile Emma Goldman's role consists largely of "watch[ing] her fellow immigrants' hopes turn to despair on the Lower East Side" (I-5). The real Goldman rejected her Jewish roots. Emma narrates Tateh's early immigrant story, but breaks off when he achieves success. Doctorow's novel offers a far more complete characterization, but the musical positions her as merely a stand-in for Jewish social liberalism or radicalism. However, these themes were largely whitewashed from the musical.

Doctorow's grandparents were Russian Jews, and, according to Clayton, "It is to the generation of immigrant Jews that Doctorow turns for his image of what Life is about" (111). Doctorow thus grants Tateh much more time and complex consideration in the novel. Doctorow's portrayal of the immigrant experience and the potential falsities or sacrifices that come with the American Dream, are particularly simplified in the musicalization. As such, the musicalized Tateh seems less complex than his fellow characters. The vast majority of the story, certainly in terms of stage time, follows Mother, Coalhouse, and Sarah. Tateh stands for American Jews' success story, and the musical limits his portrayal to the scenes that trace the outlines of that story. Coalhouse receives a more nuanced portrayal, although it certainly could be argued that the libretto also simplifies him. Although most of the characters are purposefully iconic, Tateh seems the most sketched in. When Emma Goldman asks him his name he replies, "They gave me a name I can't pronounce so you can call me Tateh like everyone else" (27). The dialogue ascribes his namelessness to the de-culturalizing process at Ellis Island: America has robbed him of his name, leaving him a universal Jewish immigrant. Tateh means father in Yiddish. This name allows him to stand more specifically for a universal Jewish father. *Ragtime* the musical re-inscribes this universalizing. Tateh makes silhouettes as a profession, and he is a silhouetted character. He points out the denizens of the Lower East Side in terms of his profession, and we don't hear the other silhouetted immigrant stories: Tateh presents our only connection to the complexity of Jewish immigrant life. Additionally, the musical removes some of the more inconvenient aspects of Tateh's story. For example in Doctorow's novel Tateh's wife has sex for money in desperation, forcing Tateh to shun her. In the musical we assume she is dead, left in the Old Country, or killed in a pogrom. The libretto only mentions that Tateh, "would not lose [his daughter], as he had her mother" (I-3). In "Gliding," he sings of his wife to comfort his daughter, leaving us again with the impression that she has passed away, untainted with the pain of American compromise.

One of the musical's most significant simplifications involves Tateh's political loyalties. Doctorow's novel portrays Tateh as a dedicated socialist who attends political meetings. His subsequent capitalist success carries layers of resultant complexity. Tateh's sympathies are simply not present in the musical. In fact, they are actively revoked. McNally's libretto has Tateh telling Emma Goldman, "I am an artist. I work for no one. Trade unions are fine but they are not for me. [...] I was in your socialist frying pan over there; I'm not jumping into the same fire over here" (27). Tateh leaves Lawrence, Massachusetts as the strike gets out of hand, and he repeatedly refuses Emma Goldman's radical stance. Tateh's abandonment of socialism emphasizes the positivistic nature of the American dream. It allows us to think that America as a nation simply allows success — with the right work ethic and the right luck — without the messy politics of injustice along the way. While the musical purports to be politically engaged with the struggles of immigrants, depicting the evils of J.P. Morgan and his confederates, and a convincing Emma Goldman, it de-politicizes our lead Jewish character. It seems that a commercial American musical can only question the basic American mythos so far, especially one premiering in the new Ford (motor company) Theatre. (Given the subject matter, the theatre was ironically named, as the libretto also whitewashes the character Henry Ford's notorious anti–Semitism). In fact, aside from Goldman, whose socialism is essentialized, only the African-American characters are allowed to test radical views. Those views, despite their celebration in a few rousing anthems, result in defeat and death. Therefore, while the novel follows the pattern we would expect from a radical Jewish humanistic standpoint, the musical fights it. Doctorow's novel does not offer a simple nostalgic narrative, while the musical's cleaned up narrative does. A more easy understanding of the immigrant success story allows nostalgia to come into play. While *Rags* embraces labor politics, *Ragtime* de-politicizes Tateh — offering essentially a paen to capitalism instead. Perhaps some of this difference can be attributed to the changing times, although the 1980s of *Rags* would seem more likely to embrace the capitalist ethos of *Ragtime*. Authorial views, appeals to simple audience approval and various other factors likely contributed. Regardless of explanation, this difference in basic attitudes strongly differentiates these musicals.

Score

Ragtime's score offers a complex source of memory and nostalgia, appropriate for a show whose very title offers a musical genre. As in Strouse's score for *Rags*, Flaherty examines the turn of the century evolution of American music. Flaherty uses musical style and genre to illustrate Tateh's path to Americanization. At first, Tateh does not take part in the dominant ragtime style of the score. Instead Flaherty utilizes leitmotif Jewish themes, perhaps evoking fleeting nostalgia. Typical Jewish melodies and instrumentation are associated with Tateh in the opening of "Success," where he also sings in Yiddish. "Gliding," which he sings to comfort his daughter while traveling on the train, presents the most significant use of music to evoke memory traces. The B section involves his memories of his wife (the Little Girl's mother) and this section changes from a major-key, waltz A section into a more evocative minor-key "Jewish" melody. This section was added to the score later, in order to redress the absence of Tateh's wife from the musical (Breyer). This redolent Jewish melody associated with loss, mourning, and memory for a Jewish mother and family, allows a powerfully nostalgic moment. By the time Tateh moves away from his roots and attains success, all traces of Jewish music are erased. Tateh's music has shifted to a vaudeville-esque, Broadway musical style, in "Buffalo Nickel Photoplay Inc." This use of musical style to underscore Tateh's rise through the ranks doubles the thematic concerns, demonstrating that distance from ethnic roots offers the quickest path to success. Although Tateh moves away from his Jewish identity, his metaphorical descendants in the audience, safe with the success he allowed them, could reclaim his story in easy nostalgic terms.

Nostalgia of Place

The editors of *Remembering the Lower East Side*, a book that emerged from a 1998 conference of the same name, agree that a resurgence of interest in the Lower East Side took place in the 1990s. While the Doctorow novel was published in 1974, the musical opened in New York in 1998, the same year as the conference. Perhaps the portrayal of Tateh's experience on the Lower East Side was at least partially influenced by this resurgence of interest. However, in *Ragtime*, Tateh and his daughter have a horrible experience with the neighborhood, and leave as soon as they are able. After entering through Ellis Island, Tateh and the Little Girl move to the Lower East Side, Tateh to sell his silhouettes. Times get harder and harder for Tateh. Emma Goldman narrates, "The angry, fetid tenements of the Lower East Side were worse than anything Tateh and his wife and suffered in Latvia. The little girl was often sick now. Tateh wrapped her in his prayer shawl. What rabbi would disapprove?" (29). Tateh's breaking point comes when a man offers to buy his daughter. Tateh has a musical collapse, sardonically echoing his earlier confidence that he will be a "success." However, temporary setbacks or disillusionment offer an essential part of the mythic American success story. Tateh revives his determination and tells his daughter, "I promised you America / and little one... We will find it" (32). Tateh experiences the same tribulations and difficulties as Rebecca in *Rags*, but in *Ragtime* Tateh does not stay to fight the system, or to triumph over it. To find America, in this tale, it is necessary to abandon the Lower East Side, to flee destitution and corruption. The specific nostalgia of place, however much it exists within this negative treatment, thereafter ceases in this production, replaced with a consideration of the larger American dream.

American Dream

Ragtime the musical ends with Tateh, now a successful film director and married to Mother, narrating:

> One afternoon, watching his children play, Tateh had an idea for a movie; a bunch of children, white, black, Christian, Jew, rich, poor — all kinds — a gang, a crazy gang [...] together despite their differences. He was sure it would make a wonderful movie — a dream of what this country could be. He would be first in line to see it [II-114].

This vision (humorously referencing "Our Gang") has indeed come true for Tateh, prompting the question: does *Ragtime* present the path to integration and the "American Dream" as achievable or as fantasy? To investigate, we need to consider Tateh's journey, the larger arc of which offers a clichéd success story.

We first see Tateh on line to board a rag ship, *"poorly clothed and undernourished [...] Tateh looks old and we will think he is the little Girl's grandfather"* (I-3). Next we see him hopeful on the ship, passing Father in the night, excited about the possibilities for success in the new world. Father thinks he doesn't have a chance, but Tateh tells his daughter, "America is our shtetl" (12). We next find Tateh and his daughter at Ellis Island where, *"waves of immigrants are arriving and waiting for processing. They will go through a series of massive, foreboding gates"* (24). They sing "A Shtetl Is Amerike," partially in Yiddish. The nostalgic power of language combines here with other immigrants' memory, in a simultaneous section in Italian and Haitian. Like a linguistic tower of Babel, an aural melting pot, this section underscores the chaos at arrival and the myriad groups hoping to be Americanized. Tateh holds great hope for their prospects in America, and elaborates an acquisitive American dream, detailing the luxuries he will provide for his daughter. Although we fear Tateh's confidence is naïve, based on the understood story of Jewish American success, we assume he will eventually achieve the success he predicts.

First however, Tateh must be tested. Times get harder, until conditions drive him to leave the Lower East Side. We next find Tateh on a train platform, encountering Mother and The Little Boy, in the process further emphasizing Tateh's ritualized success story. At his lowest Mother would never romantically or sexually consider him, she views the very idea as impossible:

> THE LITTLE BOY: We know those people.
> MOTHER: That's ridiculous. They're poor foreigners.
> THE LITTLE BOY: Then we're going to know them [40].

Despite Mother's dismissal, Tateh ends the musical her husband, making sexualized acceptance part of his success story.

After a long break we find Tateh has made his way to Lawrence, Massachusetts, where he works in a sweatshop at the center of strike agitation and violence. The gruesome description of his desperate labors contributes to his ultimate success story. Emma Goldman tells us that he, "stands at a loom sixty-four hours a week. His fingers were bleeding. I almost did not recognize him. [...] He looked like his own daughter's grandfather" (52). Although he has already abandoned his connection to socialism, Emma uses Tateh as a universal symbol for labor agitation. However, we only have the barest sense of him in Lawrence, the mythic outlines of struggle, without its specificity. Tateh plans to send his daughter away from danger, but when violence breaks out on the platform he reaches his lowest point, shouting, "I hate you, goddamned America!" (56). He then makes the pivotal decision to join his daughter on the train, leaving his job behind. When Tateh and his daughter get off the train the conductor wants to buy his silhouette book, beginning his meteoric rise. Tateh's momentary despair and hatred of America rebounds to optimism almost immediately, and his joy echoes the commodification of the American dream, "We'll make more of these [movie books] and sell them for two dollars. [...] Everyone will want them. They just don't know that yet!" (59).

This scene underscores the subliminal message that America measures success by how far you can get from your roots, your identity, and other immigrants. Tateh's story is one of travel, of distancing, of running away. *Ragtime* presents distancing as Americanization. Tateh ends both verses of "Gliding" with the firm promise to never dwell in the painful past. When we next see Tateh he has indeed distanced himself. A famous early movie director, he now masquerades as the "Baron Ashkenazy." The name is carefully chosen, for Ashkenazic Jews are the subset of Eastern European Jews. So while Tateh hides his identity, those in the know would understand that he was Jewish, that in fact, he stands for a universal Eastern European Jewish immigrant. Now when he encounters Mother he impresses her with his status, and they exhibit immediate attraction. Tateh boasts of his financial success, telling Mother his first two picture plays were made for five hundred dollars and made ten thousand back, an ultimate expression of the capitalist ideals of the American dream. He tells of his success in cinematic terms, and his success indeed echoes a movie. Doctorow's novel presents this cinematic quality ironically, but the musical seems to take it at face value. Still in Atlantic City, the "Baron" and Mother come closer by singing, "Our Children," which again underscores Tateh's need to distance himself from his immigrant past. Tateh confesses his true identity to Mother, but only as a secret:

> I'm a poor immigrant, a Jew, who points a camera so that his child can dress as beautifully as a princess. I want to drive from her memory every tenement stench and filthy immigrant street. [...] Now you know me. Now you understand. I am no baron. I am Tateh [93].

Tateh makes his final appearance in the multi-ethnic walk into the sunset that ends the musical. *Ragtime* opens with three separate ethnic groups, but ends with imagery of inclusion, when the newly combined family, "*walks off into the future*" (II-114). Uncomplicated by the subtlety of the novel's narrative, this imagery encourages the musical's audience, telling of the potential of America, at least for Jews. In this manner the musical re-inscribes the myth of the American dream; not a myth, in fact, for many Jewish immigrants. Tateh enjoys immediate success; many immigrants had to wait for later generations to achieve the kind of financial rewards he receives in a matter of years. Still Jewish immigration to America largely tells a success story. In view of our knowledge of that achievement, the musical's final imagery of inclusion does not in fact read as fantasy, as Neil Gabler claims. Sentimental nostalgia allows hardships, waiting to exult in accomplishment, and knowledge of the modern Jewish success story colors nostalgia. In Bilik's terms, Tateh is an immigrant survivor — an easier kind of survivor, standing in for a much more painful and difficult Holocaust survivor. His immigrant pain and suffering offers a far reduced version of Holocaust suffering — more palatable, as we know he will endure and in fact flourish. As *Fiddler* implies, America offers the immigrant survivor trials and tribulations, but these obstacles are surmountable. In these musicals, America offers the solution.

Ragtime's self-aware portrayal of the turn-of-the-century, a more "innocent" time when the "crime of the century" was a murder of a lover by a husband, also senses the hovering menace of that innocence's destruction. Several times The Little Boy urgently tells Houdini to "Warn the Duke!" (4), a hint that World War I rapidly approaches, through its reference to the assassination of Archduke Franz Ferdinand. This intimation points to the horrors of the century of war and genocide that will be unleashed in 1914. The first World War's link to the second, which engendered the Holocaust, should not be overlooked here. In one other scene we sense the possibilities of the Holocaust: the song "Gliding," Tateh's lullaby sung to calm his daughter. The song is staged on the back of a train, an image staged with impressively technical skill in *Ragtime*. Can we help but to associate violence against Jews with train platforms, one of the enduring images of the Holocaust burned into modern consciousness? The possibilities are subtle, but present nonetheless. The beautiful soothing imagery of "Gliding" can be disturbing, contextualized against train imagery and its potential associations.

Conclusion

Immigrants from this early period largely present an American success story. While Jewish immigrants went through a painful hazing process including anti–Semitism and life-threatening violence, in America, they emerge a success. As with *Fiddler on the Roof*, which offered America as a solution, the obsession with the Jewish immigrant period hints at the pain of the Holocaust but offers a transference to a happy ending — an ending suitable to a commercial American art form largely created by Jews who were inheritors of those immigrants. A large-scale substitution occurs in these stories. By the 1980s and 90s, when the establishment of the Americanization of the Holocaust was firmly in place, we instead embrace these stories of an earlier period. In this safer, more sanitized era, Jewish characters leave the Europe that was to be caught in the flames of war and escape to a land where, after some pain, success was more or less assured.

We have discussed themes which *Rags* and *Ragtime* share: an examination of the American Dream, nostalgia for the immigrant past, often located in the Lower East Side, and an interest in radical Jewish humanism and the labor movement. However, the musicals treat these themes quite differently. Both attempt to present inspirational ending images, *Rags* of Americanized immigrants in front of the Statue of Liberty, and *Ragtime* of a multi-cultural family walking into the sunset. However, *Rags* tells a much darker tale of hardship than *Ragtime*. Given their respective content, *Ragtime*'s image convinces more than *Rags*. *Ragtime* presents a rosier, more attainable, and more *universal* American dream than *Rags*, and was also far more commercially successful.

This cannot be a coincidence. And yet, simultaneously *Rags* more straight-forwardly evokes Jewish nostalgic sites: the Lower East Side, the labor movement. Those nostalgic sites are critical, for they allow a virtual trip to the old neighborhood and an ethnic community that many feared was in danger of disappearing altogether. Regardless of their differences or their approaches, the two musicals both emerge from a nostalgic need to remember the immigrant period. With a firm rooting in postmemory, including cautious substitutions for the pain and agony engendered by the Nazi era, these musicals examine a time before the Jewish American success story truly took root, but where, in contrast to the Holocaust, success and triumph were imminently possible, even assured.

CHAPTER VIII

The Producers

"Don't be stupid, be a smartie, Come and join the Nazi party."
— Song lyric, *The Producers* (1968)

On March 17, 2002, the Jewish Museum in Manhattan opened an exhibition entitled, "Mirroring Evil: Nazi Imagery/Recent Art," to a maelstrom of criticism. Concentration camp survivors picketed outside the museum, protesting the exhibitions' perceived trivialization of the horrors of the Holocaust through its ironic, rebellious and at times humorous images of Nazi perpetrators. While this controversy raged, fifty blocks south Mel Brooks' smash hit musical *The Producers*, with its far from politically correct portrayal of Nazism, was running to great acclaim and virtually no protest. In fact, audiences were scrambling for tickets and paying literally hundreds of dollars for the chance to see pigeons with Nazi arm bands, a production number featuring a large twirling swastika à la Busby Berkeley, and a Judy Garlandesque Hitler. Brooks' portrayal of Nazis and Nazi themes can be argued to be vastly more transgressive than some of the art works at the Jewish Museum, and yet *The Producers* seemed to escape the anger incited by the "Mirroring Evil" exhibit. Other musicals we have examined here contain only resonances of the Holocaust, but *The Producers* approaches Nazism head on, albeit surprisingly, through trangressive humor. This chapter explores the complicated multi-layer satire in Brooks' hit, as well as its place in our culture's fascination with both the Nazi era and with one of the few fully American art forms, the Broadway musical. *The Producers'* equation of show business with fascism, and in turn, fascism with sex, presents layers of signification not fully recognized in the popular and critical response to the musical.

The Producers, in its Broadway musical incarnation, reflects a 21st century where the link between Nazi representations and the Holocaust, between

172

Nazis and anti–Semitism, has been firmly established. The period of silence regarding Nazi crimes had long since ended. In fact a veritable cultural saturation now exists. It is hard to go a week without seeing some mention of the Holocaust or Nazism, either in the press, on the television screen, at the movies, or at the theatre. Contemporary popular representations assume a high level of familiarity with the catastrophic events of the Holocaust. *The Producers* offers an example of the saturation of, and changing attitudes towards, Nazi representations in our culture.

Background

Mel Brooks, born Melvin Kaminsky in Brooklyn in 1926, began his career as a stand-up comedian, heavily influenced by both vaudeville and Borscht Belt traditions. In the 1950s and 60s he worked as a writer on such TV series as *Your Show of Shows* and *Get Smart*, and in 1963 earned critical success for his Oscar winning animated short *The Critic*. His first feature film, *The Producers*, opened on May 18, 1968, starring Zero Mostel as producer Max Bialystock and Gene Wilder as accountant Leo Bloom who together come up with a money-making scheme to over-finance "the worst show ever written," and abscond to Rio with the money. The show they choose is entitled "Springtime for Hitler: A Gay Romp with Adolf and Eva in Berchtesgaden." In the film incarnation of *The Producers*, Bialystock casts the appropriately named hippie, "LSD," to play Hitler, but LSD's unwittingly humorous performance grants the show hit status, landing Bialystock and Bloom in Sing Sing prison.

Initial response to the film varied. According to film scholar Lester Friedman, the Jewish community felt, "shock, horror, dismay and embarrassment" (188), toward Brooks' flights of comic fancy. As one would expect, *The Producers*' humorous Nazi representations were vastly more shocking in 1968, a period marked by slowly changing attitudes towards the Holocaust and the troubled moral ambiguity it evoked, than they are today. The film's distributor prevailed upon Brooks to change the title of the movie from *Springtime for Hitler* to *The Producers*, for fear of potential backlash. Roger Ebert relates a story of an encounter in an elevator between Brooks and a woman disapproving of the film who said, "'I have to tell you, Mr. Brooks, that your movie is vulgar.' Brooks retorted [...] 'Lady, it rose below vulgarity'" (quoted in Zelizer 1). Many critics attacked Brooks' bad taste in their primarily mixed reviews. Renata Adler, the *New York Times* film critic, typified such a response:

> Strangely enough, the first act of "Springtime for Hitler" [...] is the funniest part of this fantastically uneven movie [...] "The Producers," leaves one alternately picking up one's coat to leave and sitting back to laugh [Adler n. pag.].

Audiences generally accepted the film, despite its potentially shocking content. Brooks had his timing just right; many Americans were able to understand and then embrace the source of his humor. Public response to Brooks' movie mirrored the pivotal moment in the film where "Springtime for Hitler's" first night audience initially reacts with open-mouthed shock and then hilarity. The film became a commercial success, and Brooks received an Oscar that year for Best Screenplay.

Fast forward to the year 2000, when, after numerous film successes including *Blazing Saddles* (1973) and *Young Frankenstein* (1974), Mel Brooks decided to musicalize his first movie. He worked with musical supervisor, Glen Kelly, to embellish and orchestrate his newly written score, and asked Thomas Meehan, a collaborator on several of Brooks' films, to help him adapt the screenplay into a format more suitable for the musical stage. Susan Stroman directed and choreographed the production, taking on the directorial reigns after the original director, her husband, Mike Ockrent, passed away during the early stages of the process. Critics agreed that Stroman could be granted much of the credit for the success of the project, due to her inventive staging and keen eye for the requirements of the musical stage, as opposed to the cinematic demands with which Brooks was familiar. *The Producers* opened April 19, 2001. Twelve Tony Awards, two more than the previous record, record high ticket prices and sales, and virtually unanimous rave reviews kept the show running for six years, and the musical closed April 22, 2007. In 2005, Brooks' team brought their Broadway musical back to its roots in cinema, opening the new film of *The Producers*. The musical's creative team dominated the film, including Brooks and Meehan's virtually identical script, Susan Stroman as director, and most of the same cast, excepting additions Will Ferrell as Franz Liebkind and Uma Thurman as Ulla. This dizzying new phenomenon of a movie musical version of a stage musical, based on a movie, allowed imbricated layers of intertextual nostalgia.

Synopsis

The Producers' last two incarnations, in addition to further musicalizing the script, made significant plot alterations from the original film, which necessitate a synopsis here. The curtain opens as the audience for *Funny Boy*, the musical version of *Hamlet* produced by Max Bialystock, exits the theatre, exclaiming that it was "the worst show in town" ("Opening Night"). Bialystock emerges from hiding and seeks sympathy from street dwellers, singing of his past theatrical glories ("The King of Broadway"). The next morning, accountant Leo Bloom visits Bialystock's office to do his books. They are interrupted by the elderly woman Bialystock calls "Hold Me, Touch Me," one of his regular backers, who wants to play one of their "dirty little games" (82) in exchange for her financial support. After she leaves, Bloom muses offhandedly that a producer could make more money on a Broadway flop than on a hit. Bialystock seizes on this idea and tries to convince Bloom to join him in the scheme ("We Can Do It"). Bloom refuses and returns to work, where he dreams of becoming a Broadway producer, accompanied by imaginary showgirls ("I Wanna Be a Producer"). He summons up the courage, quits his job and joins Bialystock. They proceed to find the worst show ever written, "Springtime for Hitler," and rush off to get the rights from its author, Franz Liebkind. We discover Liebkind on his Greenwich Village roof, tending to his fascist pet pigeons and singing of his beloved Germany ("In Old Bavaria"). In order to grant the producers the rights to his show, Liebkind demands that they don swastika arm bands and join him in singing the Führer's favorite song ("Der Guten Tag Hop Clop"). After securing the rights, they head over to the townhouse of Roger De Bris, the worst director in town, in order to obtain his services. We meet Roger, his "common-law assistant" Carmen Ghia, and his entirely homosexual design staff who decide to take on the production under the lure of a Tony Award ("Keep It Gay"). When Bialystock and Bloom return to their office, a well-endowed Swedish blonde named Ulla has come to audition ("When You Got It, Flaunt It"). Bialystock heads to "Little Old Lady Land," trading sexual favors to septuagenarians to raise money ("Along Came Bialy").

Act II begins by exploring the burgeoning attraction between Ulla and Leo ("That Face"). At auditions for the role of Hitler, the prospects are unsatisfactory until Liebkind reveals his suitability for the role by angrily demonstrating one of the candidate's audition songs ("Haben Sie Gehört das Deutsche Band"). Several weeks later, opening night arrives. As the cast members and production staff enter the theatre, Max shouts "good luck" to all while Roger explains to Leo the perils of that phrase ("It's Bad Luck to Say Good Luck on Opening Night"). When Leo instead states "Break a Leg" to Liebkind, the author/star does that very thing, and Carmen exhorts Roger to take over the eponymous role. Finally the curtain opens on the centerpiece show within a show and we witness "Springtime for Hitler" in all its glory, including showgirls with sausage, beer, and pretzel headdresses, a challenge tap between Hitler and the Allied leaders, and a Busby Berkeley production number crowned by a swastika reflected in a giant mirror ("Springtime for Hitler"). After the show becomes a surprise hit, Bialystock and Bloom run to their office in shock and terror ("Where Did We Go Right?"). Liebkind bursts in with a gun but the police interrupt, and cart Franz and Bialystock to jail. Ulla enters and convinces Leo, who has escaped, to flee to Rio with her and

the money. Weeks later, the incarcerated Max receives a postcard from the lovers and recounts his bitterness ("Betrayed"). At Max's trial, Leo and Ulla make a surprise appearance and Leo sings of how Max changed his life ("Till Him"). Leo accepts responsibility and goes to jail with Max. In Sing Sing the producers put on a musical ("Prisoners of Love"), and are released on its merits to bring the show to Broadway where it becomes a smash hit ("Leo and Max").

Nostalgia

Although initially *The Producers'* nostalgia appears less specifically Jewish themed than in the other musicals we have examined, the nostalgic locus evoked can be read in Jewish terms. *The Producers* offers communal memory for a specifically Jewish site such as Israel, the shtetl or the Lower East Side: the golden age Broadway musical. Andrea Most tells us:

> We have learned how to "see" Jews by seeing musical theater and that the musical theater exists because of the unique historical situation of the Jews who created it. The social reality of being a Jew in America is fundamentally inscribed in the form of the American musical theater [7].

In other words, *The Producers* recalls a Jewish musical theatre glory age. Here again, Bial's double coding proves helpful. Wider audiences can nostalgically embrace the memories of Broadway's heyday for its general cultural resonances, while Jewish audiences can recall that the vast majority of the form's authors in that period (and today) were Jewish. Those authors allowed their specifically Jewish sensibility to shine through their work, even in a subtle way. Jewish audiences therefore are afforded a particular source of memory and cultural pride within the larger nostalgic context.

The Producers contains a double layer of parody, first of Nazism, secondly of the Broadway musical. Brooks parodies the form of musical theatre while working within it. As Ben Brantley states, "*The Producers* is more packed with steals and references than a deconstructionist's college term paper" ("Scam" E1). Virtually the entire musical delights in its status as meta-theatre, in its gloriously abandoned self-referential theatricality, from the allusion to *Fiddler on The Roof* in "The King of Broadway," to a dancing Hitler audition scene à la *A Chorus Line*; to set designer Robin Wagner's homage paid to the latter show's tilting mirror (which he himself designed) and to *Guys and Dolls* and *Follies*; to Brooks' tribute to *42nd Street* where Carmen convinces Roger to

OPPOSITE: *The Producers* (2005). (Film) Directed by Susan Stroman. Shown: "Springtime for Hitler" production number. Shown center left, standing: Cady Huffman as Ulla; center: Gary Beach as Roger DeBris; center right, standing: John Barrowman as Lead Tenor.

take over the role of Hitler by inspiringly stating, "You're going out there a silly hysterical screaming queen and you're coming back a great big passing-for-straight Broadway star!!" (178). Critics have also pointed out allusions to "Rose's Turn," from *Gypsy* and *How to Succeed in Business Without Really Trying*, among others.

To begin, the premise and execution of the 1968 film illustrates this nostalgic love of show business. As film reviewer A. O. Scott tells us in the *New York Times*, "Some of the big laugh lines have been provoking groans since the first, nonmusical *Producers* movie way back in 1968, and probably even longer, since even that film was a fond, nostalgic embrace of a dying show business tradition" (10). With the passage of time, the 2001 stage version allows the original film to in turn act as a focus for self-referential metatheatre. While Brooks felt comfortable enough to change various plot points, he still made sure to offer fans of the film enough references and in-jokes to make them happy. For instance, in response to the opening number "King of Broadway," one of the ensemble offers the aside, "It's good to be the King," famous from Brooks' film *History of the World* (1981). *The Producers* even included an actor lip-synching to a stage recording of Brooks' voice on the famous line, "Don't be stupid, be a smartie, come and join the Nazi party" (182). By offering glimpses of himself and his past work, Brooks encouraged intertextual memories and never allowed the audience to forget the musical's origins.

Although an extended analysis of the 2005 filmic *The Producers* lies outside the scope of this work, it is necessary to acknowledge that the movie increased the self-referentiality already present in the multiple incarnations of Brooks' work. The 2005 film followed quickly on the heels of the 2001 stage musical and took an extremely faithful, if not slavish adherence to details of the stage musical. The 2005 film also made a case for a more potent source of nostalgia: old Hollywood movie musicals. The latest film resonates more strongly with old Hollywood than the 1968 film and the 2001 musical, allowing persuasive cinematic nostalgia. Busby Berkeley references, for instance, have power on stage, but on film the relationship encourages direct memory. Director Stroman, new to the film genre, purposefully used techniques and visual choices inspired by classic movie musicals. Brooks underscores this emphasis on golden age Hollywood musicals and demonstrates his artistic intentions and inspirations by the simple statement, "I think we're right up there with *Singin' in the Rain*" (quoted in Arnold n. pag.).

Nostalgia for a musical golden age, be it stage or screen, intimately ties to the Jewish roots of musical theatre. Brooks' work demonstrates his pride in his Jewishness, according Michael Elkin in the *Jewish Bulletin*, "Sure it's good to be king, but, according to Brooks, it's even better to be Jewish: 'If You're Jewish, you have a small smile on your face'" (quoted in Elkin n. pag.).

Judaism maintains a presence in *The Producers*; both the eponymous characters are clearly, although never explicitly stated, assimilated New York theatre Jews, in the fashion of Mel Brooks himself. The happy ending of the show displays a lit up marquee of Leo and Max's future Broadway hits, all Judaized version of famous shows including: *Katz*, *High Button Jews*, *She Schtups to Conquer*, and *A Streetcar Named Murray*. In fact, *The Producers*, particularly the 1968 film version, has been accused of perpetuating negative Jewish stereotypes. Scholar Lester Friedman comments that, "the two failed impresarios embodied a virtual compendium of negative Jewish clichés and were willing for their own purposes to put a spectacle about Hitler on stage to make a few bucks" (188). *The Guardian*'s Michael Billington, however, argues that the titles are, "Tasteless? Possibly. But I suspect it is Mel Brooks's final comment on Broadway's ability to turn everything into show business" (n. pag.). Regardless of potential offense, Brooks clearly intends these titles and *The Producers*' Jewish context to affectionately evoke nostalgia for a period he loves and glorifies.

Comedic Nostalgia

Brooks' use of comedic genres intimately ties into the Jewishness of *The Producers*. Brooks came from the "Borscht Belt" school of comedy, a tradition of Jewish comics who performed in New York's Catskill Mountains, a Jewish summer vacation region at its peak from the 1920s through the 1960s. Comics such as Sid Caesar, Alan King, Buddy Hackett, Jackie Mason, Joan Rivers, Danny Kaye, Jerry Lewis, and Milton Berle all shared a formative experience in the Borscht Belt and similar comic stylings of the "set it up, knock it down" school. This specifically Jewish sensibility also combined with roots in vaudeville and burlesque, as these influences moved into the musical theatre. Brooks' bio for the show points out that he is a, "Comedy writer-director whose satiric tough and farcical stylings are influenced both by vaudeville and Borscht Belt shtick" (producersonbroadway.com). The musical embraces Brooks' background with recognizable jokes and set-ups from those traditions. These influences combine to provoke nostalgic associations with many of these old forms, kept alive by Brooks' success on Broadway. These comedic traditions, most particularly the Yiddish theater, Catskills comedy, and the 1950s variety show, are largely Jewish created forms. *The Producers* allows nostalgia for Jewish old-school humor genres not in circulation in their pure forms anymore. Audiences can appreciate this humor, while groaning at its age, feeling a wistful twinge of memory for the more innocent age these genres flourished, and for the Jewish community they evoke. The Catskills resorts and the early age of television existed in the same era as the golden age of the Broadway musical, an age *The Producers* hearkens back to on several levels.

Mel Brooks combines this comedy background with his own particular brand of over-the-top, far from politically correct humor. As Brustein points out, "Let us concede that insensitivity and bad taste are inseparable from the production. [...] Let us also concede that Brooks's willingness to give offense is the primary reason why this event is proving so exhilarating" (1). Brooks himself, when working on the musical version of *The Producers* states, "I have never been politically correct. I'm not going to change my spots and become a nice person in my old age. I'm working hard so that sensitive souls will be outraged" (quoted in Mesic 2). *The Producers* employs all-purpose offense to every group it addresses: homosexuals, women, Jews and even old ladies. By doing so in such an unabashed manner, Brooks aims, and primarily succeeds, at offending no one. Brooks' methods include "slamming over corny jokes, puerile double entendres, and silly sight gags" (www.theproducersonbroadway.com). Indeed, the vast majority of *The Producers* takes place on a purely comedic level, including slapstick, sight gags and "in-jokes" for fans of Brooks' films. But these farcical stylings are not the only form of humor in the piece. Brooks makes use of satire against Nazis in order to provide deeper resonances not always noted in *The Producers*.

Nazi Humor and Postmemory

Theorists have begun to examine the use of humor in response to the Holocaust, yet how can we examine this issue after discussing the nostalgic elements of *The Producers*? How can nostalgia be present alongside transgressive subject matter? As Fred Davis tells us in his study of nostalgia:

> Almost anything from our past can emerge as an object of nostalgia, provided that we can somehow view it in a pleasant light. (This effectively eliminates from nostalgia's universe such grotesque possibilities as a "nostalgia" for the ovens at Auschwitz or for the bomb at Hiroshima) [Davis viii].

No one longs to return to the Holocaust, or feels bittersweet recollections of horrific events like those that occurred at Auschwitz; the very idea offends. However a work like *The Producers* approaches the perpetrators of the Holocaust, in the context of a highly nostalgic musical. How can these two sides of the musical be joined or explained? In order to answer this question we must discuss Brooks' use of transgressive humor.

Satire has been one of Brooks' favored methods throughout his career, particularly against Nazism. In addition to *The Producers*, he wrote many anti–Nazi pieces in the 1950s for *Your Show of Shows*, ridiculed Nazis in his remake of the film *To Be or Not to Be* (1983), and wrote a video, *The Hitler Rap*, for MTV. He makes no bones against making fun of Germans:

> Why should I not like Germans? Just because they're arrogant and have fat necks and do anything they're told so long as it's cruel and killed millions of Jews in concentration camps and made soap out of their bodies and lampshades out of their skins? Is that any reason to hate their guts? [quoted in Elkin n. pag.].

Brooks further states, "If you can laugh at your enemy, you've won" *(Recording The Producers)*. Brooks had early practice at writing German buffoons in *Your Show of Shows*, and he continues that trend in *The Producers*, where he uses laughter as a weapon to exorcize any lingering power or allure of fascism. By doing so, *The Producers* flies against traditional comic theory. Plato states that "the object of ridicule must not have the power to harm, or else fear will prevent laughter" (quoted in Gerould 4). W.H. Auden also famously argued that Hitler cannot be humorous, that we cannot find an object of hatred comic (Gerould 4). Brooks, on the other hand, opines, "You can't compete with a despot on a soapbox [...] The best thing is to make him ludicrous" (quoted in Zoglin n. pag.). This attitude places Brooks' work within the tradition of comedy of tyranny, as examined by Daniel Gerould, which includes such plays as Jarry's *Ubu Roi* (1896) and Brecht's *The Resistible Rise of Arturo Ui* (1941). Gerould states, "comedy [...] is the best antidote to the tyrant's pretenses to grandeur because the comic spirit revels in universal pettiness and vulgar complicity, reducing the mighty dictator to a properly banal, everyday plane" (9). Brooks manages to make petty, banal fools of Hitler and his followers, using a wide range of comic techniques.

The central conceit of *The Producers* depends on the shocking idea of Nazis in a musical, so shocking in fact that Max and Leo can assume with justification that "Springtime for Hitler" will offend absolutely everyone and close right away. However, in the show within a show, the audience loves "Springtime for Hitler," just as in the real world, people have joyously accepted and loved *The Producers*. There has been, however, a sense of unease on certain fronts, from several critics, and, in my own completely unscientific survey of audience members, from several attendees of *The Producers*. What exactly are we laughing at?

Holocaust Humor

A summation of academic and critical response to Holocaust humor outside the musical genre will contextualize our study of *The Producers*. Sidra

DeKoven Ezrahi, in her article, "After Such Knowledge, What Laughter," divides two competing forms which address Holocaust art: "those who deny the value of any representation that does not confront its audience with raw suffering and unmediated evil agency, and those who countenance what I would call a more liberated and mediated engagement with history" (295). The comic fits into the second category. Comedy certainly presents a problematic genre from which to confront horrific events. Terrence Des Pres, in his article on "Holocaust Laughter," remarks on the three unwritten rules of Holocaust literature and study: first that the Holocaust must be referred to as an entirely unique event which admits no comparisons, second that representations must be unfailing in their factualness, unerringly faithful to the details of the events, and most importantly, that, "the Holocaust shall be approached as a solemn, or even a sacred event, admitting of no response that obscures its enormity or dishonors its dead" (278). Comedy breaks each of these rules and proves highly problematic. Despite these complications, Des Pres surmises that in some ways the comic offers an effective means of representation, "Comic works, on the contrary, make no attempt at actual representation. Laughter, in this case, is hostile to the world it depicts. It is free as tragedy and lamentation are not" (280). Des Pres refers here to humor in the absurd vein, one of the few comic styles applied directly to the Holocaust. He discusses Art Spiegelman's "comix" rendering of his father's Holocaust experience in *Maus* (1986), and Leslie Epstein's *King of the Jews* (1979), a "comic" Holocaust novel. Given these examples, Des Pres goes on to argue the viability of a comic treatment of the Holocaust, which distances the traditional tragic emotions of pity and fear:

> The paradox of the comic approach is that by setting things at a distance it permits us a tougher, more active response [...] they give us laughter's benefit without betraying our deeper conviction. They foster resilience and are life-reclaiming [286].

Sander Gilman emphasizes the distinction between the "comic" and laughter, arguing that most Holocaust comic representations, including fiction, choose not to provoke actual laughter, arguing that, "all assume that the author and the reader [...] will not laugh, even at the comic turns of the fiction" (283).

What about other uses of the comic and the Holocaust, representations which intentionally cause laughter? In *The New Yorker*, Peter Schjeldahl, referring to both the stage and film versions of *The Producers*, argues one explanation for laughter, "as an explosive release from anxiety. We were afraid that Adolf Hitler would keep making us feel bad forever, but you know what? He's dead, and we're not" (87). Alan Cowell, writing about the differing responses to Holocaust humor in Germany and America, has a slightly different take on the matter. He argues, "Humor offers Americans an easier, more liberating perspective than is available to Germans, for whom the Hitler years remain a source of deep, complex and agonized emotional entanglement" (2). He states that Americans have more distance from the events, which makes it easier to laugh at them. While this is certainly true, Americans have taken upon themselves an equal sense of holiness and sanctification around the Holocaust that continues to make the comic problematic. We do not consider the Holocaust, and by extension, Nazi representations, to be funny. Or at least, we believe they *shouldn't* be, despite examples that *are* demonstrably funny. As Sheng-Mei Ma states, "A sense of moral indignation shrouds the Holocaust, precluding certain approaches to this subject in both artistic expression and scholarly pursuit" (49). Due to this constraint, Ma argues, comic treatments of Nazism and Hitler that were possible before the facts of the Shoah were known, or even perpetrated such as Charlie Chaplin's melodramatic yet light-hearted satire of Hitler, *The Great Dictator* (1940), are now impossible.

Ma ignores post-war popular representations that are very similar to Chaplin's, for instance Brooks' *The Producers.* This scholarly absence points to the necessity of distinguishing between two types of Holocaust comic representations. First are the comic representations of which the scholars speak, humor which directly address the grimmer realities of the Holocaust. This tradition includes work on concentration camp prisoners' "gallows humor" and continues into the realm of higher culture. Art Spiegelman's comic book renderings of his father's concentration camp experience, in *Maus* (I in 1986, and II in 1991) are most often mentioned in this category. Although critics discuss Spiegelman's work in the context of mass culture, it is certainly not sold next to "Superman" or "X-Men." *Maus* fits more clearly into the genre of high culture Holocaust literature addressed by critics of humor of the Holocaust, including Tadeusz Borowski's *This Way for the Gas, Ladies and Gentlemen* (1948), Jurek Becker's *Jakob the Liar* (1969), and Leslie Epstein's *King of the Jews* (1979). Although these works are much studied, they are less present in the general public's awareness. An example of perhaps the first direct *popular* comic reaction to the Holocaust, Roberto Benigni's film *Life Is Beautiful* (1997), ignited much controversy. Maurizio Viano, in his article, "Life Is Beautiful: Reception, Allegory, and Holocaust Laughter," perceived a critical split in reaction to the film, "An examination of the critical judgments on *Life is Beautiful,* conventionally framed within a low-, middle-, and highbrow hierarchy, reveals that, [...] the higher the re/viewer's position, the more negative the re/view" (28). Musicals are often placed in the "low-brow" category although they are often granted higher status than media forms such as television and popular film.

This split in critical reaction brings us to the second category of comic representations, ignored by critics as irrelevant and trivializing, because of its "low-brow" classification. This second category does not address the Holocaust directly, but rather deals with its fringes, usually ridiculing Nazis in general, or Adolf Hitler specifically. These popular culture representations are nevertheless complicated by the previously addressed link in modern culture between Nazism and the Holocaust. It is this category that has been labeled the "trivialization" of the Holocaust. In this category belongs humor such as the series of YouTube videos comically dubbing in Hitler's rant from the film *Downfall*, *Hogan's Heroes*, *Saturday Night Live*'s recurring character, Gay Hitler, and much of Mel Brooks work, including the "Hitler Rap" on MTV, the "Naughty Nazis" number in the film *To Be or Not to Be* (1983) and *The Producers*, in each of its incarnations.

In a discussion of *Life Is Beautiful*, Sander Gilman argues that only in film are comic representations of the Holocaust and Nazis allowed. He reasons:

> The comic in the cinema from its very origin is coupled with laughter [...]. Our sense of distance is much greater than when we, face to face with another, are told a joke or read a novel. We are isolated in the cinema while still part of a collective [286].

With this emphasis solely on filmic or literary representations, Gilman demonstrates the critical disregard for a popular theatrical response to the Holocaust. In a manner representative of most scholars of the subject, he does not choose to recognize examples of the comic outside his own circumscribed field. Gilman describes a set of conditions that could easily be applied to the theatre, ignoring the existence of a one particular theatrical reaction, a genre often appropriately titled musical *comedy*. Much of musical theatre's response defies the critical statements of scholars who ignore that this response even exists. How might the Holocaust related comic context of *The Producers* function?

Although critics reacted negatively to the film's Nazi subject matter in 1968, the healing passage of time and transference of *The Producers* to another artistic medium seems to have softened the protests. Even a Rabbi, Gerald L. Zelizer, when writing on a conservative Jewish website about the 2000 opening of the musical, states:

> I believe that after an adequate period of time comedy actually can become a healthy outlet to help people cope with even heinous crimes [...] as World War II recedes further into history, comedy becomes a [...] more legitimate coping mechanism, a catharsis for the victims of the 20th century's most vicious mass killers [n. pag.].

New York Magazine's John Simon, in perhaps the only non-rave review for the musical, underlines this argument in a less positive manner:

With the passage of time having made Nazi jokes less disturbing and audiences less discerning — the show within the show couldn't help being a hit, which makes the eponymous producers into even bigger fools than intended [n. pag.].

Not everyone agreed that passage of time made Nazi humor acceptable. Some angry letters to editors of New York publications appeared after the opening of *The Producers*, but these seemed to be in the vast minority. At least according to box office and critical reactions, most people seemed to find the musical an entirely acceptable forum for dealing with the Nazi past.

Mel Brooks has explained:

[I don't] make fun of the Holocaust. It's too large, too heartbreaking. You can't really deal with it, it's too earth-shattering. But I do use Hitler and the Nazis and the guys who perpetrated the outrage. I make fun of them, showing what brutes and pigs they were [quoted in Elkin n. pag.].

Brooks' show makes no mention of the Holocaust specifically, and indeed its Nazi representations are confined to a show within a show context, as "staged Nazis" in a meta-theatrical space, thus avoiding many of the difficulties of Holocaust related humor. I question however if it is possible to ignore the link which has been established in America between Nazi imagery and mass death, between a swastika and anti–Semitic hatred. The implications of laughter at Nazi imagery, of a comic Hitler, encompass the shock and discomfort of the knowledge that one is laughing at the perpetrators of one of the most horrific crimes in the history of the human race. This fact should be faced in order to fully unpack *The Producers'* sources of laughter and the ensuing implications for American society.

It would be misguided not to fully admit and embrace *The Producers* as a comedy first and foremost. It was intended to elicit humor, and certainly seems to have been taken on most fronts as pure comedic fun. I am interested, however, in exploring the extent to which the symbols, imagery and content allowable within the musical context has completely shifted over the years since the first Nazis appeared on the musical stage in *The Sound of Music*. In 1959, swastikas were considered to be too much for audiences to accept, and as much as possible the Nazi characters and any presence of Judaism or possible overtones of the Holocaust were firmly excluded. By 1966 in *Cabaret*, swastikas were allowed in moderation, and Nazi characters were allowed to be fairly central. In *The Producers* (2001), swastikas are ubiquitous — including on pigeons — in a humorous context. For instance, after Franz Liebkind has forced Leo and Max to wear swastika armbands, they leave to visit Roger De Bris, forgetting they have them on. Carmen Ghia invites Leo and Max in and politely asks, "May I take your hat, your coat and your swastikas?" (122). All the trappings of Nazism appear in glorious show business style, showgirls in pointe shoes as German tanks, parachuting Nazi soldiers, tap dancing Nazis, and a cabaret-style Hitler. We find the high point of Nazi regalia in the over-head mirror image of a swastika spinning Busby Berkeley style. The saturation of these images and the extent to which they have become normalized in our society seems to be apparent through their use for comedy in *The Producers*.

Leo and Max are not threatened by the Nazis, indeed, not only do they have the potential to "win" in Sander Gilman's sense; they have already "won." The war is over; they are taking advantage of Hitler for their own financial gain. In Brooks' world laughing at Hitler deflates him and his evil; Brooks uses laughter as a weapon. Brooks, and therefore the audience, do not judge Leo and Max's similar strategy, to take advantage of Hitler, and to "win," or defeat him through glorious bad taste. Their reaction when they are forced to put on swastika armbands by Franz Liebkind can therefore be used to comedic purpose. A horrified Leo attempts to stand against the Nazi, but Max knows they must humor Liebkind in order to get the rights to his show. After they hand Liebkind the contract he states:

> FRANZ: You may produce my play [...] but only if you vil take the Siegfried Oath.
> LEO: The Siegfried Oath? What's that?
> FRANZ: A pledge of eternal allegiance to our beloved Führer!
> LEO: Never... *(Max gives him a painful poke in the ribs)* ... took that oath before.
> FRANZ: *(taking out three Nazi armbands from his pocket, hands one to each)* Gut!
>   Von for me, von for you, und von for you!
> LEO: *(looking aghast at his armband)* Never... *(as Max again pokes him in the ribs)* ... had one on before. Thank you.
> FRANZ: You're welcome.
> MAX: Nice colors [116–7].

Leo's horrified reaction and Max's businesslike acceptance are played for laughs. The eponymous producers are not threatened, and in fact they show their dominance of the insane Franz by switching their raised finger for the Siegfried Oath to their middle fingers, taking advantage of Franz's oblivious-ness, gaining an additional, though childish, "win" over Nazism.

Despite the fact that our sympathies clearly lie with Max and Leo, Lester Friedman points out: "Brooks's characters are a compendium of ethnic clichés that, in the past, might well have been attacked as blatantly anti–Semitic" (188). Patricia Erens elaborates these stereotypes from the original film:

> As Leo Bloom, Gene Wilder personifies the Jew as Man-Child — a frightened, hysterical adult, with multiple phobias [... .] In addition, Max represents the scheming money-hungry Jew, always looking for a deal. He is a modern-day Shylock, obsessed with money [267].

As in *The Rothschilds*, the stereotype of money-loving Jews takes center stage in Brooks' work. Similar dissonances to Bock and Harnick's musical circulate in *The Producers*. But the show takes on these stereotypes within a comic frame. Whereas a portrayal of a Jew interested in money has the potential to be taken hatefully in *The Rothschilds*, a dark and fully serious musical, Brooks' humor complicates the reception of anti–Semitic clichés. As Friedman asks, "So why is all this so funny? What Brooks does in *The Producers* is to create a film in which the Jewish characters, however unappealing they may be, are far more attractive and loveable than the people they exploit" (188). In particular, these characters are vastly superior to their perceived enemy, the Nazi, Franz Leibkind. Through these victorious parodic stereotypes, through "defeating" the real Nazi on stage by showing him a buffoon, Brooks allows a warmer realm where nostalgia can also circulate.

Staging Nazis

Liebkind presents an anomalous example of the staged Nazi within *The Producers*. Unlike the examples of the Nazis in "Springtime for Hitler," who are merely chorus members masquerading as Nazis in the show within a show, Liebkind is an actual member of the party, a Hitler lover hiding out in Greenwich Village. The first words out of Franz's mouth, after Max and Leo come upon him on his roof, wearing a German helmet and Lederhosen, are a frenzied denial:

> FRANZ: I vas never a member of the Nazi party. I only followed orders. I had nossing to do with the war. I didn't even know there vas a war on. Ve lived in the back. Right across from Svitzerland. All ve heard vas yodeling. *(he yodels a bit to prove his point)* [112].

Brooks characterizes Franz as completely unhinged, and entirely defeated. Despite his angry ramblings against Churchill, and in favor of the Third Reich, Franz presents no threat. The action of *The Producers* takes place in 1959, and so Franz has therefore presumably been hiding in New York for the fourteen years since the war. We are introduced to him on the roof with his pigeons, named, "Otto, Bertha, Heidi, Heinz, Volfgang ... Adolf!" (112), and he sings his first song, a hymn to "Old Bavaria" (with pigeons cooing backup, ending with the tune of "Deutschland über Alles"). This combination of Nazi sentiments with vaudeville flourishes typifies the portrayal of Liebkind. Obsessed with show business, musicals, and Hitler, and very excited that he will have the opportunity to glorify the Führer through song, he tells his pigeons:

> FRANZ: Do you hear? Ve are going to clear the Führer's name! Ach, Broadvay! Lights, music, happy tippy tappy toes. You know, not many people know it, but the Führer vas a terrific dancer [113].

As Mel Brooks states in the stage directions, Franz is indeed "more than slightly nuts" (112). Brooks' portrayal of the only real Nazi character as an aging, overweight, insane buffoon undercuts the fear and foreboding inherent to most Nazi representations. Hans Christoph Kayser writes of a perceived shift in the American media's portrayal of the Nazi, from sadist to clown. Kayser describes the shift from sexualized Nazi figures in so-called stag magazines of the 1960s, to the figure of the bumbling inept Nazi depicted in the popular TV series of the 1970s, *Hogan's Heroes*. The trend in musical theatre also seems to follow this sequence, from offstage menace in *The Sound of Music*, frightening and sexualized Nazis in *Cabaret*, to the buffoonery of Brooks' Nazis in *The Producers*. In the style of *Hogan's Heroes*, Franz's buffoonery marks a change from representations of all Nazis as, in the words of Josef Joffe, German editor of *Die Zeit*, "icy cold machos in black SS uniform, [to] bumbling incompetent figures who were always outwitted by the allies" (quoted in Cowell 2).

Franz's three songs are therefore presented in a very different context from our earlier musicals. As in *Cabaret*, a Nazi sings, but this is no co-opting of the moral power of music. In this case Franz's three songs, all mock German numbers, including the Führer's "favorite," "Der Guten Tag Hop Clop," are used to purely comic effect. The latter presents a satire of German polkas where the dancing gets increasingly violent, against Leo in particular. Both other numbers mix vaudeville style with German elements and Nazi sentiments. "In Old Bavaria" has a big vaudeville finish, as discussed, while "Haben Sie Gehört das Deutsche Band" combines show biz with gibberish German to hilarious effect. As in the show within a show, "Springtime for Hitler," Nazi regalia and sentiments are undercut by their connection with show business.

Fascist Aesthetics

Aside from Franz Liebkind, all other Nazis in this piece exist only in the musical within a musical, "Springtime for Hitler." Were they meant to be actual Nazis, the humor would be dissipated. *The Producers* exists at a safe remove from the actual period of the Third Reich, portraying a fully deranged and defeated Nazi, Liebkind, hiding out with his pigeons. *The Producers* therefore lends credence to Sander Gilman's proposition that the victim's "winning" offers a condition necessary to Holocaust related humor. In *The Producers*, the win has already occurred; victory has been so ingrained that we may now laugh at all the trappings of a defeated regime. The most effective means of laughing at that regime are through the self-referentiality in Brooks' central metaphor, Nazis represented (or misrepresented) through musical theatre. Here meta-theatre serves a larger purpose, to equate Hitler and the fascists with theatre, and by naming this as a source for potential allure, further debasing their source of power. Robert Brustein, in his article entitled "The Jew Who Buried Hitler," states, "nobody can touch Brooks when it comes to letting the air out of evil icons [...] generally by exposing how much they have in common with showbiz" (Brustein n. pag.).

What *do* fascists have in common with showbiz? Susan Sontag, in her article entitled "Fascinating Fascism," writes of the allure of Nazi aesthetics and their connection to theatre:

> The fascist dramaturgy centers on the orgiastic transaction between mighty forces and their puppets, uniformly garbed and shown in ever swelling numbers. Its choreography alternates between ceaseless motion and [...] "virile" posing [...] The rendering of movement in grandiose and rigid patterns [...] rehearses the very unity of the polity. The masses are made to take form, be design [91–92].

Sontag's makes a deliberate choice of the words *choreography* and *movement*. Removing the political associations in this quotation arguably leaves a definition of a musical production number, with ever swelling numbers of chorus members dancing in unison, often around a leader figure, making "form and design" out of bodily movement. Sontag herself states that "[Fascist aesthetic] art is hardly confined to works labeled as fascist or produced under fascist governments" (91). She cites a Busby Berkeley film, *The Gang's All Here* (1943), as an example. This reference presciently invokes the pivotal moment in "Springtime for Hitler," where chorus members dressed as black leather clad storm troopers enter, each flanked by two identical full sized human puppets. These units of three join in formation, and through a massive mirror that lowers from the flies, we see their configuration into a large rotating human swastika, with Hitler in the central point. Director Susan Stroman recognizes the parallels, "[The moment] became a perfect statement of what the Nazis were like, actually, these indistinguishable storm trooper puppets" (quoted in Singer 12). The phenomenological rush of associations at this moment defies quantification. The image calls into mind a Berkeley style extravaganza, and also invokes associations with *A Chorus Line*, which similarly draws the comparison of dancing chorus members to fascist style automatons. The moment also draws allusions to Boris Aronson's tilted mirror in the original set design for *Cabaret*. As this association demonstrates, the darker implications inherent in *Cabaret* are not absent from *The Producers*. In fact the swastika moment presents a disturbing mix of the humorous and the frightening. Mel Brooks maintains he does not make fun of the Holocaust, merely Nazis. But how well is this distinction maintained? Can we look at the massive swastika formation on the stage and not automatically summon to mind images of death camps and enormous human suffering? Though popular response to *The Producers* would seem to argue yes, the implications of this response throw light on our culture's darker obsessions and urges. Brooks states, "Comedy must be daring [...] It must skirt the edge of bad taste. If it doesn't, it's not challenging or exciting" (quoted in Gardner 1E) Brooks walks this razor's edge between humor and disgust and fear more closely than we might initially discern.

The complicated nostalgia and darker implications of Holocaust humor in *The Producers* complicate musical theatre's typical "fluff" label. Why does *The Producers* thrive without protest while the "Mirroring Evil" exhibit became bogged in a swamp of controversy? Perhaps because humor holds the power to overcome not only protest, but also evil itself. Brustein states:

> The Jew who finally buried Hitler, Mel Brooks demonstrates that comedy is not only capable of exposing stupidity and pretension. At times it can also exorcize and nullify evil—not as powerfully, but sometimes more lastingly than a hundred Sherman tanks, a thousand B-42s, or a million GIs [n. pag.].

The Producers presents the Jewish eponymous producers "winning" and uses comedy to exorcize the evil of Hitler. In the ultimate thumbing of his nose at evil, Brooks' went so far as to thank Hitler, in his Tony speech, "for being such a funny guy on stage" (quoted in Nisse 3). Brooks allows this humor through joyous show biz references and hearkening back to the glories of golden age musical theatre, creating nostalgia for a parallel universe in the 50s where the Holocaust wasn't traumatic to Jewish characters like Leo and Max; where swastika armbands were appalling but not so much that singing and dancing can't overcome them. Leo and Max, and the musical *The Producers* as a whole, has carnivalistic fun at Hitler's expense. Gilman's "winning" affords nostalgia, and by remembering a golden era, we forget, at least momentarily, a horrific one. Where other musicals contain nostalgia for clear sources of Jewish community: Israel, the shtetl, the Lower East Side; *The Producers'* nostalgia for golden age Broadway's Jewish community is expansive enough to allow dissonant transgressive humor. Brooks' celebration of the Broadway musical demonstrates Jewish success, rather than victimization. What better symbol of the American Jewish success story, than the Broadway musical, created, honed and perfected by American Jews?

CHAPTER IX

Conclusion

Musical theatre, while popular with the general public, has only recently begun to be explored by the academy. Now that scholars have begun to plumb the depths of this rich field, we can begin to understand just how much these works tell us about changing American values. Numerous scholars have explored the politically and culturally sensitive shift that has occurred in America towards Nazism, within the fields of film, television, and drama. Musical theatre, the most American of our theatrical forms, has been left out of this consideration. I have attempted to redress this absence here.

Direct Musicals

As we have seen, only three musicals in this study directly portray the Nazi era. In *The Sound of Music, Cabaret* and *The Producers* I have identified two distinct and yet interlocked trends in the representation of Nazism in American popular culture, and more specifically on the American musical stage. These trends mark the progression towards a grimmer realism and towards comedy, or to return to scholar George Mosse's terms, towards sanctification and trivialization. Although these three musicals are very different works, seemingly united only in the basic fact of their presentation of Nazism on the musical stage, both trends, while different in style, scope, genre and tone, can be traced in all three of these works. Ultimately both these trends can also be united in their source: collective memory and trauma.

Parallel with the ever increasing trend towards Holocaust claiming in America is a feeling that artistic representation should be more specific: face the era head on, accept more fully what was ignored for so long, and strengthen early tentative attempts to address the subject matter. This first trend, towards

191

what I have termed a grim realism, can most clearly be seen not in the individual productions of the three works I examine, but traced as a whole when examining their various incarnations simultaneously. Therefore when we place the original production of *The Sound of Music* next to its film version and 1998 Broadway revival, we can trace an increasing interest in the imagery and regalia of Nazism, a growing use of swastikas, and an escalation in numbers of staged Nazis. *Cabaret* demonstrates this same trend, not necessarily in the number of swastikas or Nazis, but in their dramatic impact and in their sexualization. *The Producers* follows this last trend in particular, intertwining sexuality and fascism to an almost startling extent, and doing so far more strongly in its Broadway musical form than in the original film. *The Producers*, however, must be acknowledged to fall more strongly into the second trend I discuss, towards comedy.

All three of these productions utilize some form of comedy, whether connected to or firmly distanced from Nazi imagery. In fact we can trace a clear line in comic use of the Nazi figure in these musicals from a careful lack of humor regarding Nazism, to the opposite, Nazism as the main source of comedy. In *The Sound of Music*, Nazis are completely non-comic, albeit within a "musical comedy" format, which makes the imposition of figures of evil rather surprising in the piece. In *Cabaret* the Nazi characters, most specifically Ernst, start as mildly comic, until their views become known, whereupon they become fully serious, non-humorous characters. The Emcee, although complicating this trend through his complicity with the Nazis — to various levels in different productions — also more or less follows this trend, becoming more and more troubling and less and less comic as he moves towards Nazism. In both these musicals then, Nazi characters are not treated as fodder for comedy. *The Producers* reverses the idea of the non-comic Nazi character. Through the one true Nazi character, the buffoon Franz Liebkind, and through the seemingly bizarre juxtaposition of Nazism with show business, Nazis are no longer forbidden to be funny; indeed at a safe remove of fourteen years from the war, they are the most comic figures in Brooks' zany world.

A consideration of singing Nazis must go along with the discussion of comic Nazis. Once again a clear line can be traced from the moral clarity of *The Sound of Music* where no Nazi characters are permitted to sing, and where singing represents freedom and goodness, to *Cabaret* where the joy of singing is co-opted and corrupted by the powers of Nazism, to *The Producers* where fascism and show business have become so intertwined that singing seems a natural activity for the ridiculed Nazis. This consideration of singing is vital to the exploration of the portrayal of Nazism in musicals, where the power of song is paramount. The aesthetic use of song therefore offers a key to understanding the works' stance towards the Nazi threat.

Indirect Musicals

The remaining musicals considered here do not directly address or portray the events of the Nazi era. Instead, *Milk and Honey, Fiddler on the Roof, The Rothschilds, Rags* and *Ragtime* substitute or sublimate their Holocaust encounters through nostalgia. Despite their presence together in this work, these five musical case studies have contrasting origins, concerns, and themes. Each musical focuses nostalgic representations on a different site: Israel, the shtetl, the Lower East Side and Old Europe, and makes use of different methods to provoke wistful memory: restorative nostalgia, nostalgia of place and family, and intertextual nostalgia, all in a postmemory context. Many of the musicals take more than one of these sites or methods in their nostalgic evocations, but focus on one. The dramatic forms of these musicals also greatly differ, encompassing *Milk and Honey*'s light musical comedy, *Fiddler*'s golden age integrated musical, *The Rothschilds*' darker anti-nostalgia, *Rags*' hearkening back to the classic American musical form and *Ragtime*'s postmodern musical epic. Additionally, the nature of Holocaust references in these musicals change through time, in keeping with the "Americanization of the Holocaust" and our increasing ability to discuss the Holocaust in grimmer detail, while simultaneously taking transgressive, even humorous stances in response to that event. These musicals progress from sublimating responses into an emphasis on vigorous life in *Milk and Honey*, through successively more explicit Holocaust echoes or substitutions in *Fiddler, The Rothschilds, Rags*, and *Ragtime*. Lastly, the extent to which these musicals vary in their use of nostalgia also potentially contributed to their commercial success. *The Rothschilds*, the most anti-nostalgic musical, was not commercially successful, while *Fiddler on the Roof* and *The Producers*, the most successfully nostalgic pieces examined here, were smash hits. Clearly, effective use of sentimentalized memory does not hurt a musical's box office.

Each of these musicals makes use of most of the nostalgic categories, even when not central to their narratives. For instance, although *Fiddler* takes place in the shtetl and does not explicitly focus on Jewish humanism and liberalism, it clearly points to these values through its crusading character Perchik. Restorative nostalgia for biblical Israel can be seen briefly in *The Rothschilds* and *Fiddler*. Nostalgia for the Jewish family unit can be found in all of these projects. "Nostalgia for Place" — most particularly the Lower East Side, but also for biblical Israel — also suffuses each of these musicals. For example, *Fiddler on the Roof* by implication references the Lower East Side as a place of refuge for Tevye and his family, more explicitly so in drafts. We find nostalgia for the golden age of Broadway musical theatre in both *Rags* and *The Producers*. Intertextual nostalgia for other musicals, particularly *Fid-*

dler, is at work in almost all of these shows. In fact a true common thread for each of these musicals since *Fiddler* has been their constant comparisons to that piece. When it comes to Jewish themed musical theatre, the success of *Fiddler* will inescapably define the genre into the foreseeable future.

JUDGING NOSTALGIA

In 1989, David Lowenthal argued that nostalgia has become a "social pariah" (18) in modern society, "Diatribe upon diatribe denounce it as reactionary, regressive, ridiculous [...] "Nostalgia" [...] now ranks near the top [...] in the vocabulary of political abuse" (20). Nostalgia has become more and more a "widespread cult" (21) in recent popular culture according to Lowenthal, encouraging distaste and disapproval for three reasons: nostalgia often takes a reactionary political slant, the commercialization of nostalgia implies lack of authenticity, and the pervasiveness of nostalgia throughout the media adds to its unreality. Lowenthal argues, however, that critics overstate the matter, defending nostalgia against the most stringent of accusations. He points out, "It is wrong to imagine that there exists some *non*-nostalgic reading of the past that is by contrast 'honest' or authentically 'true'" (30 orig. emphasis). Lowenthal's last point is crucial to remember when examining these musicals' nostalgia production. While it is easy to condemn them for presenting the "shtetl we've never had" (Howe 74) or for cleaning up the harshness of immigrant life on the Lower East Side, we should recall that understanding history is a subjective endeavor, and that perhaps a reading or examination of *why* these musicals may distort the Jewish past is more instructive than an easy condemnation of their doing so.

COMMUNITY

These indirect musicals' focus on vibrant Jewish communities in Israel, the shtetl and the Lower East Side, offers their central commonality. The musicals' authors demonstrate awareness of these communities' difficulties, but as secondary to a hazy superior yesteryear where community was not challenged as it is today. Even in *Ragtime* where Tateh leaves his Lower East Side community, he is consistently staged as a part of a larger, tight-knit immigrant community. The exception proves the rule, for *The Rothschilds*, the least nostalgic musical examined here, presents an isolated family within a small and fragile community. Scholar David Lowenthal argues, "The diverse goals of contemporary nostalgia do have one point in common. They mainly envisage a time when folk did not feel fragmented [...] in short, a past that was unified and comprehensible, unlike the incoherent, divided present" (29). The loss of the steadying force of community makes the present seem divided or incoherent.

The musicals' communities are stable, even if events surrounding them are not. For example, although changing times challenge Tevye's traditions, Anatevka's residents are close, fulfill traditional roles, and even as they are being broken apart, maintain their Jewish identity and their intimate ties. While *Fiddler* dramatizes the testing of traditions, for the majority of the piece, it displays the strengths of community. These musicals' secure communities contrast with Lowenthal's "turbulent and chaotic present" (21), with the immense challenges posed to Jewish community in modern America. The pressures of Americanization, integration, and the Holocaust combine to underline American Jews' loss of community. For one, Jews are intermarrying at such a rate that many fear the community will disappear altogether. In a 1990 survey on intermarriage rates, we find that before 1965, Jews in America only married outside their faith 9 percent of the time. Between 1965 and 1974 that rate rose to 25 percent, and from 1985 on the intermarriage rate has risen to 52 percent (Waxman 30). Although studies differ in their findings, jewishfederations.org claims that the intermarriage rate since 1985 has stabilized in the 40 percent range. The fact that almost half of the time American Jews choose to marry outside the faith has caused consternation in many circles, and fear that the children of these marriages will not only fail to meet conservative law's definition of Jewishness, but will lose even their most secular Jewish identity. Because Jews do not encourage conversion, but pass on community only through children, an extrapolation of these intermarriage rates leads to fear of the Jewish people's disappearance, both ethnically and religiously. Many scholars also believe that Americanization and secularization contribute to the shrinking of the Jewish community, responding to the seemingly inescapable fact that the Jewish community shrinks as it assimilates. Fear of disappearing community remains a widely held concern in modern fragmented society.

As Bial states, "The experience that this generation of American Jews shares is not the densely packed memory of their parents and grandparents; instead they share the anxiety that comes from an unfulfilled, and perhaps unfulfillable, desire to remember" (110). The combination of these factors leads both to yearning for community and a search to find it in the past: the perfect breeding ground for nostalgia. In postmodern America, community no longer defines our lives, instead we search for its meaning. Through acceptance in America, Jews have faced new concerns. Each of the threads these musicals have in common — particularly their use of Jewish or "Hebraic" music, and interest in Jewish rituals — emerge from a nostalgic need to focus on past communities, in order to counter the perception of disintegrating present community. Music's evocative power makes its calls to memory stronger. When composers include a suggestive Jewish melody in these scores, they appeal to audiences' memories and shared experiences. They might evoke religious memories, or merely paint an aural picture of longed-for community. Additionally, each of the rituals examined share their emphasis on the collective Jewish experience they evoke and underscore. The weddings in *Milk and Honey* and *Fiddler*, the Sabbath prayer in *Fiddler*, *Rags'* funeral, and the various rituals cut from *The Rothschilds* all have in common their highlighting of the community that performs them. The power of the community pulling together to perform these rituals doubles any feeling of sacred power attendant in their performance onstage.

These musicals' focus on Jewish family, on Jewish tropes like the labor movement and progressive humanism, and their use of Holocaust resonances also underscores the importance of shared experience. The family unit offers the foundation for community, and is of utmost importance to the Jewish faith. In *The Rothschilds* family ties offer the main source of community, but family figures strongly in the other works as well, most clearly *Fiddler*, but also *Rags*, *Ragtime*, and *Milk and Honey*. *Rags* and *Ragtime* most clearly demonstrate an emphasis on Jewish liberal humanism, but we also find this concern in the other musicals, underscoring the importance of coming together for a common goal. Fighting larger injustice grants a sense of kinship and closeness vital for collective experience. Finally, the Holocaust was arguably the defining event for American Jewish identity in the 20th century, challenging community both through the destruction it wrought, and by emphasizing the importance of community in the wake of disaster. Only through valuing history, coming together to remember and move forward can we fight the horrors of tragedy. In the wake of tragedy, we must move on but also to remember "better" times before calamity struck.

Holocaust Aesthetics

I have chosen to avoid aesthetic or moral judgments as much as possible in this work, as artistic valuations are not important in a cultural studies context, and moral concerns can stand in the way of a clear headed examination of the implications of these works. But it may prove useful to outline these concerns briefly, in order to avoid accusations of blindness. Alvin Rosenfeld, one scholar who has raised moral objections to the proliferation of Hitler imagery in popular culture, writes in his *Imagining Hitler*:

> The release of these images [of Hitler and Nazis] across all the media of culture does not in and of itself mean an instant return to bad times, but it does suggest a rapid removal of the fear of those bad times and the moral disgrace that once attended them [17–8].

When Hitler and Nazis become the easy shorthand for evil, when representations are carelessly scattered across our culture, it perhaps becomes easy to be blind to the enormity of Nazi crimes. The troublesome implications of this possibility resonate with the hoards of people coming to the "Sing-a-long *Sound of Music*" dressed in Nazi regalia, gleefully and carelessly booing the Nazis. It also extends to the huge popularity of *The Producers* where tap dancing Nazis and swastika wearing pigeons are applauded without worry for the implications. This argument projects the worst possible outcome, that a constant barrage of representations can cause people to emotionally shut down, allowing history to repeat itself more easily.

A similar argument presented by critics of our current Nazi fascination contends that when Nazism acts as an easy shorthand for evil, we may then use Hitler and Nazi imagery to overlook more difficult and more current evils in the world. It would be an interesting future study to note whether Nazi and Hitler imagery increases in times of intense current conflicts. If relative artistic silence regarding September 11, 2001, prevailed for several years afterward, did representations of a more removed situation of evil, the Nazi era, proliferate in order to take up the slack? In this period of intense moral ambiguity and confusion, the simple, clear-cut case of pure evil, which Hitler presents for our society, becomes appealing. But it certainly may be problematic if our fascination with Nazism serves to dull our interest in issues of immediate import. Additionally, if Hitler presents a black and white case of pure insane evil, then the Holocaust becomes by association a historical anomaly, something that will not and cannot happen again and therefore may be dwelled upon in an unconsidered and uninformed way.

Rosenbaum also points out that our barrage of cultural representations and images may chip away at the link between Nazism and the Holocaust on which I have based much of my analysis. The effect of Nazi obsession, says Rosenbaum, "is to undermine any sane vision of culture and ultimately to erase the fingerprints of Hitler from a history of mass murder. To popularize the man and his crimes is to trivialize them and, in time, to render them almost invisible" (105). Rosenbaum is not alone. This feeling that popular culture representations are morally harmful presents part of the reason for the critical focus on "high art" representations of Nazism and the Holocaust to the exclusion of the popular. Rosenbaum states:

> Laugh at Hitler often enough, dress him up as a stage villain, convert him into a cartoon of frightful or ridiculous demeanor, and in time you will no longer know who or what he was. Play with the symbols of his Reich as if they were harmless toys and before long the distractions of mind generated by the pleasures of lighthearted amusement weaken the sanctions of historical memory [104–5].

Finally, by culturally obsessing on Nazi imagery and Hitler stories, many argue that we are correspondingly belittling the indescribable pain, agony and suffering of millions upon millions of people. Not only are we denigrating the pain of the survivors, those who remain to see the popularization of the movement which tortured them, but more importantly dishonoring the memory of the millions who died at the hands of the regime whose symbols and stories are now so recklessly told. Because of the immediate connection between Nazism and the Holocaust which today is so accepted and apparent, all images of Nazis, including Rolf in *The Sound of Music*, Ernst in *Cabaret* and especially Adolf Hitler in *The Producers*, according to this argument, can conceivably contribute to the dishonoring of the millions of victims of the Holocaust.

This truth about our perceptions of Nazism and the Holocaust makes the choice of method of artistic representation a theoretically difficult question. Highly influential scholar Theodor Adorno famously stated in 1955, "To write poetry after Auschwitz is barbaric" (quoted in Cole 100). His statement started the debate regarding Holocaust art that has continued with fervor to this day. Theatre presents a particularly challenging case, with its live actor / audience relationship complicating the representation of tragedy. As Isser states, "Theater is even more problematic, [...] because of the physical presence of actors in a space shared with an audience. The spectators are confronted by the material without insulation or mediation" (21). Dramatic artists must therefore find Lawrence Langer's "aesthetic of atrocity." This aesthetic may take any number of theatrical forms; however, scholars have questioned the efficacy of traditional theatrical realism to examine events as intensely shocking as those of the Nazi era. As we have come to realize in our postmodern era, realism often implies a positivist universe, where meaning is stable. Realism presupposes rationalism and impartialness, and thus, states Skloot, "it becomes increasingly clear why some artists and critics reject as inappropriate any realistic treatment of the most hope-defying and irrational event of modern times" (*Four Plays* 17). Susan Sontag agrees: "To simulate atrocities convincingly is to risk making the audience passive, reinforcing witless stereotypes, confirming distance and creating meretricious fascination" (quoted in Skloot *Four Plays* 17). If realism is fraught with difficulties, abstraction does not present a simple answer either. By distancing the audience from the material through abstract means, the artist risks losing all connection to horrific reality and thus betraying the truth of the events.

If most methods of representation are problematic, and mass cultural representations are stigmatized, what formats must Nazi or Holocaust representation then take? Scholar Geoffrey Hartman, siding with abstract representations of the Holocaust against realism in mass culture, has argued that, "most of the time, [...] transmissibility and truth move in opposite directions" (quoted in Landsberg 68). Alison Landsberg disagrees, stating:

> Not only does Hartman's dichotomy tend to rearticulate a kind of high/low distinction where mass culture, precisely because of its power to transmit, gets relegated to the "low" end, but it also takes the Holocaust outside the realm of representability [68].

Despite the many objections to proliferating Holocaust and Nazi representations discussed above, Landsberg's point must be considered closely. Although most American representations of the Nazi era and the Holocaust have been accused of "Americanizing" something which is not ours; adding happy endings, laughing at, simplifying, many of these representations need to be more fully explored in order to understand the implications of this Americanization. This is particularly true of the musicals I have discussed. Many of these pieces are more complex than they are given credit for, and exploring them tells us about our attitudes towards not just anti–Semitism and fascism, but on sexuality and gender and other issues central to our conception of ourselves and our culture.

Moving Forward

As this work went to press, a new musical attempting to address this material opened, and shortly thereafter closed, on Broadway. *The People in the Picture*, starring Donna Murphy, book and lyrics by Iris Rainer Dart of *Beaches* (the 1988 film) fame, music by Mike Stoller (of Lieber and Stoller) and Artie Butler, was produced by the Roundabout theatre, opening April 28th, 2011 and closing less than two months later on June 19th, 2011. Following the story of Raisel Rabinowitz, a Yiddish actress in Warsaw 1935–1946, and then jumping to her life in America in the 1970s, this musical combined both approaches examined here — nostalgia for Borcht Belt Jewish humor through the Yiddish theatre troupe, nostalgia of family through following the generational dynamics of Raisel as a survivor and her daughter and granddaughter, and attempts to directly address Holocaust material through a musical comedy / drama format. Reviews were generally lukewarm to unfavorable, many citing the saccharine book, and the clash of the serious material with the borscht belt style humor. Ben Brantley held, in the *New York Times*, that, "the music tends to trickle, avoiding the big crescendos of Broadway showstoppers. This tonal uncertainty may reflect the problems of combining peppy folk humor and death-camp fears into one package" (C1).

While unfortunately a detailed analysis of this musical will have to wait for future work, *The People in the Picture* demonstrates that this material will continue to be examined on the popular Broadway stage. Far from dissipating, our fascination with this era and its implications continues. Some questions to close: Does our society use theatre to attempt to free itself from remembering and re-experiencing the pain of the Nazi era? Do we invent new ways to keep the subject fresh, to never forget, lest it happen again? Are these positive motivations entirely straightforward, or is our fascination with evil perhaps connected to darker forces within ourselves? Approached with more questions than answers, the musical may be able to contribute a forum for the examination of these most complex of issues.

Works Cited

Adler, Renata. Rev. of *The Producers*, dir. Mel Brooks. *New York Times*. 19 March 1968: n. pag. Rpt. in *New York Times Film Reviews*. Vol. 5. New York: New York Times and Arno Press, 1970. p. 3742.

Aleichem, Sholem. *Tevye the Dairyman and The Railroad Stories*. Trans. Hillel Halkin. New York: Schocken Books, 1987.

American Musicals: Bock and Harnick. Time-Life Records, Time Incorporated 1982. n.a.

Appell, Don, and Jerry Herman. *Milk and Honey: A Musical Play*. New York: Tams-Witmark Music Library, 1961.

_____. *Shalom: A Musical Play*. Early draft of *Milk and Honey*. Author's personal collection.

Arnold, Thomas K. "Brooks raising the curtain on his favorite 'Producers.'" *The Hollywood Reporter* 11 May 2006, *Lexis-Nexis*. 9 November 2006.

Backhaus, Fritz. "The Last of the Court Jews — Mayer Rothschild and His Sons" in *From Court Jews to the Rothschilds*. Vivian B. Mann and Richard I. Cohen eds. Munich: Prestel, 1996.

Bial, Henry. *Acting Jewish: Negotiating Ethnicity on the American Stage and Screen*. Ann Arbor: University of Michigan Press, 2005.

Bilik, Dorothy Seidman. *Immigrant-Survivors: Post-Holocaust Consciousness in Recent Jewish American Fiction*. Middletown: Wesleyan University Press, 1981.

Billington, Michael. "Happy Days Are Here Again." *The Guardian Unlimited* 21 July 2001. 18 April 2002 <http://www.guardian.co.uk/Distribution/Redirect_Artifact>.

Boyarin, Jonathan. *Storm from Paradise: The Politics of Jewish Memory*. Minneapolis: University of Minnesota Press, 1992.

_____, and Daniel Boyarin, eds. *Jews and Other Differences: The New Jewish Cultural Studies*. Minneapolis: University of Minnesota Press, 1997.

Boym, Svetlana. *The Future of Nostalgia*. New York: Basic Books, 2001.

Brantley, Ben. "A Cozy Little McShtetl." *New York Times*. 27 February 2004: E1, E4.

_____. "An Exotic Tevye in Anatevka." *New York Times* 21 January 2005: E1.

_____. Rev. of *Cabaret* by Joe Masteroff, John Kander and Fred Ebb. Kit Kat Klub Theatre, New York. *New York Times* 19 March 1998 n. pag. Rpt. in *New York Times Theatre Reviews* pp. 249–250 New York: New York Times & Arno Press, 1998. Vol. 22.

_____. Rev. of *Ragtime* by Terrence McNally, Stephen Flaherty and Lynn Ahrens. Ford Center Theatre, New York *New York Times* 19 January 1998 n. pag. Rpt. in *New York Times Theatre Reviews* pp. 203–204. New York: New York Times & Arno Press, 1998. Vol. 22.

_____. "A Scam That'll Knock 'Em Dead." *New York Times* 20 April 2001: E1, *Lexis-Nexis*. 18 April 2002.

_____. "What Bubbie Did During the War." Rev. of *The People in the Picture* by Iris Rainer Dart, Mike Stoller and Artie Butler. Studio 54, New York *The New York Times* 29 April 2011: C1.

Brenner, Lenni. *Jews in America Today*. Secaucus: Lyle Stuart, 1986.

Brooks, Mel, and Tom Meehan. *The Producers: How We Did It.* New York: Hyperion, 2001.

Brustein, Robert. "The Jew Who Buried Hitler." The New Republic Online 28 May 2001. 18 April 2002 <http://www.thenewrepublic.com>.

_____. "A Revived 'Cabaret' That Feels Brand-New." *New York Times* 28 March 1998 n. pag. Rpt. in *New York Times Theatre Reviews* pp. 257–258 New York: New York Times & Arno Press,1998. Vol. 22.

Bryer, Jackson R., and Richard A. Davison. *The Art of the American Musical: Conversations with the Creators.* New Brunswick: Rutgers University Press, 2005.

Canby, Vincent. "Big and Beautiful, 'Ragtime' Never Quite Manages to Sing." Rev. of *Ragtime* by Terrence McNally, Stephen Flaherty and Lynn Ahrens. Ford Center Theatre, New York *New York Times* 19 January 1998 n. pag. Rpt. in *New York Times Theatre Reviews* pp. 203–204. New York: New York Times & Arno Press, 1998. Vol. 22.

_____. "The Hills Are Alive Again, and It's Quite O.K." Rev. of *The Sound of Music* revival, by Howard Lindsay, Russel Crouse, Richard Rodgers and Oscar Hammerstein. Martin Beck Theatre, New York. *New York Times* 22 March 1998 n. pag. Rpt. in *New York Times Theatre Reviews* pp. 250–251 New York: New York Times & Arno Press, 1998. Vol. 22.

_____. "A Revived 'Cabaret' That Feels Brand-New." Rev. of *Cabaret* by Joe Masteroff, John Kander and Fred Ebb. Kit Kat Klub Theatre, New York. *New York Times* 28 March 1998 n. pag. Rpt. in *New York Times Theatre Reviews* pp. 257–258 New York: New York Times & Arno Press, 1998. Vol. 22.

Carr, Jay. "Musical 'Rothschilds' Opens at the Fisher." *The Detroit News* 12 August 1970 n. pag.

Cashman, Greer Fay. "A Musical Saga in Yiddish." *The Jerusalem Post* 6 December 2000, Lexis-Nexis. 30 November 2006.

_____. "Too Ambitious for the Stage." *The Jerusalem Post* 4 January 2001, Lexis-Nexis. 30 November 2006.

Citron, Stephen. *Jerry Herman: Poet of the Showtune.* New Haven: Yale University Press, 2004.

Clayton, John. "Radical Jewish Humanism: The Vision of E.L. Doctorow." In *E.L. Doctorow: Essays and Conversations.* Richard Trenner, ed. Princeton: Ontario Review Press, 1983.

Coffin, Rachel W., ed. Reviews of *Cabaret*, by Joe Masteroff, John Kander and Fred Ebb. Broadhurst Theatre, New York. *New York Theatre Critics Reviews*, New York: Critics Theatre Reviews, Vol. 21: 1966. 240–243.

_____. Reviews of *The Sound of Music*, by Howard Lindsay, Russel Crouse, Richard Rodgers and Oscar Hammerstein. Lunt-Fontanne Theatre, New York. *New York Theatre Critics Reviews*, New York: Critics Theatre Reviews, Vol. 17: 1959. 227–230.

Cole, Tim. *Selling the Holocaust: From Auschwitz to Schindler, How History is Bought Packaged and Sold.* New York: Routledge, 1999.

Corrigan, Robert W. *Comedy: Meaning and Form.* San Francisco: Chandler Publishing Company, 1965.

Cowell, Alan. "The World; Germans and Hitler Jokes: He Who Laughs Last..." *The New York Times on the Web.* 9 Sept. 2001 23 Sept. 2001 <http://www.northernlight.com>.

Davis, Fred. *Yearning for Yesterday: A Sociology of Nostalgia.* New York: The Free Press, 1979.

Des Pres, Terrence. "Holocaust Laughter" in *Writing Into the World: Essays: 1973–1987.* New York: Viking Press, 1991.

Diner, Hasia R., Jeffrey Shandler and Beth S. Wenger, eds. *Remembering the Lower East Side.* Bloomington: Indiana University Press, 2000.

Disch, Thomas M. "*The Rothschilds.* (Circle in the Square, New York City)." The Nation.

The Nation Institute. 1990. Highbeam Research. June 25, 2012 <http://www.highbeam.com>.

Elkin, Michael. "It's Springtime for Mel Brooks, with a Broadway Hit." *Jewish Bulletin* n.d. 18 April 2002 <http://www.jewishsf.com>.

Erens, Patricia. *The Jew in American Cinema.* Bloomington: Indiana University Press, 1984.

Erstein, Hap. "*Rothschilds* Glitters, Though It's Not Pure Gold." *The Washington Times* 23 August 1990, *Lexis-Nexis.* 30 November 2006.

Ezrahi, Sidra DeKoven. "After Such Knowledge, What Laughter?" *Yale Journal of Criticism.* Spring 2001, 287–313.

Farber, Roberta Rosenberg, and Chaim I. Waxman. *Jews in America: A Contemporary Reader.* Hanover: Brandeis University Press, 1999.

"Fiddler on the Roof: Trivia" www.imdb.com http://imdb.com/title/tt0067093/trivia. Retrieved 2 May 2006.

Fine, Ellen S. "Transmission of Memory: The Post-Holocaust Generation in the Diaspora," in *Breaking Crystal: Writing and Memory after Aushwitz,* ed. Efraim Sicher. Urbana: University of Illinois Press, 1998.

Finkielkraut, Alain. *The Imaginary Jew.* Trans. Kevin O'Neill and David Suchoff. Lincoln: University of Nebraska Press, 1994.

Flanzbaum, Hilene, ed. *The Americanization of the Holocaust.* Baltimore: Johns Hopkins University Press, 1999.

Flender, Harold. "The Stage Reporter." *Women's American Ort Reporter.* November/December 1970, p. 11.

Franklin, Ruth. "The Sunrise and Sunset of 'Fiddler's' Old World Nostalgia." *The New York Times.* 29 February 2004. Retrieved 20 September 2005 from <http://www.nytimes.com>.

Frieden, Ken. *A Century in the Life of Sholem Aleichem's Tevye.* Syracuse: Syracuse University Press, 1997.

Friedlander, Saul, ed. *Probing the Limits of Representation: Nazism and the "Final Solution."* Cambridge: Harvard University Press, 1992.

Friedman, Lester D. *Hollywood's Image of the Jew.* New York: Frederick Ungar Publishing Co., 1982.

Furnish, Ben. *Nostalgia in Jewish-American Theatre and Film, 1979–2004.* New York: P. Lang, 2005.

Gabler, Neal. "A Story of America, Set to Ragtime." *The New York Times.* 7 September 1997, *Lexis-Nexis.* 25 July 2006.

Gans, Herbert J. "Symbolic Ethnicity: The Future of Ethnic Groups and Cultures in America" in *On The Making of Americans* Herbert Gans. Ed. Philadelphia: University of Pennsylvania Press, 1979.

Gardner, Elysa. "'Fiddler' Again Plays Its Magic." *USA Today,* 27 February 2004: 11E.

_____. "Hilarious 'Producers' Signals Springtime for Musicals." *USA Today* 20 April 2001: 1E, *Lexis-Nexis.* 18 April 2002.

_____. "Musical Mel." *USA Today Online* 11 June 2001. 18 April 2002 <http://www.usatoday.com>.

Garebian, Keith. *The Making of Cabaret.* Toronto: Mosaic Press, 1999.

Gerould, Daniel. "Tyranny and Comedy," in Charney, Maurice. ed. *Comedy: New Perspectives.* New York: New York Literary Forum, 1978.

Gilman, Sander L. "Is Life Beautiful? Can the Shoah Be Funny? Some Thoughts on Recent and Older Films." *Critical Inquiry* (Winter 2000): 279–308.

_____. *Jewish Frontiers : Essays on Bodies, Histories, and Identities.* New York: Palgrave Macmillan, 2003.

_____. "The Jew's Body: Thoughts on Jewish Physical Difference" in *Too Jewish? Chal-*

lenging Traditional Identities Norman L. Kleeblatt ed, New Brunswick: Rutgers University Press, 1996.

Gold, Gerald. "*The Sound of Music*, Without Alps." *The New York Times*. 4 March 1990, *Lexis-Nexis*. 21 March 2003.

Goodrich, Frances, and Albert Hackett. *The Diary of Anne Frank*. New York: Random House, 1954.

_____. *The Diary of Anne Frank*. "Newly adapted" by Wendy Kesselman. New York: Dramatists Play Service, 2000.

Goren, Arthur A. "'A Golden Decade' for American Jews: 1945–1955." *The American Jewish Experience,* 2nd ed. Ed. Jonathan D. Sarna. New York: Holmes & Meier, 1997. 294–311.

Green, Stanley. *The World of Musical Comedy*. New York: Da Capo Press, 1980.

Grose, Peter. *Israel in the Mind of America*. New York: Alfred A. Knopf, 1983.

Gurewitsch, Matthew. "Tradition? The Delicate Task of Returning 'Fiddler.'" *The New York Times*. 26 February 2004: E1. Retrieved 20 September 2005 from <http://www.ny times.com/2004/02/26/arts/theater/26FIDD.html>.

Gussow, Mel. Review of *Rags* American Jewish Theater, New York, Libretto by Joseph Stein, Music by Charles Strouse, Lyrics by Stephen Schwartz, Dirrector Richard Sabellico. *The New York Times*. 4 December 1991. C22.

Harnick, Sheldon. "A Conversation with Jerry Herman." *Dramatists Guild Quarterly Dramatists Guild Quarterly*. 21 (1) Spring: 1984, 26–39.

_____. An interview conducted by letter by Jessica Hillman, August 29, 2009.

"Hebrew National: Music That Answers to a Higher authority." CD, 1996. <http://www. allmusic.com/album/r239172>.

Herman, Felicia. "Hollywood, Nazism, and the Jews 1933–41." *American Jewish History* 89.1 pp. 61–89.

Herman, Jerry, and Ken Bloom. *Jerry Herman, The Lyrics: A Celebration*. New York: Routledge, 2003.

Herman, Jerry, with Marilyn Stasio. *Showtune: A Memoir by Jerry Herman*. New York: Donald I. Fine Books, 1996.

Hischak, Thomas S. *Boy Loses Girl: Broadway's Librettists*. Lanham: Scarecrow Press, 2002.

Hofler, Robert. "'Fiddler' Director, Scribe get Physical Over Column." *Variety*. 1 March 2004, Retrieved 17 May 2006 <http://www.variety.com/index.asp?layout=print_story& articleid=VR1117901030&categoryid=15>.

Holden, Stephen. "Spare Revival of a '70 Broadway Musical." *The New York Times*. 26 February 1990, *Lexis-Nexis*. 30 November 2006.

Horwitz, Simi, and Ira J. Bilowit. "Remembrances: 1960." *Backstage*. 22 December 1995, 36 (51) 20–26. Retrieved via EBSCOhost.

Howe, Irving. "Immigrant Chic." *New York*. 19: May 12, 1986, p. 76.

_____. "Tevye on Broadway." *Commentary* 38: 1964, 73–75.

_____. *World of Our Fathers*. New York: Harcourt Brace Jovanovich, 1976.

_____, and Kenneth Libo, eds., *How We Lived: A Documentary History of Immigrant Jews in America (1880–1930)*. New York: New American Library, 1979.

Hyland, William G. *Richard Rodgers*. New Haven: Yale University Press, 1998.

Ilson, Carol. *Harold Prince: From Pajama Game to Phantom of the Opera and Beyond*. New York: Limelight Editions, 1989.

Isherwood, Christopher. *Goodbye to Berlin*. London: Minerva, 1989.

Isser, Edward R. *Stages of Annihilation: Theatrical Representations of the Holocaust*. Madison: Associated University Presses, 1997.

"Jerry Herman: 'Still Goin' Strong.'" *The Dramatist*. 1 (1): 1998, 10–19.

Jones, John Bush. *Our Musicals, Ourselves: A Social History of the American Musical Theatre*. Waltham, MA: Brandeis University Press, 2003.

Kerr, Walter. Review of *Fiddler on the Roof*, by Sheldon Harnick, Jerry Bock and Joseph Stein. Imperial Theatre, New York. *New York Theatre Critics Reviews*, 25: 19 (1964): 214–217.

Keyser, Hans Christoph. "The Sadist and the Clown: The Changing Nazi Image in the American Media." *Journal of Popular Culture* Spring 1977: 448–851.

Klein, Alvin. "After Anatevka: Dark Look at a New Land." Review of *Rags* The Papermill Playhouse, New Jersey. Libretto by Joseph Stein, Music by Charles Strouse, Lyrics by Stephen Schwartz. *The New York Times*. 21 November 1999, *Lexis-Nexis*. 25 July 2006.

_____. "A Conflict Develops Over a Musical." *The New York Times*. 10 June 1990, *Lexis-Nexis*. 30 November 2006.

_____. "Hoping to Turn 'Rags' into Riches." *The New York Times*. 17 August 1986, *Lexis-Nexis*. 25 July 2006. p. 21.

_____. "The Musical (and the Clothes) That Refused to Die." *The New York Times*. 7 November 1999, *Lexis-Nexis*. 25 July 2006.

Knapp, Raymond. *The American Musical and the Formation of National Identity*. Princeton: Princeton University Press, 2005.

Koenig, Rhoda. "Musical: Papa Don't Preach." *The Independent*. 6 November 2001, *Lexis-Nexis*. 25 July 2006. p. 11.

Krefetz, Gerald. *Jews and Money: The Myths and the Reality*. New Haven: Ticknor & Fields, 1982.

Kuchwara, Michael. "Broadway Musical May Reopen Next Month Despite Negative Reviews." *Associated Press*, 25 August 1986, *Lexis-Nexis*. 25 July 2006.

_____. "Broadway Musical 'Rags' Will Not Reopen in September." *Associated Press*, 28 August 1986, *Lexis-Nexis*. 25 July 2006.

Landsberg, Alison. "America, the Holocaust, and the Mass Culture of Memory: Toward a Radical Politics of Empathy." *New German Critique*. Spring-Summer 1997, 63–86.

Lang, Berel. *Holocaust Representation: Art within the Limits of History and Ethics*. Baltimore: Johns Hopkins University Press, 2000.

Langer, Lawrence L. "The Americanization of the Holocaust on Stage and Screen," *Admitting the Holocaust*. New York: Oxford University Press, 1995.

_____. *The Holocaust and the Literary Imagination*. New Haven: Yale University Press, 1975.

Lawrence, Greg. *Dance with Demons: The Life of Jerome Robbins*. New York: Berkley Books, 2001.

Levine, Paul ed. *E.L. Doctorow: Three Screenplays*. Baltimore: Johns Hopkins University Press, 2003.

Lifson, David S. *The Yiddish Theatre in America*. New York: Thomas Yoseloff, 1965.

Lindsay, Howard, Russel Crouse, Richard Rodgers and Oscar Hammerstein II. *The Sound of Music: A New Musical Play*. New York: Random House, 1960.

Lowenthal, David. "Nostalgia Tells It Like It Wasn't" in *The Imagined Past: History and Nostalgia*. Christopher Shaw and Malcolm Chase, eds. Manchester: Manchester University Press, 1989.

Ma, Sheng-mei. "The Great Dictator and Maus: 'The Comical' Before and After the Holocaust." *Proteus: A Journal of Ideas*. Fall 1995, 47–50.

Mandelbaum, Ken "The Rothschilds" Yellen, Sherman, Jerry Bock, and Sheldon Harnick. *The Rothschilds CD*. Thomas Shepard, producer. Sony Music: 1970.

Mann, Abby. *Judgment at Nuremberg*. New York: New Directions Books, 2002.

Masteroff, Joe, John Kander, and Fred Ebb. *Cabaret*. New York: Random House, 1967.

_____, _____ and _____. *Cabaret: The Illustrated Book and Lyrics*. New York: Newmarket Press, 1999.

McNally, Terrence, Stephen Flaherty, and Lynn Ahrens. *Ragtime*. New York: Music Theatre International Licensing Agency.

_____, _____ and _____. *Ragtime CD.* Jay David Saks, producer, Livent Music: 1998.

"Mel Brooks — Bio." *"The Producers" Website* n.d. 18 April 2002 <http://www.producersonbroadway.com/flash.html>.

Miller, Arthur. *The Portable Arthur Miller.* New York: The Viking Press, 1949.

Miller, Stuart. "New Milk and Honey." *Theater Week.* 7 (42): 23–25.

Mintz, Alan. *Popular Culture and the Shaping of Holocaust Memory in America.* Seattle: University of Washington Press, 2001.

"Molly Picon." *Universal Jewish Encyclopedia,* Vol. VIII, Varda Books, p. 530, 2009.

Mordden, Ethan. *One More Kiss: The Broadway Musical in the 1970s.* New York: Palgrave Macmillan, 2003.

_____. *Open a New Window: The Broadway Musical in the 1960s.* New York: Palgrave, 2001.

_____. *Rodgers and Hammerstein.* New York: Harry N. Abrams, Inc., 1992.

Morton, Frederic. *The Rothschilds: A Family Portrait.* Greenwich: Fawcett Publications Inc., 1961.

Most, Andrea. *Making Americans: Jews and the Broadway Musical.* Cambridge: Harvard University Press, 2004.

Nadel, Norman. "'Fiddler on the Roof' is Humorous, Tender Musical." Review of *Fiddler on the Roof,* by Sheldon Harnick, Jerry Bock and Joseph Stein. Imperial Theatre, New York. *New York Theatre Critics Reviews,* 25: 19 (1964): 214–217.

Nisse, Jason, and Hannah Cleaver. "Showtime of Hitler in Germany; The Producers: Mel Brooks's Classic Musical Spoof of the Nazi Era is to be Staged in Berlin" *The Independent.* 3 March 2002, *Lexis-Nexis.* 9 November 2006.

"NJPS: Rates of Intermarriage." The Jewish Federations of North America, Inc. 2011 http://www.jewishfederations.org/page.aspx?id=46253.

Nolen, Frederick. *The Sound of Their Music: The Story of Rodgers and Hammerstein.* New York: Walker and Company, 1978.

Novick, Peter. *The Holocaust in American Life.* Boston: Houghton Mifflin, 1999.

Patraka, Vivian M. *Spectacular Suffering: Theatre, Fascism, and The Holocaust* Bloomington: University of Indiana Press, 1999.

Peretz, Martin. "Identity, History, Nostalgia." *The New Republic.* 200 (6), 1989, p. 43.

Picon, Molly, with Jean Grillo. *Molly! An Autobiography.* New York: Simon and Schuster, 1980.

Picon, Molly, and Eth Clifford Rosenberg. *So Laugh a Little.* New York: Julian Messner, Inc., 1962.

Plagens, Peter. "A 'Sensation' About Nazis." *Newsweek.* 28 January 2002: 73.

Raczymow, Henri. "Memory Shot Through with Holes." *Yale French Studies.* 85 (1994), pp. 98–105.

Raphael, Marc Lee. "From Marjorie to Tevya: The Image of the Jews in American Popular Literature, Theatre and Comedy, 1955–1965." *American Jewish History,* 74 (1984): pp. 66–72.

Rawson, Christopher. "JCC Turns Lively 'Rags' to Riches." Review of *Rags.* Jewish Community Center Theater, Pittsburg, PA. Libretto by Joseph Stein, Music by Charles Strouse, Lyrics by Stephen Schwartz. *The Pittsburg Post-Gazette.* 15 February 1994, *Lexis-Nexis.* 25 July 2006.

_____. "'Rags' Counts Big Cast Among Riches" Review of *Rags* Stage 62, Pittsburg, PA. Libretto by Joseph Stein, Music by Charles Strouse, Lyrics by Stephen Schwartz. *The Pittsburg Post-Gazette.* 7 November 2001, *Lexis-Nexis.* 25 July 2006.

Recording "The Producers": A Musical Romp with Mel Brooks. Prod. Susan Froemke and Peter Gelb. By Mel Brooks, Thomas Meehan. DVD. Sony Classical, 2001.

Reviews of *Cabaret,* by Joe Masteroff, John Kander, and Fred Ebb. Broadhurst Theatre, New York. *New York Theatre Critics Reviews,* New York: Critics Theatre Reviews Inc., Vol. 21: 1966. 240–243.

Reviews of *Fiddler on the Roof*, by Sheldon Harnick, Jerry Bock, and Joseph Stein. Imperial Theatre, New York. *New York Theatre Critics Reviews*, New York: Critics Theatre Reviews Inc., Vol. 25: 1964. 214–217.

Reviews of *Milk and Honey* by Don Appell and Jerry Herman. Martin Beck Theatre, New York. *New York Theatre Critics Reviews*, New York: Critics Theatre Reviews Inc., Vol. 22: 1961. 238–241.

Reviews of *Rags* by Joseph Stein, Charles Strouse, and Stephen Schwartz. Mark Hellinger Theatre, New York. *New York Theatre Critics Reviews*, New York: Critics Theatre Reviews Inc., Vol. 47: 1986. 238–243.

Reviews of *The Rothschilds* by Sheldon Harnick, Jerry Bock, and Sherman Yellen. Lunt-Fontanne Theatre, New York. *New York Theatre Critics Reviews*, New York: Critics Theatre Reviews Inc., Vol. 31: 1970. 181–182, 184–186.

Richards, David, "Amorous Adventures From a Simpler Time." Rev. of *Milk and Honey*. *New York Times* 20 May 1994. 22 June 2006 <http://theater2.nytimes.com/mem/theater/treview.html?res=9906E2D61238F933A15756C0A962958260.>.

Rosen, Jonathan. "Beyond Nostalgia." *The Forward*. N. 30, 25 May 1990, p. 768.

Rosenbaum, Thane. "A Legacy Cut Loose." *Los Angeles Times*. 15 February 2004.

Rosenfeld, Alvin H. *Imagining Hitler*. Bloomington: University of Indiana Press, 1985.

_____, ed. *Thinking About the Holocaust: After Half a Century*. Bloomington: Indiana University Press, 1997.

Roskies, David. *The Jewish Search for a Usable Past*. Bloomington: University of Indiana Press, 1999.

Rothstein, Mervyn. "In Three Revivals, the Goose Stepping is Louder." *New York Times* 8 March 1998, *Lexis-Nexis*. 5 September 2001.

Sanders, Ronald. "The Rothschilds on Broadway: Jews, History, and Musical Comedy." *Midstream: A Monthly Jewish Review*. Vol. 16 (10) December 1970. pp. 23–31.

Schjeldahl, Peter. "The Hitler Show: The Jewish Museum revisits the Nazis." *The New Yorker*. 1 April 2002, 87.

Schwartz, Stephen. "In Conversation with Jerry Herman." *The Dramatist*. 7 (3) January/February 2005, 16–18.

Scott, A. O. "'The Producers,' Again (This Time with Uma)." *The New York Times*. 16 December 2005, *Lexis-Nexis*. 9 November 2006, p. 10.

Shipow, Sandra. "Depression-Era Trends in Popular Culture as Reflected in the Yiddish Theatre Career of Molly Picon." *Theatre Studies* 30: 43–55.

Simas, Rick. "Ragtime." Review of *Ragtime*. Ford Performing Arts Center, New York City. Book by Terrence McNally. Music by Stephen Flaherty, Lyrics by Lynn Ahrens. *Theater Journal* 50.4 (1998) 540–542.

Simon, John. "Blazing Twaddle." *New York Magazine Online*. 30 April 2001. 18 April 2002 <http://www.nymag.com>.

Singer, Barry. "A Crash Course in the World of Mel." *New York Times*. 20 May 2001: 2:12, *Lexis-Nexis*. 18 April 2002.

Skloot, Robert. "Introduction" in Skloot, Robert, ed. *The Theatre of the Holocaust: Four Plays*. Madison: University of Wisconsin Press, 1982.

_____. "Introduction" in Skloot, Robert, ed. *The Theatre of the Holocaust: Volume Two*. Madison: University of Wisconsin Press, 1999.

Smith, Starla. "Holding It Together: A Conversation with Paula Kalustian, 'The Only Straight Answer in Town.'" *TheaterWeek* (13), 1987, pp. 22–24.

Smurthwaite, Nick. "Rags and Riches" in *The Stage Newspaper*. 1 November 2001, *Lexis-Nexis*. 25 July 2006. p. 8.

Solomon, Alisa. "Fiddling with 'Fiddler.'" *Village Voice*. 21 January 2004. Retrieved September 20, 2005 from http://www.villagevoice.com/issues/0403/solomon.php.

Sontag, Susan. *Under the Sign of Saturn*. New York: Farrar, Straus, Giroux, 1980.

Sorin, Gerald. *Tradition Transformed: The Jewish Experience in America*. Baltimore: Johns Hopkins University Press, 1997.

"Sound of Music: It's a Wrap." *The Sound of Music Film Website* n. date 21 February 2003 www.foxhome.com/sounofmusic/wra/wram.html.

Spencer, Charles. "Laughter all the way as Hitler's troupers go down a storm." *The Daily Telegraph* 10 November 2004, *Lexis-Nexis*. 9 November 2006. p. 3.

_____. "Ragged Riches." *The Daily Telegraph*. 6 November 2001, *Lexis-Nexis*. 25 July 2006. p. 21.

Spiegelman, Art. *Maus: A Survivor's Tale*. New York: Pantheon Books, 1973.

Stein, Joseph. *Rags*. New York; Rodgers and Hammerstein Theatre Library, 1986.

Stein, Joseph, Jerry Bock, and Sheldon Harnick. *Fiddler on the Roof CD*. Thomas Z. Shepard, Reissue Producer. Sony Music: 2001.

Stein, Joseph, Charles Strouse, and Stephen Schwartz. *Rags CD*. Robert Sher, producer. Herrick Theatre Foundation, Sony Music: 1987.

Steyn, Mark. *Broadway Babies Say Goodnight*. New York: Routledge, 2000.

Stone, Peter, Jerry Bock, Sheldon Harnick and Joseph Stein. "Landmark Symposium: *Fiddler on the Roof*." *Dramatists Guild Quarterly*. Spring 1983: 10–29.

Trapp, Maria Augusta. *The Story of the Trapp Family Singers*. New York: Harper Perennial, 1949.

"Trapp Family Museum." *The Trapp Family Lodge Website*. n. date 12 February 2003 www.trappfamily.com/history.html.

Viano, Maurizio. "Life Is Beautiful: Reception, Allegory, and Holocaust Laughter." *Film Quarterly*. Fall 1999, 26–34.

Waxman, Chaim I. *Jewish Baby Boomers: A Communal Perspective*. Albany: State University of New York Press, 2001.

Wenger, Beth S. "Memory as Identity: The Invention of the Lower East Side" *American Jewish History* 85.1 (1997) 3–27.

Whitfield, Stephen J. "Fiddling with Sholem Aleichem: A History of Fiddler on the Roof" in Jack Kugelmass, ed. *Key Texts in American Jewish Culture*. New Brunswick: Rutgers University Press, 2003.

_____. *In Search of American Jewish Culture*. Hanover: Brandeis University Press, 1999.

Wiesel, Elie. "Stage View: Treasured Family Is the Secret Wealth of 'The Rothschilds.'" *The New York Times*. 23 September 1990. Accessed 14 February 2007. http://theater2.ny times.com/mem/theater/treview.html.

Winer, Linda. "Fiddler on the Roof" (review). *New York Newsday*, 27 February 2004. Retrieved 20 September 2005 from <http://www.newsday.com/entertainment/local-guide/ny-etledew3687277feb27,0,7112695,print.story?coll=ny-guide-rail>.

Winn, Steven. "Attuned to the Century: 'Ragtime' Strikes Rich if Uneven Chords of Earlier America." Review of *Ragtime*, Shubert Theatre, Los Angeles, CA. Book by Terrence McNally. Music by Stephen Flaherty. Lyrics by Lynn Ahrens. *The San Francisco Chronicle*, 17 June 1997, *Lexis-Nexis*. 25 July 2006.

Wolf, Matt. "London Maverick Arrives For First (and Second) Time." *The New York Times*. 1 February 1998, *Lexis-Nexis*. 25 September 2001.

_____. *Sam Mendes at the Donmar: Stepping into Freedom*. New York: Limelight Editions, 2002.

Wolf, Stacy. *A Problem Like Maria: Gender and Sexuality in the American Musical*. Ann Arbor: University of Michigan Press, 2002.

Wolnitz, Seth L. "The Americanization of Tevye or Boarding the Jewish 'Mayflower.'" *American Quarterly*, December 1988: 514–536.

Yellen, Sherman, Jerry Bock, and Sheldon Harnick. *The Rothschilds CD*. Thomas Shepard, producer. Sony Music: 1970.

_____, _____ and _____. *The Rothschilds: A Musical*. New York: Rodgers and Hammerstein Theatre Library, 1970.

Young, James E. Foreword. *Mirroring Evil: Nazi Imagery/Recent Art Catalogue*. n.d. 20 April 2002 <http://www.jewishmuseum.org/Pages/Exhibitions/Special_Exhibitions/mirroring_evil/excerpts.html>.

_____. *The Texture of Memory: Holocaust Memorials and Meaning*, New Haven: Yale University Press; 1994

Zelizer, Rabbi Gerald L. "Is 'The Producers' Tasteless?" *United Synagogue of Conservative Judaism* 31 May 2001. 18 April 2002 <http://www.uscj.org/njersey/metuchen/zel6/html>.

Zoglin, Richard. "Brush Up Your Goose Step." *Time Pacific Magazine Online* 20 April 2001 18 April 2002 <http://www.time.com/time/pacific/magazine>.

Index

211